INCOME REDISTRIBUTION

A conference sponsored by the
American Enterprise Institute for Public Policy Research
and the
Hoover Institution on War, Revolution and Peace

INCOME REDISTRIBUTION

Edited by Colin D. Campbell

American Enterprise Institute for Public Policy Research
Washington, D.C.

Library of Congress Cataloging in Publication Data

Main entry under title:

Income redistribution.

    Papers presented at a conference held in Washington,
D.C. from May 20 to May 21, 1976.
    Includes bibliographical references.
    1. Income distribution—United States—Congresses.
I. Campbell, Colin Dearborn, 1917–   II. American
Enterprise Institute for Public Policy Research.
III. Stanford University. Hoover Institution on War,
Revolution, and Peace.
HC110.I5I516   339.2′0973   77-6342
ISBN 0-8447-2099-2
ISBN 0-8447-2098-4 pbk.

Printed in the United States of America

MAJOR CONTRIBUTORS

Henry J. Aaron
Professor, University of Maryland
and Senior Fellow, The Brookings Institution

Walter J. Blum
Professor, University of Chicago

Robert H. Bork
Solicitor General of the United States

Edgar K. Browning
Professor, University of Virginia

Oswald H. Brownlee
Professor, University of Minnesota

James M. Buchanan
Professor, Virginia Polytechnic Institute and State University
and Adjunct Scholar, American Enterprise Institute

Colin D. Campbell
Professor, Dartmouth College
and Adjunct Scholar, American Enterprise Institute

Rita Ricardo Campbell
Senior Fellow, The Hoover Institution

Marshall Cohen
Professor, City University of New York

Wilbur J. Cohen
Dean, University of Michigan School of Education

Barber B. Conable, Jr.
United States Congressman, New York

George H. Dixon
Deputy Secretary of the Treasury, Department of the Treasury

James S. Duesenberry
Professor, Harvard University

Martin Feldstein
Professor, Harvard University

Irving J. Goffman
Deputy Assistant Secretary for Income Security Policy,
Department of Health, Education and Welfare

Irving Kristol
Professor, New York University
and Resident Scholar, American Enterprise Institute

CONTENTS

PART THREE
The Case for the Progressive Income Tax
Easy or Uneasy?

PART FOUR
Where Do We Go from Here?

PART FIVE
Welfare Reform: Why?

INTRODUCTION

Colin D. Campbell

A conference on income redistribution jointly sponsored by the American Enterprise Institute for Public Policy Research and the Hoover Institution on War, Revolution and Peace was held in Washington, D.C., from May 20 to 21, 1976. The seven papers presented, together with the commentary on the papers and selected portions of the discussion and questions from the floor, are included in this volume. The volume also includes the conference luncheon address by Deputy Secretary of the Treasury George H. Dixon and a paper by Professor Walter J. Blum, which he has generously given us permission to include.

The conference was divided into five sessions. The first session was chaired by Professor Herbert Stein and was on the topic "Equality and Efficiency—What Is the Optimum Equality in Incomes?" The second session was "Income Maintenance and the Economy," chaired by me. The third session, "The Case for the Progressive Income Tax: Easy or Uneasy," was chaired by Dr. Dan Throop Smith. The fourth, chaired by Dr. Thomas G. Moore, was "Where Do We Go From Here?" and the fifth, a round table, "Welfare Reform: Why?"

The conference showed clearly a very wide division of opinion on the subject of income redistribution. The principal areas of disagreement were whether people want equality, whether the end result or the process of income distribution is what matters most, what the effects of income redistribution are on efficiency and liberty, whether the United States today is effectively redistributing income, and whether the social security program is essentially one to equalize incomes. Each of these areas of disagreement is briefly summarized in this introductory chapter.

Do People Want Equality?

The paper presented by Arthur Okun is based on his book, *Equality and Efficiency: The Big Tradeoff*.[1] Its basic premise is that people want equality. Okun himself is not certain how intensely people want equality. He feels certain, however, that people want more equality of income than would be generated by the market. To Okun, the steps that have been taken by government toward equalization are convincing evidence that people want equality. In addition, he points out that rights

---

[1] Arthur M. Okun, *Equality and Efficiency: The Big Tradeoff* (Washington, D.C.: The Brookings Institution, 1975).

shared equally by all have been firmly established in many of our social and political institutions—for example, one person one vote, one person one spouse, equal justice, universal freedom of speech and religion, universal immunity from enslavement, and equal claims for public services. He infers from these equal social and political rights that persons would also prefer equality in the economic sphere.

Others at the conference disagreed. Irving Kristol believes that the majority of the American people do not want a government that imposes a high degree of equality. To him, the distribution of income is not a problem in the United States today, and he is critical of egalitarians for not specifying the degree of inequality that they consider inequitable.

Similarly, Martin Feldstein does not believe that the social security program and progressive income taxes are evidence of the public's desire for equality. Instead, he believes, the social security system is evidence of the public's desire to assist persons in various types of catastrophies—retirement, disability, death, sickness—and progressive income taxes are evidence of the public's desire to achieve equal sacrifice rather than income redistribution.

Irving Goffman notes that federal income transfers are mainly for social insurance functions rather than for welfare. He believes that equality for equality's sake is not a strong force because the United States is a middle-class society that has already achieved a great deal of income equality.

A discrepancy between the views of most people and those of educated elites is highlighted by Robert Lampman and Robert Nisbet. Many academics, according to Lampman, have asserted that reducing inequality is an implicit goal of government tax and transfer programs, yet this is not explicitly the goal of any government legislation. Nisbet states that income equality has become the predominant goal in the social philosophy of most intellectuals, though the majority of the people are not interested in equality of income. Incomes are being redistributed by the government, Nisbet says, only because of the disproportionate political influence of intellectuals.

Wilbur Cohen too believes that there is little popular support for measures to equalize income—but a great deal for governmental programs to improve equality of opportunity.

While James Duesenberry believes that there was not a consensus for egalitarianism in the United States when progressive taxation was adopted, he predicts that there will be political conflict over equality in the future, as career opportunities for young men and women become increasingly restricted.

Robert Nozick criticizes Okun for not explaining in greater detail what he means by the social preference for equality. In his discussion of Okun's paper, Nozick assumes Okun to mean majority preference. As noted by Nozick, recent studies have concluded that the aggregation of individual preferences is a difficult problem and may be impossible.

Both Marshall Cohen and Nozick criticize the importance Okun gives to his premise that the majority of people want equality. Marshall Cohen expresses the belief that moral judgments are involved and that equality of opportunity and a decent minimum standard of life are moral rights. Nozick asks, even if a majority prefers income redistribution, is that sufficient reason to justify government programs to redistribute income? He argues on ethical grounds that persons have a right not to have certain sorts of things done to them and that there are moral limits to what governments can do—whether or not anyone agrees to them and even if a majority says there are no limits. Property and other rights, Nozick believes, place limits on governmental redistributive activities.

There was some difference of opinion in regard to Nozick's and also probably Marshall Cohen's conception of rights. James Buchanan questions whether such rights should be determined individually. Instead, he argues, people must collectively determine what they can agree on and this should be formally established as in a contract.

James Tobin expresses concern about the inequality that is the result of genetic differences and inherited wealth and that gives the children of successful parents a head start. On the other hand, Blum points out that correcting for differences in original endowments is a difficult problem. He notes that, in addition to wealth and income, qualities such as beauty, leadership, and artistic ability are unevenly distributed. If the government effectively redistributed income and wealth, he says, it is questionable whether much would be gained because differences in social status would then depend on the unequal distribution of these other qualities, and, in addition, the opportunity to achieve status through earning large incomes and accumulating wealth would be diminished.

Kristol is the most outspoken defender of inequality. To him, status differentials reflect real differences in character, ability, and talent; they are interesting, and they should not be discouraged. Allen Wallis too is opposed to government policies that would take away the high incomes of rich persons. He notes that in some cases very rich persons have used their wealth in ways that are unusually creative and have contributed much to human welfare. On the other hand, Marshall Cohen and Richard Musgrave contend that unless there is a rough equality of opportunity, inequalities could be unjust. Most participants are in favor of assuring all persons some minimum level of income.

The Process of Income Distribution versus the End Result

A second major topic of discussion concerns the emphasis on equality of results attributed to Okun. Others state that the *process* by which income is distributed is more important than the end result.

Warren Nutter, a critic of Okun's paper, argues that the good society is one that maximizes the use of voluntary arrangements in organizing social activity rather than one that maximizes the equality of income or circumstance. To Nisbet, the proper goal for a democratic society is equality before the law, and he considers equality of opportunity to be a corollary of equality before the law.

Nozick, another critic, states that instead of asking how things should be distributed or how things end up, we should ask, What method is appropriate for distributing things? To him, an acceptable distribution of income would be whatever resulted from that mechanism. Buchanan agrees with Nozick, insisting that the important question is what type of system of income distribution we can agree on at some sort of basic constitutional level. There is no point, he says, in discussing the particular results.

Nozick also argues against the view that all that matters is how people end up. This view neglects ethical questions raised by the efforts required to achieve such results. Futhermore, there is a significant difference between an end result that is decreed by the government and involves coercion and one that occurs unintentionally as the result of the economic system. The concluding recommendations of Okun and Nozick reflect the difference in their views. Okun urges wider discussion of people's views about equality of income, while Nozick urges economists to redirect their discussion to evaluating the method by which income is distributed.

Along these lines, Kristol argues that there is a relationship between a liberal society and a system of distribution in which persons are paid in accordance with their productive input as determined by the market. This is based on Kristol's conception of a liberal society as one in which people are skeptical of anyone's ability to know the "common good" and thus to distribute income on that basis. (In such a society, authorities should not even try to define the "common good.") Instead, people are expected to pursue their own material interests and to engage in mutually advantageous transactions. Thus, Kristol believes that if persons think a liberal society is a good society, they will consider fair the distribution of income that comes about in such a society. Kristol does not believe that the market system of distribution is necessarily superior. The way a society distributes income depends on its history and traditions. He also believes that a society in which authorities distributed income in accordance with their conception of the common good might be a good society—although it would not be a liberal society. In his opinion, a liberal society would be destroyed by a strong egalitarian movement. The individualism of a liberal society would be replaced by some type of idealism such as egalitarianism and by a strong government.

In response to these objections, Okun is critical of the market system of income distribution. He believes that the market method need not fairly reward persons for their contributions to production and that there are ways in which people might be paid other than in accordance with their contributions to production. Tobin agrees with Okun that in an interdependent economy, the incomes that people receive need not be just deserts for their efforts—but instead depend on specialization and trade, governmental policies toward property and contracts, and the shared benefits of science and technology. He believes it is not possible to distinguish sharply between incomes earned as a result of voluntary agreements and incomes earned as a result of government coercion and the particular way in which governments enforce contracts.

In his essay on "The Uneasy Case for Progressive Taxation in 1976," Blum agrees with Okun and Tobin concerning the deficiencies of the market mechanism in distributing income. However, he does not believe that an alternative to the market mechanism has been clearly developed. In his opinion, an alternative to the prevailing view that persons are entitled to what they own must become widely accepted if it is to be the basis for an effective way of organizing the economic system.

Henry Aaron criticizes Kristol's belief that there is a relationship between the market system and a liberal society. Aaron believes that Kristol's approach to income distribution is too abstract and that discussion of income distribution should concern specific government policies. He also believes that experience in various countries, including the United States, shows that governmental efforts to redistribute income are compatible with a liberal society.

Efficiency

A third major topic of discussion concerned the trade-off between equality and efficiency. The thesis of Okun's book on this subject is that, given that people want more equality than market-determined incomes provide and given that there is a cost of altering the market-determined distribution of income, government programs to redistribute income force a trade-off between equality and efficiency. There are various possible costs of government programs to redistribute income— a reduction in saving, a decline in labor force participation, and a slackening in experimentation and innovation, as well as the additional costs of administering such programs. Okun believes that by far the most important costs are those affecting experimentation and innovation. He believes that reduced work effort is not a major problem and that the government can control the rate of saving regardless of the distribution of income through control of both public capital expenditures and fiscal and monetary policy. Furthermore, Okun is not convinced that a higher saving rate would be desirable. Although he believes that the overall costs of income redistribution are small, he urges economists and other social scientists to measure such costs more accurately.

Tobin's view of the trade-off between inequality and efficiency is similar to Okun's. He believes that governmental efforts to reduce inequality through progressive taxation must be limited because they may foster tax-avoiding behavior that deprives society of potential resources. In his opinion, a decline in the work ethic would be harmful. Like Okun, however, he believes that we do not know much about the strength of the disincentives caused by egalitarian policies. In his opinion, although the choice between equality and efficiency is an ethical decision, the nature of the trade-off may be examined empirically and analyzed.

Feldstein disagrees with Okun's opinion that government programs to re-distribute income have had only a slight impact on the efficiency of the economy. He believes that Medicare and Medicaid have caused a sharp rise in health-care costs, that the payroll taxes financing old-age and health benefits have reduced work effort, that unemployment insurance has created substantial unemployment, and that old-age insurance has depressed saving and induced retirement. A major problem, as he sees it, is that these adverse effects are ignored or denied by those responsible for these programs. Feldstein's paper includes an analysis of the harmful effects on the economy of these programs, and he summarizes the results of empirical research done by him and by others to estimate the magnitude of these effects.

Feldstein also disagrees with Nancy Teeters's point of view that social se-curity has simply replaced family responsibility for the elderly who can no longer work. Teeters argues that because of this, social security has only a small effect on the saving rate. Feldstein notes that a dramatic increase in retirement has occurred during this century. While most persons used to expect to work in their later years, because of their growing affluence they now save for retirement. In his opinion, there would have been a rise in the saving rate if it had not been for social security.

Feldstein believes it would not be easy politically to encourage saving through fiscal policy as suggested by Okun because the federal government would have to have budget surpluses. In his opinion, it would be easier to achieve budget surpluses through the social security system than in other ways. He notes that an attractive alternative method of increasing private saving would be to adopt the decoupling proposal suggested by the Consultant Panel on Social Security, chaired by William Hsiao.[2] This proposal would encourage saving by reducing social security replace-ment rates in the future as real incomes rise.

Wallis's principal criticism of progressive taxation is the growing administrative complexity of the tax law—a cost of redistribution mentioned by Okun. Wallis believes that Blum and Kalven's degressive tax proposal in *The Uneasy Case for Progressive Taxation* would alleviate this problem.[3] A degressive tax is one in which a certain amount of income is exempt from taxation and all income above that is taxed at a uniform rate. In his opinion, the argument in favor of a degressive tax is stronger today than when it was originally proposed because of the increased complexity of the tax law and because of the expansion in welfare programs such as Medicare, food stamps, and housing subsidies. The government may now directly redistribute income through these welfare transfers rather than through progressive

[2] See *Report of the Consultant Panel on Social Security to the Congressional Research Service,* Joint Committee Print, 94th Congress, 2nd session, prepared for the Use of the Committee on Finance of the U.S. Senate and the Committee on Ways and Means of the U.S. House of Representatives, August 1976.

[3] Walter J. Blum and Harry Kalven, Jr., *The Uneasy Case for Progressive Taxation* (Chicago: University of Chicago Press, 1953).

taxation. Wallis also believes that the large inequities in the progressive income tax—which result in different treatment for persons with the same income—will eventually weaken popular compliance and respect for the tax system and undermine the finances of the federal government.

In his comment on Wallis's paper, Oswald Brownlee expresses doubt that Blum and Kalven's degressive tax proposal would accomplish as much as Wallis suggests. In his opinion, it is high tax rates rather than progressive tax rates that have resulted in political pressures to create loopholes and complicate the income tax.

In his paper, "The Uneasy Case for Progressive Taxation in 1976," Blum distinguishes between the use of progressive taxation to finance governmental services and the use of such taxes to finance transfers to the poor. He discusses the various ways in which welfare payments to the poor may be financed—by highly progressive income taxes, mildly progressive income taxes, or proportional taxes on all incomes in excess of the minimum level. He enumerates the reasons for believing that the reduction in efficiency would be greater if highly progressive taxes were used to finance a welfare program rather than to finance governmental services.

Okun's idea of a trade-off between equality and efficiency, especially in regard to equal political and social rights, is rejected by Marshall Cohen. Cohen believes that the reason for equal political and social rights is that these rights are based on important human values. In his opinion, people would not be willing to sacrifice such rights even if maintaining them were costly in terms of efficiency.

Nozick criticizes Okun's belief that there is equality in the political and social systems but not in the economic sphere because of the greater costs of reduced efficiency in the economic system than in the political and social systems. He believes that the reason why there is equality in the political realm is the desire to give each person one vote in controlling the coercive power of the government.

Feldstein suggests that there is an important need to balance the goals of protection and efficiency in the social security system, rather than the goals of equality and efficiency. To him, the unemployment insurance system, for example, should balance the protection from a loss of earnings against the incentive to be unemployed.

Liberty

The relationship between income distribution and liberty was also explored. Nisbet believes that governmental efforts to achieve equality of condition, if carried far enough, will destroy political freedom. His point of view is similar to Kristol's conception of the relationship between a liberal society and the market system of distribution. Nisbet believes the dogma of equality carries with it the same kind of moral fervor as religious movements have in the past, and he believes such

7

dogmas are important. In his essay, Nisbet discusses why most intellectuals are egalitarians and why the egalitarian movement is likely to grow.

Aaron criticizes Nisbet for presenting the issue of redistribution as a choice between complete equality and cessation of redistribution. To Aaron, the choice is between doing a bit more and a bit less than we do now in dealing with specific kinds of problems. Also, Aaron argues that government spending and taxing unavoidably affect the distribution of income, and he criticizes Nisbet for appearing to suggest that we blind ourselves to these redistributive effects. Aaron does not believe that the desire to reduce inequality amounts to a religious movement. Instead, in his opinion, it reflects concern with achieving greater equality of opportunity.

Marshall Cohen criticizes Okun's view that there is little conflict between the interests of liberty and equality. Although Cohen would restrict liberties as little as possible, he believes that justice, the maintenance of equal political rights, equality of opportunity, and a decent minimum standard of living may require restrictions on the freedom to enjoy and dispose of one's property as one wishes.

Marshall Cohen and Musgrave are concerned that economic inequality could be a danger to political equality. On the other hand, Blum is concerned over the possibility that tax policies designed to reduce the income of the rich would endanger political freedom by affecting the distribution of power between those within the government and those without. He believes it is desirable to have considerable power outside of government.

In contrast to those who hold that the capitalistic economic system could be undermined by efforts to reduce inequality, Tobin believes that the system could be undermined by excessive inequality. In his opinion, to be successful, a complex interdependent market economy must avoid popular disaffection. He believes that the problems of crime, corruption, demoralization, and antisocial behavior in our cities may be caused by inequality, and that it is too much to expect that loyal consent to the rules of the game will be forthcoming regardless of the outcome of the game.

The Effectiveness of Income Redistribution

Several participants in the conference question whether governmental efforts to reduce inequality had been effective. Edgar Browning notes that no one knows with any degree of certainty how much income is redistributed annually to low-income families. His own attempts to measure income redistribution showed that when in-kind transfers were included, income redistribution from the rich to the poor had become substantial in recent years. He believes, however, that no one can understand the welfare system fully because it has become so complex. He urges that all existing programs eventually be replaced by a negative income tax.

Both Wallis and Brownlee state that there is still no conclusive evidence whether progressive taxation has in fact reduced inequality. Statistical problems in measuring inequality—such as whether to use income, expenditures, or wealth to measure economic capacity and whether to use the individual, the family, or the household as the unit of comparison—are mentioned by Blum. An issue raised by several persons was the prevailing use of annual income rather than lifetime income to measure inequality. Kristol is critical of the use of annual statistics by egalitarians to show that the distribution of income is a problem. Tobin would agree that the inequality that people are concerned about is lifetime income rather than annual income. Because capital markets are not perfect, however, he believes that progressive tax policies based on annual income may be justified. Capital markets are imperfect because some persons who are temporarily poor cannot borrow, and the poor, if able to borrow, may have to pay relatively high interest rates.

The complexity of the problem of measuring the effect of government policies on the distribution of income is illustrated by George Dixon's paper on "The Social Allocation of Capital." Henry Simons's view—that the market can be relied upon to control the allocation of resources efficiently while the federal government, through progressive income taxation, might lessen inequality in the distribution of income—has become outdated. In his paper, Dixon discusses the major ways in which the federal government now regulates the allocation of capital. Although these controls are designed to solve such ills as poor housing, inadequate rail passenger service, the financial plight of the cities, consumer ignorance, and dependence on foreign energy sources, they also may have significant effects on the distribution of income—which may or may not be egalitarian.

Norman Ture believes that the efforts of government to redistribute income through progressive income taxation have had little effect because market responses to those efforts have cancelled them out. On the other hand, Musgrave believes that, though shifting of income taxes may occur, the redistributive effects of progressive income taxation is not completely offset. Buchanan mentions another obstacle to governmental efforts to redistribute income through progressive taxation—the possibility that rich persons may move from countries with high taxes to those with low taxes.

Both Musgrave and Duesenberry state that progressive taxation may not have done much for redistribution because of the numerous loopholes, and they urge that the base of the income tax be broadened. On the other hand, Brownlee doubts that proposals to broaden the income tax base would be politically acceptable. Instead, he would have the federal government rely less on income taxation and more on an expenditure tax. Brownlee believes that an expenditure tax would be not only more egalitarian but also less costly to society because it would be less complex to administer and would not place a tax on saving.

There was also disagreement over the effectiveness of the government's anti-poverty programs. Lampman states that the war on poverty was pretty nearly won

9

as of 1972 if food, housing, and health benefits are added to cash transfers. In his paper, Kristol contends that even though statistics may show that few persons have incomes less than the poverty line, major social problems associated with poverty such as crime, drug addiction, and alcoholism continue. He believes that distributing welfare to persons who might be productive members of the community causes such persons to become idle and demoralized. He also believes that the alleviation of the major social problems associated with poverty is mainly dependent on economic growth rather than on government programs to redistribute income.

Alan Walters too is skeptical of the effectiveness of governmental efforts to eliminate poverty because the elimination of poverty is not in the self-interest of the bureaucracy. He bases his comments on the egalitarian movement in Great Britain. In his opinion, the expansion of bureaucracies depends on the creation of inequalities and new "problems." As a result, poverty is not diminished through governmental programs, despite the egalitarian claims of government spokesmen.

Social Insurance

Social insurance, the most important federal program of income redistribution, is the topic of the paper presented by Martin Feldstein. Feldstein views social insurance as a program of event-conditioned transfers, not a program of income equalization.

The discussion of social security at the conference is primarily concerned with problems of equity. Both Rita Ricardo Campbell and Nancy Teeters stress the need for more equitable treatment of married women workers. Rita Ricardo Campbell would also correct inequities resulting from the exclusion of federal government employees and many state and local government employees from the social security system. In Goffman's opinion, horizontal equity has become the most important issue facing the social security system. Removing such inequities would involve adjusting benefits so that households with similar lifetime earnings would be treated equally. Goffman doubts that the redistributional component in the current social security program will remain unquestioned by the middle class. Feldstein also is in favor of making the social insurance program a quid pro quo, an individualized account in which a person would get back what he had paid plus a rate of return that comes from the growth of the program. In his view, the Supplemental Security Income program, which is financed by general revenues, would provide welfare benefits at the bottom, and the recently adopted earned income credit would exempt low earnings from taxation.

PART ONE

EQUALITY AND EFFICIENCY— WHAT IS THE OPTIMUM EQUALITY IN INCOMES?

FURTHER THOUGHTS
ON
EQUALITY AND EFFICIENCY

Arthur M. Okun

I have recently expressed in some detail my views on the goal of equality in our society, particularly in relation to the goal of efficiency.[1] I trust that it will come as no surprise to readers of this paper that I have not yet accumulated a brand-new stock of ideas, nor am I yet ready to recant. Rather, I shall use this occasion to elaborate on some of the central issues, presenting them at a level appropriate for an audience of professionals, rather than of interested laymen.

Implicit in my book (and more explicit in this paper) is a reliance on a loose notion of "revealed preferences." I look for the rationale—the internal logic—of the institutions that actually operate in contemporary American society. In moving from the realities of institutions back to the principles, preferences, and constraints that could explain them as a reasonably rational and consistent system, my chain of reasoning reverses that of the social philosopher, who starts with his principles and attempts to derive from them the practices of a "good" society. Perhaps that makes me a backward philosopher.

Yet I too am interested in the good society, and I pursue the line of revealed preferences because I think our society is pretty good. At times, however, I depart from this approach to express my personal preferences, some of which are contrary to those of the majority as reflected in the political process. Indeed, a rigorously consistent application of revealed (rational) preferences would be awfully stuffy, since it must always conclude that whatever society does is best for it, or else it would be doing something else. The theory of efficient markets often strains my credulity, and any theory of efficient institutions would shatter it. I believe I can identify accidents of history, lags and imperfections of the democratic political process, misperceptions of costs or benefits, income effects, and technological innovations that result in policies that are suboptimal or inconsistent with majoritarian preferences. But this is a tricky game, no matter how honestly one tries to play it, and the reader should be on guard for any passages in which I might seem to lean on existing practices just because I like them or to find them irrational just because I do not.

Note: The views expressed are my own and are not necessarily those of the officers, trustees, or other staff members of the Brookings Institution.

[1] Arthur M. Okun, *Equality and Efficiency: The Big Tradeoff* (Washington, D.C.: The Brookings Institution, 1975).

The basic observation that requires explanation is that our society accepts far more inequality in the distribution of its economic assets than in the distribution of its sociopolitical assets. In interpreting that seeming inconsistency, I shall once again argue these points:

(1) The social preference for equality applies to economic as well as to "noneconomic" assets (although the intensity of those preferences may vary among classes of items).

(2) While there may be costs of equalizing distribution in any area, those costs tend to be greater for income (and wealth) than for social and political rights. Hence, it can be rational to tolerate more inequality in the economic realm than elsewhere.

(3) The major cost of equalization of income involves the sacrifice of some of the economic efficiency associated with the unaltered determination of incomes in the marketplace.

(4) On this reasoning, inequality that is economically inefficient can be explained as rational and justified only if it serves some other social goal (liberty, respect for the market, preference for lotteries, or the like).

(5) In general, since equality of income is both desirable and costly, the optimum will involve a compromise—a sacrifice of efficiency to gain more equality than would obtain in the absence of social action, but a tolerance of more inequality than would be preferred in the absence of the costs.

(6) While various aspects of the trade-off are amenable to economic analysis and even to empirical quantification, the optimal compromise must be sought through political decision making. And society has clearly stated its choice for that mechanism—democracy untainted by economic inequality.

The Preference for Equality

When an economist is asked to determine what amount of X is optimal for an individual or for a society, he immediately divides the question into two parts: (1) How much does the decision maker in question like X, in varying quantities? (2) What does it cost to get those varying quantities of X? To noneconomists, this division may appear to be an unnecessary abstraction or complication—or, as Irving Kristol has put it, a flight into "poetry or theology."[2] But it is the only way to use the tools of our trade. The strict separation of preferences and opportunities is essential in organizing the considerations that enter into rational choice.

One application of the economist's approach lies in drawing inferences about preferences from behavior with respect to close substitutes that have sharply different relative prices. Only because of a strong preference do we use any amount of the high-priced item, as we do when we put expensive gold in our teeth and TV

---

[2] Irving Kristol, "The High Cost of Equality," *Fortune*, vol. 92 (November 1975), p. 199.

sets, and make room for costly lobster in our diets. To a capitalistic nation, accepting the verdict of the marketplace on income distribution is the low-cost diet. That we leave considerable economic inequality on our menu is no more surprising or instructive than is the fact the individuals eat more codfish than lobster. What is striking is that our society takes some steps toward equalization, reflecting a preference for more equality of income among our citizens than the market would generate.

The underlying rationale of the social preference for economic equality has been propounded in many ways. I shall discuss briefly a few of the formulations: (1) my own technique of drawing inferences from the domain of rights; (2) John Rawls's "original position" formulation; and (3) the classical argument based on interpersonal comparisons of utility.

Inferences from Rights. In our political and social arrangements, society diligently pursues equality. American institutions strive for one-person/one-spouse, one-person/one-vote, equal justice, universal freedom of speech and religion, universal immunity from enslavement, and universal and equal claims for such public services as police protection and public education. They also impose on all citizens, at least in principle, some "negative rights," or duties, such as responsibility to obey the law, military conscription when imposed, and jury service.[3]

These social and political rights reveal a preference for treating people equally. This preference is embodied in the proposition that all men are created equal, a proposition obviously intended as a social principle rather than an enunciation of a biological fact. That principle in turn fits Rawls's conception that people see equality as a type of "mutual respect . . . owed to human beings as moral persons." [4]

Our institutional rules suggest that the pure preference (abstracting from costs and consequences) for social and political equality is monotonic—that is, more equality is better than less, and complete equality best of all. The costs of equalization can account for society's countenancing of some inequality of rights and its failure to achieve Rawls's "lexical ordering" which would prevent any inequality of other assets from compromising equality in the domain of basic liberties.[5] In the strict sense, precisely equal justice would require every defendant at a criminal trial to have an equal chance of being represented by F. Lee Bailey. Absolute purity of equal suffrage would involve a ban on all resource-using ways of expressing partisan political sentiments. The costs of purity justify the toleration of some impurity and the adoption of criteria for practical rather than perfect equality in the domain of rights.

To be sure, a society might adopt egalitarian sociopolitical practices even though it did not have a preference for equality. If a preferred distribution with

---

[3] Okun, *Equality and Efficiency*, pp. 6-10.
[4] John Rawls, *A Theory of Justice* (Cambridge: Harvard University Press, 1971), p. 511.
[5] Ibid., pp. 302-303.

structured inequality could be obtained only by very expensive or cumbersome methods, equal rights might be adopted rationally as the less desirable but also less costly alternative—as a purely instrumental rather than a normative choice. Thus, an individual (or a society) might wish votes to be allocated according to competence or spouses according to "need" and yet despair of any satisfactory (low-cost, operational, and objective) means of achieving that allocation. In particular, such an individual or society might see a high risk that any structured inequality would be administered by government officials in ways creating distortion and discrimination among citizens.

On this argument, the nice thing about counting heads is that the calculation is so simple and objective that it defies (or at least resists) deliberate perversion by a bureaucracy. This seems to be the source of the support of equal and universal rights by some libertarians; they turn to equality only out of dire need of an objective rule that constrains the state and the bureaucracy, or in despair of an operational rule for achieving the structured inequality they would prefer. On that line of reasoning, if there were an agreed-upon objective test of political competence, it would be used to allocate votes. I do not believe that "prediction." It is inconsistent with the way society rules out the objective test of voluntary exchange in the assignment of rights and duties, banning trades in votes, jury duty, and conscripted military service and forbidding contracts for indentured service. Deliberately, specialization and comparative advantage are ruled out of the domain of rights. There is no logical escape from the conclusion that Americans have opted for equal rights because we like equality and not because some preferred inequality is difficult to achieve.

If such a preference for equality operates in the social and political realm, it must apply to the economic realm as well. It would be hard, indeed, to imagine any set of consistent social preferences that would give great weight to each citizen's freedom of speech (or suffrage, or any other right) and none to his ability to exercise that right in the face of malnutrition or inadequate health care. Starvation would, to put it mildly, compromise "mutual respect." In practice, American society implements its preference by equalizing incomes to some degree at some costs in many ways—conferring entitlements to expensive resource-using rights like public education, imposing progressive taxation, and supplying transfer benefits in the form of social security, food stamps, and welfare. Egalitarian preferences do not—and logically cannot—stop abruptly at the boundary line between economic and noneconomic institutions. The case for economic egalitarianism can be inferred from the equality of sociopolitical rights. Of course, that inference takes as given, rather than seeking to explain, social and political egalitarianism—a delimitation of inquiry that I, as an economist, find convenient and intellectually defensible.

I would not argue that all of the economic inequality society tolerates is necessarily attributable to the perception of the costs of eliminating it. There may be a pure preference to leave some lottery—some inequality—in the income and wealth distribution.[6] Or, as I shall discuss below, there may be some value attached to the market's verdict. Moreover, the concept of complete or perfect economic equality is a will-o'-the-wisp which fortunately we need not chase.[7]

The "Original Position." John Rawls develops the general case for social, political, and economic equality by invoking a social-contract process: people in an "original position" frame a constitution in ignorance of their class position in the future society and their relative standing with respect to assets and abilities.[8] In particular, they will determine the distribution of the lottery tickets in an urn from which every individual's income will be drawn. From the vantage point of the original position, each participant must view his or her future income as a random drawing from the urn; given the absence of any clues on whether their own tickets will be high or low, all participants would be mutually disinterested. The risk aversion of individuals can then be relied on to produce a preference for equality. It can be safely predicted that the founding fathers and mothers would not design an urn that implied 50 percent probabilities of starvation and of great affluence.

I regard the "original position" as an appealing analytical device for establishing the social preference for equality. Rawls, however, goes far beyond this point by associating with that same process the "difference principle," which insists that "all social values . . . be distributed equally unless an unequal distribution of any . . . is to everyone's advantage"—in particular, to the advantage of the typical person in the least advantaged group.[9] If the difference principle (or "maximin" criterion) is intended as a prediction of how American citizens would behave in a hypothetical original position, I am confident that it is wrong. Contrary to what is implied by the difference principle, very few Americans would prefer an urn A whose tickets gave each and every family $14,000 a year to an urn B that provided 90 percent of all families with $20,000 and 10 percent with $13,900. As I interpret him, Rawls is really making a different "prediction": that, in the process of discussing the ethics under which the future society should operate, the founders would become impressed with the undesirability of taking advantage of the (unidentified) least fortunate members. Hence, they would adopt a constitutional provision against ever doing so, no matter how slightly and no matter for what benefit and return. I would doubt that prediction as well as the first (and, moreover, the principle is not ethically persuasive to me).

I would even be willing to "predict" various ways in which the original-position group would be willing to lower the minimum income in order to raise

[6] See the discussion of why people may like lotteries in Milton Friedman and L. J. Savage, "The Utility Analysis of Choices Involving Risk," *Journal of Political Economy*, vol. 56 (August 1948), pp. 279-304. Their model implies local areas of increasing marginal utility in the individual's utility function.

[7] Okun, *Equality and Efficiency*, pp. 70-73.

[8] Rawls, *Theory of Justice*, Chapter 4.

[9] Ibid., p. 62.

17

mean income, in violation of the difference principle. I suspect that they would behave in Rawlsian fashion insofar as it was necessary to insure against starvation, recognizing that the belly they fill may be their own. I would expect them to demand a large—but still finite—gain in mean income if they were to impose deprivation of a cultural (as well as a strictly physiological) character on the least fortunate members of society. There is even evidence on that issue: a sociological survey shows a widespread perception that the threshold of deprivation lies around half of the average income of the society.[10] I would expect them to show some special concern for the welfare of children. On the other hand, as I noted above, I would not be surprised if even their *ideal* embodied some lottery; for a given average, they might prefer the majority of people to be a little below the mean so that a few could obtain some worthwhile prizes. In principle, psychologists could take some of the conjecture (and some of the fun) out of this range of issues by designing experiments in which people selected the urn from which their "living standard" would be stochastically determined for a short period—if not for the lifetime of a society.

Interpersonal Comparisons? Both the inferences from rights and the original-position formulation are alternatives to the traditional foundation of economic egalitarianism—a foundation based on interpersonal comparisons of utility.[11] According to that line of reasoning, individuals experience diminishing marginal utility of income, as is demonstrated by their risk-avoiding behavior. When their incomes double, their economic welfare increases but does not double—as is evidenced by the fact that they will not bet their entire income double-or-nothing on the flip of a coin. If each individual experiences diminishing marginal utility of income, then the maximum utility for the whole society must be obtained when the marginal utility of all individuals is equated. And if all individual utility functions are the same, that must occur with complete equality of income.

The last assumption—that all individual utility functions are the same—is the critical one in this chain of reasoning. Since such a proposition about interpersonal comparisons of utility is not empirically verifiable, it must stand as a value judgment —all individuals *should* be treated as though they have the same utility functions. But that in itself is an egalitarian judgment; it "sneaks" an assumed preference for equality into the argument designed to establish that very preference. As Henry Simons once pointed out, that argument could prove treacherous to egalitarians.[12] Imagine a technological breakthrough in utility measurement: a new "utilometer"

[10] Lee Rainwater finds that the public's subjective attitudes correspond to this criterion. See *What Money Buys: Inequality and the Social Meanings of Income* (New York: Basic Books, 1974), pp. 41-63, 110-17.

[11] The interpersonal-comparison approach (and its doctrinal history) is discussed in Walter J. Blum and Harry Kalven, Jr., *The Uneasy Case for Progressive Taxation* (Chicago: University of Chicago Press, 1953), pp. 49-63.

[12] Henry C. Simons, *Personal Income Taxation* (Chicago: University of Chicago Press, 1938), pp. 10-14.

gives readings consistent with all other observations on any individual and yet different readings across individuals with identical incomes. The social-utility maximizers would then be committed to give especially large incomes to those citizens who are found to be efficient generators of utility. If the empty box of interpersonal comparison were ever filled, the contents might be explosive.

The appeal of the original-position approach is that it can rest its case on diminishing marginal utility without invoking interpersonal comparisons. It focuses on the way one individual would choose among urns that have large or small variances in payoffs, and relies on the well-established diminishing marginal utility of the individual to predict a preference for low variance or equality. But the "intrapersonal" comparison it requires is strained and artificial: Its "veil of ignorance" about one's own capacities introduces an element of split personality. To ensure that the participants are truly disinterested, they are not allowed to "know themselves." But that still seems analytically preferable to interpersonal comparisons.

The new egalitarian literature should render obsolete the approach based on interpersonal comparisons. Yet it is clear why the traditional approach dies hard. With interpersonal comparisons, it becomes possible to rank various Pareto-optimal states (that is, situations where no reallocation can make some better off without making some worse off) in terms of aggregate or social utility, with the higher rankings going to the more nearly equal distributions. By that standard, society misallocates resources when it distributes badly, much as it misallocates resources when it produces badly. It may then legitimately be called "waste" when the garbage of the rich contains better food than the diet of the poor, or when more land is devoted to one private estate than to the homes of a thousand average families.

In contrast, the inferences-from-rights and original-position approaches impose on us an awkward two-stage process of defining optimality. In the first stage, those approaches must accept any and all Pareto-optimal distributions as "efficient" (in terms of preferences revealed through voluntary exchange or dollar-voting)—none involves waste. In the second stage some will be judged better than others insofar as they are more consistent with society's preference for equality—a preference that is exhibited through ballot voting and that is not readily quantifiable in dollars. The analysis must grapple with two sets of considerations—one associated with economic efficiency and the other with the preference for equality. Clearly, this is more cumbersome than the one-step approach of interpersonal comparisons—sufficiently more cumbersome to make me wish I could accept the latter. But I cannot.

The Cost of Equalization

In our capitalistic economy, the marketplace determines the prices of factors of production—labor and various types of physical property. Given the ownership of the productive factors (which is itself strongly influenced by the market over the longer run), the factor prices in turn determine the incomes of the citizenry. That market-determined incomes provide incentives and signals that contribute to efficiency has been the main story told by the economics profession for two centuries. But market-determined incomes also generate the economic inequality we dislike. Equalizing income thus implies modifying, vetoing, or supplanting the market determination, and therein lies its cost.

Doubters raise many searching questions about the efficiency of the real-world (as distinct from the competitive-model) marketplace. Does more real gross national product really mean more welfare? How seriously are consumer choices distorted by misinformers and "hidden persuaders"? How important is monopoly, which confers income as a reward for promoting scarcity rather than productivity? How serious are uncorrected externalities, excess supplies and demands? These issues are crucial, but I will ignore them in this paper—because they are so broad and complex.

All in all, I find the efficiency arguments in favor of the marketplace persuasive. These arguments have both a static and a dynamic component—getting the right things produced today and achieving progress tomorrow. The dynamic component can be further split into two parts: the importance of market incentives to accumulate physical capital (save and invest) and to innovate. I see the dynamic considerations as more important than the static considerations, and innovation as far more significant than accumulation.

Indeed, I believe that concern about accumulation incentives is grossly over-emphasized in debates on redistribution.[13] The national saving-and-investment rate is, in fact, a result of political decisions—and should be explicitly faced as such. Society can have the saving-and-investment rate it wants with more or less inequality of income, so long as it is willing to twist some other dials, involving the capital-building component of public budgets, the mix of fiscal-monetary policy, and the taxation of middle-income savers and investors. In the area of innovation, collective action (such as publicly financed basic research) is essential to rescue the market from the appalling inefficiency of private property in knowledge.[14] Yet the market does provide vital incentives for experimentation and innovation that cannot be replaced on a collectivized basis. That is where the really large dynamic costs of any drastic income redistribution are likely to be found.

The basic technique of redistribution actually employed in our society lies in the tax-transfer reshuffle. It appeals to me in principle and in practice. It allows a first-round distribution of income that is dictated by market verdicts and then modifies the results by imposing progressive taxation and by supplying resource-using rights (public goods) to all and transfer benefits (the equivalent of negative taxes) to the poor. With very few exceptions, this second-round redistribution

---

[13] Okun, *Equality and Efficiency*, pp. 98-100.
[14] Ibid., pp. 57-60.

cannot be carried out costlessly: as I like to put it, we can transport money from rich to poor only in a leaky bucket.[15] Some obvious leakages include administrative and compliance costs of implementing both tax and transfer programs, altered and misplaced work efforts resulting from them, and distortion of innovative behavior as well as saving and investment behavior. The most insidious attacks on an equalization program are those that view the discovery of any leakage as prima facie evidence against the desirability of the program. Holding it up to a standard of perfection, or zero leakage, guarantees a negative verdict. A social preference for equality implies a willingness to pay some costs for equalization.

Given (1) a social preference for equality (or at least for more equality than market-determined incomes provide), and (2) a cost of altering the market-determined distribution, society faces a trade-off between equality and efficiency. The resulting optimum will normally be a compromise.[16] Some efficiency will be sacrificed by altering the market's verdict through a second-round redistribution in the direction of greater equality. But some economic inequality will be left because it preserves economic efficiency (or some other social value, a point discussed below). Thus, society will carry the leaky bucket to pursue equality up to the point where the added benefits of more equality are just matched by the added costs of lesser efficiency.

These formal principles have significant implications. For one thing, they put into perspective the often-asked question, "How much equalization of income is enough?" That issue is no different from how large a capital stock or how large a police force or how large a computer is "enough." For all, the optimal "enough" is reached when the next unit costs more than it is worth. So long as benefits and costs are continuous, both fanaticism and complacency about equalization are ruled out of bounds. Second, the principles supply sufficient grounds for society's acting to alter the results of the income distribution. In particular, the preference for equality implies that the overall tax structure must be progressive and not proportional.[17] As Henry Simons suggested long ago, the case for progressive taxes rests on the proposition that inequality is "unlovely." [18] In principle, the necessary and sufficient case for the tax-transfer reshuffle is that simple.

The formal rules do not prescribe what public policy ought to do, but they strongly suggest what public policy questions the country ought to discuss. First, the political dialogue should focus explicitly on the intensities of social preference

---

[15] Ibid., pp. 91-95.

[16] In principle, the possibility of a "corner optimum" cannot be ruled out. If the cost of even the first dollar's worth of redistribution exceeded the benefits of its added equalization, zero redistribution would be optimal. At the other extreme, if the benefits of eliminating the last dollar's worth of inequality exceeded the costs of doing so, zero inequality would be optimal. Neither of these extremes appears to have any empirical relevance, unless one invokes a "principle" against any redistribution or any inequality.

[17] Again, this assumes that there will be no corner optimum.

[18] Simons, *Personal Income Taxation*, pp. 18-19.

in favor of equality: I wish that the opinion researchers would give us the public's answers to my leaky-bucket experiment. Second, economists and other social scientists should be striving to measure the leakages and the effective equalization accomplished by various programs of taxation, transfer benefits, and public goods. The effort to quantify the trade-off ought to cover not only existing programs but also such proposals as guarantees of job opportunity, subsidization of low wages, and new forms of subsidy to higher education.

As I read the serious empirical studies of the larger and better-established programs of taxation and income maintenance, I am impressed by the small size of the leakages they find; often 80 or even 90 percent of the contents seem to stay in the bucket. I am also encouraged by the evidence that the programs can be made even more efficient; there are opportunities to plug some of the leaks. Understandably, the leakages seem especially small for aid to the aged, where disincentives to work are not a serious problem. The major leakages in our present old-age security program seem to be confined to its options for early retirement and its structure of minimum benefits (which subsidizes groups like federal workers that do not contribute during most of their careers).

One of the key unsettled empirical issues involves the effects of education on both productivity and wage differentials. The "human capitalists" and the "screeners" in the profession have been slugging it out for years on the social productivity of education.[19] According to either view, a national increase in education reduces the dispersion of labor incomes. But the size of the leakage from such a route to equality depends on how much the investment in education raises productivity. On that issue, the human capitalists are optimistic, while the screeners paint the bleak picture that the investment serves mainly private ends by providing a job-screening device based on relative education. The recent work of Tinbergen offers impressive evidence on the responsiveness of differentials between the wages of the skilled and the unskilled to increases in the supply of educated workers.[20] As he suggests, a policy of saturation of human capital—investment in human capital that is overinvestment relative to any efficiency criterion—may be an important option for reducing the inequality of labor income. Still, the size of the resulting leakage depends on the relative importance of human capital and screening—an issue on which much more research is needed.

As Jan Pen said in his review of my book, "A quantitative guess about the rate of transformation between efficiency and equality still seems beyond the intellectual capacities of our profession. . . ." [21] He is right that this was an especially "sketchy" part of my book; I claim no special expertise in the measurement of

---

[19] See the discussion in Paul Taubman and Terence Wales, *Higher Education and Earnings* (New York: McGraw-Hill, 1974), Chapters 1, 2, 9.

[20] Jan Tinbergen, *Income Distribution: Analysis and Policies* (Amsterdam: North-Holland, 1975).

[21] Jan Pen, "Review/Equality and Efficiency: The Big Tradeoff," *Challenge,* vol. 18 (January-February 1976), p. 61.

leakages or benefits. Hence, my main message remains an appeal to the public and to the profession to sharpen the focus on the trade-off.

The Puzzle of Inefficient Inequality

By the reasoning above, since inequality and inefficiency are both undesirable, society should not be expected to tolerate an arrangement that exacerbates both (unless the arrangement happens to promote some other social goal). Yet, there are uncorrected situations that contribute to both inequality and inefficiency. One of the clearest and most significant is the disadvantage low-income citizens suffer in access to capital. Clearly, the poor face effective interest rates higher than those faced by the rich. This inequality in turn increases the inequality of the income distribution, particularly by discouraging investments in human capital by the poor.[22] The discrimination by lenders can arise from their natural self-interest— the invisible hand; it does not *necessarily* reflect any intended bias on their part. The risk to the lender depends on the borrower's total ability to repay, on the reliability of his signature. Hence, to the lender, a loan to a low-income person is riskier than one to a high-income borrower, even if the former is proposing to use the money for a project with a distinctly higher probability of success. But the risk to society lies in the use of resources for unproductive projects, and this is quite separate from the question of whether the lender is repaid. Thus, a socially efficient allocation of capital would require that funds flow to the particular projects that are most likely to succeed, regardless of the wealth of the prospective entrepreneurs. The market's result, therefore, involves misallocation—inefficiency as well as inequality.

Why does society tolerate such a source of additional inefficiency and additional inequality? Surely, the discrimination does not promote other social values. Indeed, it is not condoned: witness the hortatory speeches by public officials asking bankers to take care of the poor; consider the specific social programs designed to ameliorate this bias—the Federal Housing Administration, Small Business Administration, student loan programs, and the rest. I think that the real answer lies simply in the limitations of public-sector technology: it is not easy to design effective, low-cost, public programs that would improve the access of low-income groups to capital. Innovations by social scientists in this area could help to reduce both inefficiency and inequality.

The more complex case of job discrimination based on race or sex presents similarities as well as instructive contrasts to discrimination in the access to capital. Both biases misallocate and distort investments in human capital. For example, the woman who knows she will be unlikely to get a management job has no incentive to invest in training to qualify as a manager. But the effect on income

---

[22] Okun, *Equality and Efficiency,* pp. 79-82.

inequality of job bias is not necessarily as pronounced as the effect of the lending bias. Because disadvantage in access to capital is geared directly to low income and low wealth, it must increase inequality; that need not be the case for ethnic job discrimination. For example, the average income of Jews exceeded that of other Americans at times when anti-Semitic job discrimination was widespread. In such exceptional cases, equalizing opportunity (and enhancing other social values such as fairness) may actually increase the inequality of income.

Furthermore, job discrimination (unlike the lending bias) could *conceivably* be "perfect," in the same sense that monopolistic price discrimination can be perfect, altering distribution but avoiding inefficiency and leaving social surplus intact. Under conditions of perfect job discrimination, blacks and women (and other victims of prejudice) would get exactly the same jobs they would obtain if not disadvantaged but would merely receive less pay for them. In fact, however, the prevalence of exclusion from good jobs (rather than exploitation involving lower wages) as the technique of discrimination makes substantial inefficiency a by-product of inequality.[23]

Finally, unlike the case with lending, some people *must* have preferences for discrimination when job selections are biased sexually or ethnically.[24] Those discriminators obviously lost welfare when legislation enforcing equal employment opportunity was enacted, at the same time that real GNP was increased and the welfare of the victims of discrimination was enhanced. But I do not believe that the legislation should be interpreted as the embodiment of a new conviction that the welfare gained by others outweighed the welfare lost by discriminators. The legal ban on stealing a loaf of bread does not imply a judgment that the bread stealer would gain less utility than would be lost by the potential victim. The relevant social judgment is that he would be violating the rights of others and that his own utility from such activity should be disregarded. Indeed, any system of law involves decisions that certain types of preferences are inadmissible elements in a social utility function and should not be allowed to influence allocation. The political decision outlawing job discrimination reclassified preferences for discrimination as inadmissible—placing them with preferences in favor of bread stealing. By that interpretation, an appraisal of the social pluses and minuses of equal employment opportunity should not subtract from its total benefits the welfare loss imposed on those with preferences for discrimination. But here again the technology for ruling out such preferences is sorely inadequate, as is evidenced by the

---

[23] Taking account of such dynamic influences as the costs and benefits of education and training, I doubt that long-run "perfect" job discrimination is possible; but I also doubt that any perfectly discriminating monopolist can avoid dynamic inefficiency in the face of long-run substitution options.

[24] So-called statistical discrimination may provide an exceptional unintended rationale for job bias. For example, an employer finds that women statistically have higher quit rates and he gives preference to applicants who are likely to have low quit rates.

inefficient reliance on job quotas for implementing equality of employment opportunity.

In general, a clear case of inequality of opportunity emerges whenever anyone who comes to the marketplace is confronted with a "specially" unfavorable opportunity locus because of his or her personal characteristics rather than any peculiar properties of the package that he or she is offering to buy or sell. Insofar as that discrimination is practiced "imperfectly" and operates to push the person to the lower part of the income distribution, it contributes to both inequality of income and inefficiency of allocation. Wherever the social technology is available, rooting out such inequalities of opportunity offers a promising improvement in both equality and efficiency.

To the extent that inequality of opportunity breeds both inequality of income and inefficiency, there is a clear case for corrective social action that does not depend on a distinct preference for equality of opportunity. Yet, of course, society does have such a preference—a desire for fairness—which reinforces the case for correction. The social goals include both equalizing opportunity and equalizing results. Most Americans would agree that even fair races should not result in inhumane penalties on losers or unreasonable prizes for winners. In any case, the achievement of reasonable equality of opportunity in our society requires narrowing the inequality of results in which the current inequalities of opportunity are so deeply rooted.

The Relativism of the Market's Verdict

Throughout the analysis this far, I have assumed that citizens have preferences about the *results* of the economic process—the distribution of command over goods and services—that are distinguishable from their feelings about the method by which those results were obtained. This is a crucial assumption. Indeed, every serious analysis that urges society to cease modifying the income distribution is based on the contention that the market method is so good, or any method of modification so bad, that the market's verdict should be left intact.

In some important noneconomic areas, we do regard whatever results emerge as untouchable, because they are generated by an explicitly accepted ideal process. I do not believe that the winner of an election is always the best candidate, but I believe that it would be wrong to overturn the results. Similarly, I do not care whether a jury finds a particular defendant guilty or not; I care only that justice be done. And I am prepared to respect the jury's verdict, unless I learn that the intended process was violated by tampering or the like.

Unlike the jury's verdict, the market's verdict is not accepted as necessarily ultimate. The second-round "reshuffle" is established precisely to allow political decision making to second-guess the market. As revealed by our laws, the first-round process is not regarded as sacred, nor the second-round process as sinful.

25

The Market as Ideal. To be sure, generations ago the marginal productivity theory of factor pricing was invoked by some economists to demonstrate the justice of the income distribution generated by a competitive market economy. I know of no proponent of that view within the economics profession today (though Milton Friedman is ambivalent).[25]

That normative view dissolved in recognition of the enormous distinction between effort and output, of the accidental ("unmerited") variations in the value of marginal product stemming from shifts in demand, and of the dependence of each unit's marginal product on the inputs of other units, which implies the omnipresence of joint inputs (and really makes the social environment a basic joint input in everybody's production process). These considerations effectively rule out the attribution of merit or desert to the market outcome. The results of the first-round income distribution cannot be defended as fair rewards for personal contribution.

The concept of reward for contribution has an even more fundamental defect. It is the logic—perhaps the magic—of capitalism to make distribution a by-product of production; the value of products determines factor prices which in turn determine incomes. Thus, the value of extra marketable output created by the labor and property inputs of any producer is supposed to be returned to that producer in the form of command over marketable output. In that sense, each contributor takes out what he puts in; and it all appears very natural, very fair, and almost inevitable. But that appearance is convincing only in the narrow cultural context of a market economy.

Until the seventeenth century, productive contribution was not viewed as the key to income distribution. For militaristic, marauding, and slave-owning societies, the name of the game was obtaining command over goods and services *without* engaging in the labors of production. In both feudal and monastic societies, the carving up of the pie was governed by rules and customs that did not have much to do with contributions to the baking of that pie. Across the range of human societies, the penalty for slackers was often ostracism, physical punishment, or the threat of divine retribution, rather than deprivation from consumption. The notion that income rewards geared to productive contribution is a natural or self-evident principle is a symptom of market myopia; an excellent treatment for that disease is a careful reading of the works of Karl Polanyi.[26]

[25] See Milton Friedman, *Capitalism and Freedom* (Chicago: University of Chicago Press, 1962), pp. 161-65. For a sampling of libertarian authors who explicitly reject the ethical rationale for income distribution based on marginal productivity, see Frank H. Knight, *The Ethics of Competition and Other Essays* (New York: Harper, 1935), pp. 54-58; and F. A. Hayek, *The Constitution of Liberty* (Chicago: University of Chicago Press, 1960), pp. 93-100.

[26] See Karl Polanyi, "Our Obsolete Market Mentality," in George Dalton, ed., *Primitive, Archaic, and Modern Economies* (Boston: Beacon, 1971), esp. pp. 65-67; and *The Great Transformation* (New York: Farrar, 1944; Boston: Beacon, 1957). Another type of historical perspective on the evolution of market ideology in the nineteenth and twentieth centuries is provided by R. A. Gordon, "Adam Smith in the Twentieth Century," in Leonard S. Silk, ed., *Readings in Contemporary Economics* (New York: McGraw-Hill, 1970), pp. 37-44.

An appreciation of the relativism of market rewards can also be gleaned from contemporary noneconomic institutions. Students, soldiers, amateur athletes, club members, friends, and family members are not rewarded with a command over resources geared to their contribution to the "output" of the relevant community. The laissez-faire market economy is unique in presuming that people *should* take out the value of what they contributed.

The Specter of the State. Most contemporary arguments that oppose altering the market's verdict do not rely on enthusiasm for the market, but instead stress the negative aspects of the political second-guessing process. Rather than deifying the market, these theories vilify political decision making. Such arguments are deeply rooted in basic philosophical conceptions of the desirable role of the state. Two modern laissez-faire theories, developed by Friedrich Hayek and by Robert Nozick, can serve to illustrate the nature of the critical issues in this huge area.

According to Hayek, the function of government is to root out the evil of coercion, but the only way it can carry out that mission is "by the threat of coercion. Free society has met this problem by conferring the monopoly of coercion on the state and by attempting to limit this power of the state to instances where it is required to prevent coercion by private persons." [27] Moreover, except in the case of the monopoly of an essential service, market arrangements do not involve coercion, according to Hayek; they may impose hardship on individuals but not "true coercion." [28] Hence, any policies requiring coercion by the state to mitigate such noncoercive hardships would be improper, since they would serve purposes other than preventing coercion by private persons.[29] In Hayek's view, it is clearly appropriate for the citizens to authorize coercion by the state to keep them from killing one another: but it is wrong to empower the state to exercise coercion in order to prevent death by starvation that is imposed impersonally by the market. Our society is not impressed by that distinction, and neither am I.

In his presentation of the case against redistribution, Nozick offers an even more restricted concept of the desirable role of the state. He develops an invisible-hand explanation of the state: it arises from individuals hiring protective agencies to help enforce their rights; as a result of economies of scale, a single protective agency becomes dominant in the territory and thus achieves a monopoly position. Such a state could emerge "without violating anyone's rights," and only such a state can be justified.[30] The resulting "entitlement theory" of distributive justice

---

[27] Hayek, *Constitution of Liberty,* p. 21.

[28] Ibid., pp. 136-38.

[29] Hayek even manages to justify public services (and the coercive taxation to finance them) as coercion to prevent greater coercion: "We need only remember the role that the assured 'access to the King's highway' has played in history to see how important such rights may be for individual liberty." Ibid., pp. 141-42.

[30] See Robert Nozick, *Anarchy, State, and Utopia* (New York: Basic Books, 1974); a brief summary is presented on pp. 118-19.

makes the appropriateness of any distribution of assets depend entirely on the justice of their acquisition and transfer, and not at all on the dispersion of material welfare among individuals.[31]

Like John Locke, Nozick depends heavily on a concept of natural rights. Indeed, he concedes candidly that, to him, it is an assumption rather than a conclusion that "there is some set of principles obvious enough to be accepted by all men of good will, precise enough to give unambiguous guidance in particular situations, clear enough so that all will realize its dictates, and complete enough to cover all problems that actually will arise." [32]

That assumption about natural principles or laws is indispensable to Nozick's theory. The state obviously punishes people for breaking rules. Such law enforcement can be noncoercive (not violating anyone's rights) only if the rules are "natural"—prior to and independent of the state. Thus, it can be argued that, because of natural rights, no one has the right to steal property from his neighbor: hence, when the government enforces laws against theft, it is not infringing on any right.

Frankly, I find the natural-law approach mind-boggling. One of the many questions that mystify me is how John Locke and his disciples acquired the franchise for stipulating the set of natural laws. (Was that "just acquisition"?) Suppose, for a moment, that some intruder into this game advances, as a principle "obvious enough to be accepted by all men of good will," that no citizen of an affluent society should ever be seriously deprived of material sustenance. Thus he can claim that the state is merely enforcing natural law when it carries the leaky bucket. On what basis can he be told that he is wrong? More generally, why should natural laws restrict the state's function to that of a protective association, rather than including a role as an insurance association or a mutual benevolent association?

Varying Normative Attitudes toward the Market. Empowering the political process to second-guess the market does not imply complete neutrality—a purely instrumental attitude—toward the market. People can have preferences about the dispersion of incomes and still have preferences about the process by which income is obtained. Clearly, many Americans are market fans, who like a recognition of success that takes the form of additional command over material output; others are offended by the reliance on greed and competition, rather than fraternity and cooperation, as the key motivating forces in economic life.

The market fans would pay something (but not an unlimited amount) in terms of both efficiency and equality to extend the scope of market determination, while the others would make some sacrifice to narrow it. My own value judgments come out essentially neutral: I like the impersonality of the market process, and I become

---

[31] Ibid., pp. 150-53.
[32] Ibid., p. 141.

attached to instrumentalities that work well, but I have some negative feelings about greed and competition.

I prefer exceptionally good plumbers to average plumbers—no matter whether they are better because they are more energetic, or better trained, or better endowed genetically. But I personally want average plumbers to get less steak and smaller homes only insofar as such a structure of rewards and penalties elicits better productive performance. I believe, nonetheless, that the majority of my fellow citizens are market fans. Popular expressions of concern about work incentives, handouts, and welfare ripoffs go beyond regrets about waste in the tax-transfer reshuffle, implying some attachment to the market's principles of distribution. Suppose, for example, that the voters were offered two alternative programs that would achieve exactly the same total GNP with the same income distribution. Program A would increase transfer benefits, while program B would establish an inefficiently large subsidy for the training of unskilled workers, thus permitting some of them to earn higher pay in the marketplace. Even if it could be demonstrated that the two involved the same government expenditures, the same tax burdens, and the same leakages, I would predict that program B would be preferred by an overwhelming majority—both of those who would be taxed to finance the programs and of those who would be recipients of the benefits. Equalization that raises the wage income of the poor is more popular than transfers unconnected to work effort, and it would remain so even if it were demonstrably no more efficient.

The development of such attitudes is easy to understand. Once our laws permit affluence and poverty to coexist, our attitudes must allow the wealthy to enjoy their rewards without personal guilt and must countenance the poverty without social guilt. We become committed to make a judgment that the rich and the poor deserve what they get, or else we would feel morally obliged to narrow the disparities. In effect, the rules of the game legitimatize inequality and, at the same time, reinforce pecuniary incentives with invidious socioeconomic distinctions between productive and unproductive citizens. When it rewards success in the marketplace with social approval as well as with affluence and penalizes failure with social disapproval as well as with deprivation, society marshals a broad set of incentives for market-oriented behavior.

The market ethic has been sold to a mass market. Getting paid is "belonging" in the minds of most citizens. Sociological studies reveal that the poor really do want to work and would strongly prefer higher incomes that come from better-paying jobs rather than from more generous transfer benefits.[33] The surprisingly small disincentive effects of some income-maintenance programs may reflect the motivational force of the market ethic. That, in turn, cuts two ways. On the one hand, fairly generous transfers can be provided without encountering major leakages. On the other hand, the more general and generous the transfer programs

---

[33] Leonard Goodwin, *Do the Poor Want to Work?* (Washington, D.C.: The Brookings Institution, 1972), p. 112.

become, the more nonmarket income is legitimized, thereby ultimately weakening the market ethic and increasing the size of the leakages. By that reasoning, welfare checks delivered with a smile may be a dangerous product. Indeed, many affluent voters want to keep the frown in transfers that go to people who, in principle, could work. On the other hand, the careful design of a contributory theology—even mythology—in old-age insurance keeps the frown out of that program, as seems appropriate for recipients for whom work disincentives are not a serious problem. Whether or not he shares them, no egalitarian can afford to ignore these market-oriented ethical attitudes when designing and promulgating proposals for carrying the leaky bucket.[34]

Decentralization and Freedom

Beyond the realm of economic efficiency, the market serves a valuable function by diversifying power in the society and, in particular, by providing a counterweight to the power of the state. Following the principles of portfolio diversification, a sound and viable society will not put all its eggs in one basket. It will rely on many mechanisms for decision making, including the formal political process, informal voluntary associations, and organized systems of nonmonetary awards, as well as the market. That is, society strives for balance: giving the market its place and at the same time keeping it in its place.

Trade-off with Liberty? By providing for diversification and decentralization, the market contributes to personal liberty. I attach great importance to this contribution, as should be evident in several passages in my book.[35] But I do not see a general trade-off between equality and liberty, so long as equalization is pursued through the tax-transfer reshuffle and the other mechanisms that I recommend—which do not include extended government control over employment or greater public ownership of the means of production. In insisting that the second-round redistribution need not compromise liberty, I believe that I am making the same distinction that Henry Simons intended in the following passage: "What is important, for libertarians, is that we preserve the basic processes of free exchange and that egalitarian measures be superimposed on those processes, effecting redistribution afterward and not in the immediate course of production and commercial transactions." [36] Yet, I have been frequently criticized for my position on this issue. As Irving Kristol put it, ". . . the more fundamental antithesis, the real

[34] Although I mentioned this range of issues in *Equality and Efficiency* (pp. 48-49, 100, 116), I now think they deserve even greater emphasis. I have benefited from the comments of Daniel Yankelovich at the Public Affairs Outlook Conference of the Conference Board (New York, March 17, 1976).

[35] Okun, *Equality and Efficiency*, pp. 21-22, 38-40, 60, 119.

[36] Henry Simons, *Economic Policy for a Free Society* (Chicago: University of Chicago Press, 1948), p. 6.

tradeoff, is not between equality and efficiency but between equality and liberty." [37]
I believe that this disagreement is rooted in a confusion between liberty and private
property rights.

Of course, the size and scope of redistribution affect the level of tax rates in
our society (just as do the size of the defense and highway budgets). And, in a
meaningful sense, higher tax rates narrow the scope of private property rights. At
one extreme, absolute rights to private property imply zero taxation; and, at the
other, 100 percent taxation is just a polite description of confiscation. Thus, there
is a trade-off between the size of the tax-transfer reshuffle and the scope of private
property rights.

But even by the libertarian's "negative" definition of liberty—"the absence
of . . . coercion by other men" [38]—maximum liberty cannot be equated with the
maximum scope of private property rights, inasmuch as the latter extends the police
power of the state. Private property rights are exercised through voluntary exchange
in the marketplace, which in turn depends critically on the state's enforcement of
contracts. To be sure, contract enforcement may be viewed as refereeing rather
than policing, because it "merely" requires people to abide by their own voluntary
decisions. That is a valid distinction, although it must be applied consistently: if
laws that require voluntary exchange to be based on truthful statements do not
trespass on liberty, then regulations for accurate labeling and advertising, as well
as the legal enforcement of contracts, are exonerated from the charge of trespass.

The major exercise of coercion by the state applies, however, to people who
are *not* party to the particular contract. The protection of private property rights—
the enforcement of the "Keep-Off" sign—is the most pervasive encroachment on
liberty (in the sense of minimum coercion) in our society. I want the state to
exclude everyone else from the use of my toothbrush, and I would crusade for laws
enforcing the private ownership of toothbrushes, but I must concede that such
laws represent an extension of coercion by the state. However justified and self-
evident the case for promarket coercion may be, it is still coercion. The inability
of some libertarians to recognize coercion when it is exercised in behalf of the
market is an incomprehensible blind spot in their analysis.

The conflict between liberty and private property is dramatically evident for
those private property rights that are created out of thin air by the state—patents
and copyrights, common-carrier and broadcasting certificates, and, most significantly, the limited-liability joint-stock corporation. I favor all of these useful institutions, but they all extend the exercise of coercion by the state. When the government grants an exclusive patent to one agent for a promising new antibiotic like
Minocin, it is broadening the scope of private property rights; but it is imposing

[37] Kristol, "High Cost of Equality," p. 200. See also James Grant, "Government in Exile?
The Brookings Institution Wields Tremendous Clout," *Barron's*, vol. 55 (October 27, 1975),
p. 17; and M. Bronfenbrenner, "Book Reviews, Equality and Efficiency: The Big Tradeoff,"
Journal of Economic Literature, vol. 13 (September 1975), pp. 917-18.
[38] Hayek, *Constitution of Liberty,* p. 19.

coercion on everybody else—on 99.99999953 percent of the population. By comparison, when the government bans the sale of a dangerous chemical like Kepone, it removes a private property right, opposite to the Minocin case; and it applies coercion to 100 percent of the population—only trivially different from the former case. Clearly, if all society cared about was maximizing liberty (minimizing coercion), the state should keep its hands off both Minocin and Kepone.

The cases of the altered and unaltered income distribution are to me like the Kepone-Minocin pair in these respects: the altered distribution significantly narrows the scope of private property, but does not significantly enlarge the scope of coercion. The trade-off arises between the maximum scope of private property rights on the one hand and both liberty and equality on the other, not between liberty and equality.

Maximizing the scope of private property does not maximize efficiency any more than it maximizes liberty. Within even the narrowest purview of the most abstract model of a competitive economy, efficiency requires public actions to deal with externalities, public goods, pervasive economies of scale, and incentives to destroy competition. The scope of private property rights is clearly reduced by even these minimal requirements, like public ownership of lighthouses and navigable rivers, smoke-abatement action, antimerger legislation, and regulation of the telephone company.

In my view, we can afford to deal pragmatically with the modifications of property rights required both to enhance efficiency and to increase equality, so long as the balance between the political system and the market system stays in the zone that ensures decentralization. When technology opens new areas of potentially important externalities (like the noise of SSTs and the locations of nuclear power plants), and when our affluence and our attitudes enlarge the tax-transfer reshuffle, a gradual expansion of the scope and size of the public sector is a rational response that leaves us well within the safety zone.

Democracy, Discretion, and Demagoguery

There is no Lorenz curve that I or anyone else could unveil as the optimal target for the society. I was not bashful about spelling out my personal preferences in my book, although there is no reason why they should appeal to others. I do, however, hope to persuade others to share my views about the preconditions for optimization—a more focused public dialogue on the intensities of preferences for equality and a greater research effort by social scientists on the measurement of the leakages. In short, I am pleading for us all to face up to the trade-off between equality and efficiency.

In aiming for a crystallization of social attitudes toward the trade-off and in aiming for their implementation, I am counting on effective, enlightened, democratic political decision making. I am well aware that such a course has its dangers.

One is the danger of big and erratic changes in the rules of the game. In a majoritarian political system with two political parties, the tax-transfer reshuffle and the scope of resource-using rights might undergo a drastic overhaul whenever power changed hands. Extreme uncertainty about the future levels and progressivity of taxes, for example, could pose a serious threat to efficiency. Moreover, abrupt shifts would raise questions of fairness to those people who had accumulated wealth with a reasonable expectation that the general levels of taxation imposed on property income and wealth transfer would continue.

Obviously, one sure remedy for the concern that anything might go is the establishment of a principle that nothing goes. But the need for predictability cannot justify that solution. A constitutional amendment that established extremely high and progressive rates for income and estate taxes would provide as much certainty as one that repealed them. In fact, taxes and transfers have been treated as standard kinds of legislation, enactable by simple majorities of both houses of Congress and subject to veto by the President. Yet, those laws have been subject to remarkable continuity rather than to erratic fluctuation. Major structural changes in the tax base or the scope of transfer programs have at times been phased in gradually, often with a grandfather clause. Unlike some other nations, we have not imposed federal taxes on the holding of wealth (as distinguished from property income or the transfer of wealth), in part because the initiation of such a tax might be "retroactive." The political process has displayed a great respect for continuity; on the whole, I find that reassuring.

The much graver danger is that the democratic process may become myopic in confronting the trade-off between equality and efficiency. Much of the gain from a redistributive program is immediate, while many of the efficiency costs are delayed and, indeed, less obvious than the gain. When the lowest 51 percent of families in the distribution have only a quarter of all income and only one-twentieth of all wealth, is there an adequate safeguard against a demogogue who might irresponsibly promise a majority of voters a "fair share" of the pie?

Some market enthusiasts have a recurrent nightmare in which the mob wrecks the bakeries in its quest for bread. As I see it, that nightmare has not materialized in American political and economic life, but I suspect that the security of the wealthy has been ensured because money has bought political power. Indeed, I believe that the use of money to acquire voting rights has blunted the political expression of majoritarian preferences for equality. As a result of recent legislation to curb the counterfeiting of votes, we will get a test of the operation of a more democratic political process.

At the moment, we are experiencing a disturbing divisiveness of attitudes. Recent efforts to curb the market's transgression on equal political rights have frightened those who hold the bulk of the wealth (and think that they therefore hold the bulk of the truth), and have aroused antidemocratic political sentiments. There is a more obvious growth of anticapitalistic sentiments by the nonaffluent.

Profits and *rich* are often dirty words in the halls of Congress. The rationing and allocative functions of the price system are blithely ignored by many of our legislators. Instead of blending the values of capitalism and democracy, many are pitting them against each other. Instead of compromising, we are polarizing. The nation sorely needs a serious dialogue and a major educational undertaking to develop the enlightened attitudes of compromise, and I hope that this conference will help meet that urgent national need.

THOUGHTS ON EQUALITY AND EGALITARIANISM

Irving Kristol

Is There a "Problem" in the Distribution of Income in the United States Today?
We are frequently assured that there is, and are confronted with Census Bureau
statistics to prove it. Those statistics, widely quoted, show that the top 20 percent
of American families get 40 percent of the national income, while the lowest
20 percent of the population get only 5 percent. The statistics are accurate
enough—but they are also widely misleading.

One reason they are misleading is that they refer only to cash income. They
omit in-kind transfers (such as Medicare, Medicaid, food stamps, and subsidized
housing)—and it is precisely such in-kind transfers that have characterized most
social reforms of the past fifteen years. Edgar K. Browning has shown that, once
such in-kind transfers are included, the lowest 20 percent of American families get
almost 12 percent of the national income, the top 20 percent about 33 percent.[1]
That is still a good distance short of absolute equality, of course. But very few
of those who express concern about inequality think that absolute equality is a
reasonable ideal. In what sense, then, is it a "problem" for our society if the
distribution of income is such that the top 20 percent of the population gets 33 percent of the income?

Moreover, even this revised picture grossly exaggerates the degree of income
inequality because the statistics are not corrected for age. Clearly, young people
who have recently entered the labor force and old people who have left it will
have significantly lower incomes than those in mid-career. Even in a strictly egalitarian society, where everyone's lifetime income is equal, a cross-cut statistical
snapshot at any one moment will show substantial inequality.

The statistical problems involved in correcting the picture of income distribution for age are formidable, and there are no meaningful percentages to be quoted.
But where statistical precision is lacking, common sense will take us at least part
of the way. Let us assume that any revision which takes account of age has only
modest effects—that, perhaps, it will show the top 20 percent of the population
receiving 28 to 30 percent of the national income. Does this degree of inequality
represent an "inequity"? Is it a "problem"? What percentage will a "moderate"

---

[1] Edgar K. Browning, "How Much More Equality Can We Afford?" *Public Interest,* no. 43
(Spring 1976), pp. 90-110. See also idem, *Redistribution and the Welfare System* (Washington,
D.C.: American Enterprise Institute, 1975).

35

egalitarian (or a "moderate" inegalitarian—it comes to the same thing) like Arthur Okun be satisfied with? One really does need to know the substance of such moderation, if one is to pass a sensible judgment on it.

What Is the Relation between Poverty and Income Inequality? A major source of the interest in equality arises from the desire to eradicate, or at least alleviate, poverty. The notion that income redistribution is the effective means to this end is age-old: one finds it expressed in the civil strife of the Greek city-states, the medieval peasant rebellions, the Socialist movements of the past 200 years. But if the modern science of economics has taught us anything, it is that the connection is usually spurious.

The redistribution impulse is most powerful today in those poor countries— the so-called less-developed countries—where it makes least sense. In such countries, the alleviation of poverty is *utterly* dependent on economic growth. There never is enough money among the small number of wealthy citizens to make a significant dent in the poverty of the masses. When the rich are expropriated in such countries, everyone becomes equal in poverty—though the political authorities who do the expropriating usually end up being more equal than the rest.

Even in affluent developed societies, where the poor are a minority, the alleviation of poverty is mainly—though not absolutely—dependent on economic growth. The one instance where it makes sense to think of income redistribution as a cure for poverty involves the aged and infirm—that portion of the population who are not and never will be in the labor force because they are by nature dependent. If, over these past fifteen years, we had concentrated our attention and resources on these people, all of them would be well above the poverty level by now. This would have only a slight—but not negligible—effect on the statistics of income distribution, and would not make our radical egalitarians any happier. But it would make the aged and infirm happier.

The idea of "abolishing poverty" generally through income redistribution, however, turns out to be a will-o'-the-wisp, even in our affluent United States. It is not a statistical will-o'-the-wisp, only an actual one. It is indeed *easy* to "abolish poverty" statistically. But one then discovers that this statistical achievement is quite meaningless, in human terms.

Let us draw the poverty line at a fairly high level—at one-half the median income. (This is the level preferred by most liberal reformers, as distinct from the official "subsistence" level fixed by government.) In New York City, where the politicians are notoriously compassionate, we have achieved even that high level. A family of four on welfare receives, in cash and kind, between $7,000 and $7,500 a year. The median household income in the United States is about $12,500 annually.) *We have abolished poverty in New York City!* So why hasn't anyone noticed?

The reason is that, for many of the nonaged and noninfirm, poverty turns out to be more than a simple shortage of money. Poverty as a human condition, as distinct from a statistical condition, is defined to a substantial degree by the ways in which one copes with poverty. A visitor to the Greek islands, or to an Italian village, is impressed first of all not by the poverty of the people there—which is acute—but by their cheerfulness, their determination to make the best of things, and their extraordinary ability to do so. The world of yesteryear portrayed in the movie *Fiddler on the Roof* is another such instance: those East European Jews were as poor as synagogue mice, but their poverty was less significant to them than their religious life, their family life, their communal life. And the United States, at this very moment, is populated by several thousand "communes" whose residents voluntarily (sometimes eagerly) accept a standard of living far below the average.

And what is true for poverty is also true for the abolition of poverty: *the way in which poverty is abolished turns out to be more important than the statistical abolition itself.* In New York, we have tried to abolish poverty through a generous welfare program, and have therewith rediscovered the truth of an old adage: dependency tends to corrupt and absolute dependency corrupts absolutely. Our welfare population, statistically lifted out of poverty, has actually and simultaneously sunk to various depths of social pathology. It is largely a demoralized population, with higher rates of crime, juvenile delinquency, drug addiction, teenage pregnancy, and alcoholism than when their welfare checks were less generous.[2] It is not at all implausible to think that, had we been less generous in our welfare program, these people would now be better off. Some black nationalists, who see welfare as a "neocolonialist" conspiracy, have come to think this, and one need not accept their premises to agree with their conclusions. After all, are the poor blacks in Birmingham, Alabama (where welfare is stingy), really worse off—do they even think of themselves as being worse off—than the poor blacks in Bedford-Stuyvesant or Harlem? No comprehensive, comparative study has been made. Indeed, liberal scholars, liberal politicians, and liberal foundation officials will fight vigorously against the very idea of such a study—which in itself is a kind of answer.

Meanwhile, of course, there are many poor people (including, of course, poor blacks) in this country who are too proud to go on welfare, who prefer to work hard at low-paying jobs, earning less than if they had gone on welfare—and whose spirits are undestroyed, whose lives are less afflicted, and whose children are less likely to "get into trouble." Here again, one would like to see a comparative study

---

[2] The reason for this demoralization is obvious enough, though scholars with a middle-class background have difficulty in perceiving it. Being a "breadwinner" is the major source of self-respect for a man or woman working at a tedious low-paying job that offers few prospects for advancement. It is also the major source of such respect as he (or she) receives from family, friends, and neighbors. When welfare provides more generously for his (or her) family than a breadwinner can, he (or she) becomes a superfluous human being. Both self-respect and respect soon crumble, family ties unravel, and a "culture of poverty" sets in that has more to do with the welfare system than with poverty itself.

of those two groups of poor people. But when the state of California tried to sponsor one, liberal academe and the liberal media denounced and killed the idea.

The trouble with any massive scheme of income redistribution as a way of "abolishing poverty" is not merely its impact on marginal rates of taxation for most Americans, and hence its negative effect on efficiency and economic growth—an effect that is generally conceded even if its importance is debatable. One could contemplate, in good conscience, a somewhat lower standard of living for the average American family if this would result in a more contented political community. But the evidence is clear that trying to abolish poverty through income distribution results in nothing of the sort. The evidence is also clear that when poverty is abolished through economic growth, something real and desirable has occurred. The history of the United States since 1940 testifies to the truth of this latter proposition. What happened to the "Okies" that Steinbeck and others wrote so poignantly about? What happened to the poor whites who, in most American cities (and all American movies), lived on "the other side of the tracks"? And what is happening in Appalachia today, where a boom in coal mining is accomplishing what a dozen government programs failed to do?

However, the antithesis between equality and efficiency is real enough where redistribution has become an end in itself and egalitarianism has become fanatical. This is evidently the case in the United Kingdom today, where a massive redistribution has indeed taken place, and where the society as a whole is getting poorer with every passing year. Twenty years ago, there was no noteworthy "poverty problem" in Britain. As things are now going, however, there will surely be one tomorrow.

On "Fairness" as "Equal Sacrifice." Most of us would agree that a progressive income tax is inherently "fair"—even Adam Smith was of that opinion. But it is important to understand *why* it is fair. In recent years, the idea has been propagated and popularized that it is fair because it makes for greater after-tax equality of condition. But that was not the original purpose of the income tax, or the original conception of "fairness" behind it.

The original purpose of the income tax was to raise revenues for increased public expenditure—more often than not, increased military expenditures, but in any case expenditures deemed to be necessary. Now, taxation is a hardship for the citizenry, and increased taxation is an increased hardship. Under these circumstances, "fairness" can legitimately be equated with *equality of sacrifice*—which, in the case of taxation, means distributing the burden according to one's "ability to pay." [3]

---

[3] In my opinion, it is the huge level of the military budget that justifies a *progressive* income tax as distinct from a *proportionate* income tax (in which everyone above a certain level pays the same proportion of his income as tax). In wartime, it is generally agreed that "fairness" requires everyone to be equally inconvenienced, and it is the progressive income tax that incorporates this consensus. A large peacetime military budget (or a large public debt resulting

Equality of sacrifice is "fair," is a valid principle, in preparing for moments of crisis, in enduring moments of crisis, or in coping with the consequences of moments of crisis. It is also a valid principle when the citizenry commissions the government to achieve certain extraordinary objectives. But "equality of sacrifice" is *not* a valid principle when casually applied to the everyday life of a society and the normal transactions, especially economic transactions, among the citizenry. To insist on applying this principle indiscriminately, as if it were the quintessence of "fairness" itself, is simply a devious procedure for legitimizing a dogmatic egalitarianism. This is precisely what a great many liberal and neosocialist ideologues are up to, and with considerable success.

The conventional liberal justification for the progressive income tax, as presented in most economics textbooks, is by way of appeal to "the marginal productivity of income." Any additional income to the rich is assumed to have less utility —and therefore less "value"—than any additional income to the poor. If "fairness" in taxation is "equality of sacrifice," the rich then obviously have to surrender proportionally more than the poor. There is a certain plausibility to this notion, especially when applied—as it invariably is—to the "necessities" of life (that is, food, shelter, clothing). But that plausibility vanishes once it is realized that, in real life, the rich do not spend most of their incremental income by rushing out to buy more food, shelter, or clothing. Rather, they are more likely to spend that incremental income on "superfluities" as distinct from "needs," and among such "superfluities" are to be counted philanthropy and reinvestment of capital—activities that, in the longer run, make everyone better off. If one rejects, therefore, that primitive supposition (Veblenesque rather than Marxist) that the affluent simply *consume* all their income, there is no such thing as the marginal productivity of income.

It is hardly an accident that liberal economists ordinarily scorn the distinction between "necessities" and "superfluities." When they draw a "poverty line," for instance, they do not insist that it exclude possession of a telephone, a washing machine, even an automobile. In this context they argue that "necessities" are to be defined not by biology but by social convention. It is only when they get around to discussing the progressive income tax that the distinction between "necessities" and "superfluities" suddenly appeals to them.

It is also hardly an accident that all our liberal thinkers should be crisis-mongers, always presenting our social reality to us in terms of one crisis or another (the "urban crisis," or the "ecological crisis"). They instinctively prefer "crisis"

---

from war) introduces a wartime condition into a society otherwise at peace. Were it not for this burden imposed by war and defense, I would agree that all the proper ends of government (including its "public welfare" ends) could be adequately served by a proportionate income tax —which would then be perceived as "fair" (as, in fact, it was, for many decades). Moreover, there are persuasive arguments, backed by statistical analysis, to show that a highly progressive income tax merely has the effect of putting wealthy people to the trouble of avoiding those high rates, and that even today a proportionate tax would raise just as much revenue with less bureaucratic fuss. But that is another issue.

to "problems" or "conditions" because it is in a moment of crisis that the equation, fairness equals equality of sacrifice equals equality, gains its maximum credibility.

What Is a "Fair" Distribution of Income? Capitalism has always assumed that the "fair" distribution of income is determined by the productive input—"productive" as determined by the market—of individuals into the economy. Noncapitalist societies, whether precapitalist or postcapitalist, have a very different conception of "fairness," based on one's contribution *to the society,* not merely to the economy. In such noncapitalist societies, economic rewards are "socially" justified, as distinct from being economically justified. Thus, in the Middle Ages it was thought to be "fair" to compel ordinary people to support the church, whose activities were deemed to be of major social significance and social value. Similarly, in the Soviet Union today the Communist party does not have to defend its budget on any economic grounds—the value of its contribution to the polity as a whole is put beyond question.

Obviously, there is no such pure type as "a capitalist society" or "a non-capitalist society." All noncapitalist societies recognize, to one degree or another, the importance of economic activity and material welfare. They therefore allow differential rewards—again, to one degree or another—based on one's skill at such activity. Similarly, all capitalist societies recognize, to one degree or another, that there is more to life than material welfare, and they therefore make some provision for differential rewards based on one's skill at literary criticism, music, and philosophy. Harvard University, for example, is exactly such a provision.

Still, though "pure types" may not exist, the types themselves do, in however impure a form. And one does have to choose among their different conceptions of "a good society" and the principles of "fairness" in income distribution by which they operate. In making any such choice today, three considerations are pertinent:

(1) There is no method in political philosophy which permits us to determine, *in the abstract,* which principle of distribution is superior. It is absurd to claim that capitalism, anywhere, at any time, is superior to noncapitalism—or vice versa. Any such judgment is bound to be contingent—based on the particular society's history and traditions, on the habits of mind of its citizenry, and the like. There is no point in arguing that a particular society "ought" to be capitalist or socialist if the overwhelming majority of the people are not of a mind to be bound by the different kinds of self-discipline that these different political philosophies require if they are to work. And this, of course, holds true for all large political ideas. That is why Jefferson, living in Paris before the French Revolution, could write—in all good republican conscience—that the French people were not "ripe" for republican self-government, and that it would be a mistake for them to try to establish it immediately.[4] In short, reasonable men must recognize that they do not have a

---

[4] Marie Kimball, *Jefferson: The Scene of Europe, 1784 to 1789* (New York: Coward-McCann, Inc., 1950), p. 276.

perfectly free choice in establishing a social principle of "fairness." What ought to be must have an organic connection with what is.

(2) A distribution of income according to one's contribution to the society—to the "common good"—requires that this society have a powerful consensus as to what the "common good" is, and that it also have institutions with the authority to give specific meaning and application to this consensus on all occasions. Now, if we had such a consensus and such authoritative institutions, we would not have—and could not have—a liberal society as we understand it. It certainly could be a good society (if the values behind the consensus were good); it could be better than a liberal society; but it would not be a liberal society. The authorities representing the "common good," who distributed income in accordance with their conception of the common good, would inevitably discriminate against those who were subversive of this "common good." They might, if they were broad-minded, tolerate dissidents; but they would never concede to them equal rights—even if equality were a prime social value. The dissidents, after all, might be those who believed in inequality.

(3) A liberal society, such as we have in the United States today, is one that is based on a *weak consensus*. There is nothing like near-unanimity on what the *common good* is, who contributes to it, or how. There is not utter disagreement, of course; a liberal society is not—no society can be—in a condition of perpetual moral and political chaos. But the liberty of a liberal society derives from a prevalent skepticism of anyone's ability to know the "common good" with clear certainty, and from the conviction that the authorities should not try to define this *common good* in any but a minimal way. That minimal definition, in a liberal society, will naturally tend to emphasize the improvement of the material conditions of life—something that very few people are actually against. A liberal society, therefore, will be tolerant of capitalist transactions between consenting adults (to use Robert Nozick's marvelous phrase), because such transactions are for mutual advantage, and the sum of such transactions is to everyone's material advantage. And, consequently, a liberal society will think it reasonable and "fair" that income should, on the whole, be distributed according to one's productive input into the economy, as this is measured by the marketplace and the transactions occurring there.

In sum: the distribution of income under liberal capitalism is "fair" if—and only if—we believe that a liberal society is, under existing circumstances, a good society. If not, then not.

Egalitarianism versus Liberty. There are many people in this world—there have always been many people in this world—who do not believe that a liberal society can ever really be a good society because they think that liberty is a far less important value than other values. Sometimes they prize religious truth more than liberty; sometimes they prize philosophic truth more than liberty (as with the

Marxist philosophy); and sometimes they prize equality more than liberty. This last point of view is especially popular in some circles—mainly academic circles—in the United States today.

Thus, in a recent issue of the *New York Review of Books,* Ronald Dworkin—one of our most distinguished liberal legal philosophers—has written that *"a more equal society is a better society even if its citizens prefer inequality."* [5] From which it follows inevitably that justice may require a people, whose preferences are corrupt (in that they prefer liberty to equality), to be coerced into equality. It is precisely because they define justice as equality that so many liberal thinkers find it so difficult genuinely to detest left-wing (egalitarian) authoritarian or totalitarian regimes.

The passion for equality, then, is always dangerous to liberty because it is a passion for power: the power to impose one's ideal of justice-as-equality on other people.[6] This is the "idealism" that characterizes modern egalitarianism. It is not an idealism of self-abnegation but of massive self-assertion. It involves not giving away one's own money but expropriating other people's money, not preaching equality as an ideal for the individual but enforcing equality as a "social ideal."

Whether the conception of an egalitarian society based on compulsion will in fact improve the conditions of life for anyone may be open to dispute. What is not open to dispute is the evident fact that the kind of liberal egalitarianism so casually popular today will, if it is permitted to gather momentum, surely destroy the liberal society that gave birth to this peculiar kind of "liberalism."

---

[5] Ronald Dworkin, "The DeFunis Case: The Right to Go to Law School," *New York Review of Books,* vol. 23 (February 5, 1976), pp. 29-33. Emphasis added.

[6] An exception should be made for those cases where a group of people *voluntarily* establish equality as an ideal and freely create a political community to incarnate this ideal. The Israeli kibbutz is just such an instance, as are other Socialist "communes." But this kind of egalitarianism—to which no reasonable person can object—is of little interest to our egalitarian ideologues. The vision of John Kenneth Galbraith living on a kibbutz is a comic fantasy.

COMMENTARIES

G. Warren Nutter

There seems to be an implicit pairing of speakers and discussants so that the same arguments will not be made twice. I will therefore merely acknowledge that I agree, by and large, with Irving Kristol's remarks, and turn to Arthur Okun's paper.

As I understand it, Okun's basic argument runs as follows: There ought to be a more equal distribution of income in the United States because people like equality. We know they like equality because our political institutions over the years have come to provide for equal freedoms, equal rights, and equal obligations for all. Yet, he says, our society accepts far more inequality in the distribution of its economic assets than in the distribution of its sociopolitical assets. It accepts this inequality because equalizing incomes diminishes efficiency. But, Okun argues, the trade-off is almost certain to be small as long as the market is not destroyed in the process of redistributing income, and the market need not be destroyed. That the leakage from the redistributive bucket is low would be demonstrated if social scientists would spend more time measuring it. The American society, in deference to its preferences, would then strive for and achieve far greater equality in the distribution of incomes through government action, once it knew that the leakage was low.

Value judgments are obviously entangled with empirical propositions in the case Okun makes. I will not try to disentangle them because the whole line of reasoning is so much at odds with my own that I do not know where to begin discussing it or how to find a common universe of discourse. To Okun, the good society is one that maximizes equality of circumstance. To me, it is one that maximizes use of voluntary agreement in organizing social activity. Neither ideal accords, I suppose, with popular sentiment today, but mine surely is closer to the historical aspirations of the American people than is his. It is for this reason, I believe, that Okun so seriously misinterprets the rationale of so-called equal rights.

In our political and social arrangements, he says, society diligently pursues equality. Witness that the right to vote, speak, and worship is the same for all, as is the judicial process and every public service and obligation. Surely these institutions reveal a social preference for equality. And what difference is there between equal freedom of speech and equal health care?

In deducing equal treatment as the common essence of these diverse aspects of our political order, Okun misreads history and confuses fundamental issues.

Let me note first the rather obvious fact that our social and political arrangements are replete with unequal treatment. We treat children differently from adults, ordinary citizens differently from convicted felons, public figures differently from private citizens, challengers for elective office differently from incumbents, robbers differently from those they rob, and so on. Why not, then, infer a social preference for inequality?

The point, of course, is that our social institutions embody a host of social values and principles of equity that cannot be reduced to a single norm of equality without depriving them of meaning. There is no doubt, for example, that the adoption of the Bill of Rights was motivated by a desire to minimize coercion in the affairs of man. Our founders were certainly preoccupied with this issue, as anyone can reaffirm by taking another look at the discussions of that time. They did not concern equality but freedom, meaning freedom from government. Freedom was to be embodied in individual rights, through self-denying ordinances of government. Classical liberalism came to rest on what might be called the minimum principle: government should exercise the minimum of coercion required to minimize coercion.

Freedom of speech was not designed to give everybody equal time on a soapbox but to make sure that nobody who wanted to speak was prevented from doing so by being hit over the head, locked up, tortured, or shot. In its use of coercion, government was not to prevent speech while it was preventing others from preventing it. In contrast with this concern, Okun's treatment of the problem of coercion seems rather cavalier. What difference does it make, he asks, whether government coerces to provide for defense or to reshuffle wealth and income? Or for any other reason? Coercion is coercion is coercion. It is nothing more or less, he says, than the necessary political definition of property rights, which always involves taking from some and giving to others.

At this point I must confess that Okun loses me. He argues that, whenever government creates a property right—"out of thin air," as he puts it—everybody who does not receive that right is automatically coerced. In my opinion, this way of looking at the issue invites unbounded confusion. Okun gets off the track, I think, when he makes the very mistake he accuses his critics of making—the mistake of confusing liberty with private property. As far as I can see, he makes the same mistake in the passages of his lectures that he cites as describing the importance he attaches to liberty.

Needless to say, I do not have time here to straighten all this out. But I would say that, in a nutshell, freedom is one thing, power another, and equality something else again. The problem is to find an optimal mix of the three. Property is an aspect of power, and private property, widely dispersed, complements freedom, but the only private property implied by freedom itself is ownership of one's self. *Coercion* means use of physical force, explicitly or implicitly, by one person or agent for the purpose of altering what someone else wishes to do voluntarily with his property, including himself.

The paradox here concerns the way *property* is to be defined in the first place. Okun finds it difficult, as I do, to assign the origin of private property to natural law or natural rights. But that does not mean that one must move to the opposite extreme, as Okun does, and say that *property* should be subject to instant definition and redefinition by majoritarian will, in its crudest sense. This position is advantageous if one wants government to have unlimited power to redistribute property because it begs the question of liberty.

Our founders recognized the paradox of property and resolved it by imposing severe constitutional limits on the power of government to tax and to take. For all practical purposes, time has swept away those restraints and with the barest popular support government may now take and give whatever, whenever, and wherever it wishes. The fact that I favor restoring restraints hardly means, as Okun's line of reasoning seems to imply, that I do not care what happens to the poor, or that I am opposed to any form of coercive redistribution of income. I favor redistribution but subject to strong restraints on the taking power of government. The great question of our time is this: what is to prevent a government already taking more than 40 percent of national income for one purpose or another from becoming a leviathan that ultimately devours freedom, probably in the name of greater equality of circumstance? Might it not be better to impose some limits on the taking power of government?

Okun does not find that question interesting, but he should, because any government of a large nation with the power to provide the greater equality he considers desirable would impose greater inequality instead. At least that is the lesson of recorded history as I read it. If the American people really want more equality, not much coercion is needed to achieve substantial redistribution of income. Much will occur voluntarily and charitably. Unfortunately, what Okun sees as a revealed preference for equality is something quite different. What most people want is more than they have, and, in a majoritarian democracy, majorities will often coalesce for the purpose of getting more by taking from others. The transfer need not be from the rich to the poor, and in fact usually is not. As an empirical proposition, Aaron Director's law asserts that it is the middle class that benefits by taking from the poor as well as from the rich. Director's explanation is, I believe, closer to the truth than Okun's. Moreover, the more that government takes, the less likely that democracy will survive.

So much for the broader issues. Let me now conclude with a few brief remarks on some specific points.

The trade-off of equality and efficiency heralded by Okun becomes almost trivial once he has plugged most of the leaks in his bucket. Progressive taxes, he says, have no discernible effect on effort, and very little on investment. The latter effect does not matter anyhow, because government can make investment whatever it likes simply by twirling a few fine-tuning dials. No failures, no trade-offs, no anything. Whatever investment we want, government will conjure it up with dials (or perhaps with mirrors). I find this faith in fine-tuning astounding in the face of stagflation and all that.

While endorsing Henry Simons's principle that redistribution of income should be superimposed on a free market, Okun offers a strange proposal for subsidizing borrowing by lower-income groups. It is not clear how one learns how much of the interest premium charged to low-income borrowers is due to inability to repay and how much to relatively unproductive use of loans. But why try? The remedy is to raise income, not to subsidize the interest rate.

In passing, Okun cannot resist praising recent legislation on campaign spending as a welcome curb to the "counterfeiting" of votes and hence a boost to a more "democratic" political process. Here is another example of miscomprehension of the complex issues underlying the First Amendment, with which this legislation is wholly inconsistent, to say the least. Let me merely observe that, as far as the democratic process is concerned, there is likely to be more to fear from a silver tongue than from a gold finger.

Henry J. Aaron

Arthur Okun has posed the issue of equality in the right way, if one is interested even remotely in the affairs of this world. He assumes that, other things being equal, most people regard more equality than we have as desirable, and he concludes that, if they refrain from getting it, they must perceive that an increase in equality costs something—that other things, in fact, are not equal. Whether this cost comes in reduced economic efficiency, as Okun suggests, or in reduced freedom in some dimensions, as Kristol asserts, the point is the same. To get something we want, we must give up something we want. Because our tastes, values and philosophies differ, we will not agree on specific policies.

My own perception is that some additional redistribution will cost almost nothing in freedom, though it will cost something in efficiency, and that it is worth getting. But, the point is that Okun's approach requires us to focus on specific policies—changes in the Internal Revenue Code, cash transfers, in-kind subsidies. That is, it forces us to start from where we are and decide whether we want to trade something to get a bit more or a bit less equality. He points out that some policies promote both equality and efficiency and suggests that such policies cannot rationally be opposed.

But they are opposed, and I do not think the reason lies in ignorance of the facts. Rather, I think that many who resist egalitarian policies and assert property rights include in their inventory of property not only goods and services—income, in other words—but also status, prestige, and social position. The person who has earned income has also earned high status. Equalization of opportunity that equalizes income and improves efficiency may enlarge the economic pie, but it cannot increase the prestige pie. Indeed, to the extent that equalization of income reduces the size of status differentials, it destroys one kind of property—social status—particularly the opportunity to confer it on one's children or other heirs. I do not wish to justify this explanation of why policies are rejected that, in Okun's terms, both improve efficiency and reduce equality. Indeed, I share his regret that we give up both equality and efficiency, and I find status differentials repugnant. I advance this explanation as a possible reason for our failure to eliminate the influence of parental wealth on the opportunity of children to obtain higher education or other training.

Second, though I agree with the way Okun poses the issue of equality, I disagree that the case for equality is stronger if it rests on reasoning about the original position than if it rests on utilitarianism. He scores elegantly on the natural law theorists by asking who determines the various principles of natural law and by suggesting that equality has as much claim to inclusion among the principles the state enforces as does any other. But, if we can introduce such principles into the natural law, why can we not insist that those traveling into abstraction to contemplate the original position take with them some awareness of the actual position —the world as we know it, the history and experience of all people, their possessions and their sense of what is rightfully theirs. As Okun finds natural law mind-boggling, I find mind-boggling the idea that we should abandon all we know of existing possessions and rights in deciding how to redistribute those possessions and rights. Okun defends the veil of ignorance as essential to insure that we view outcomes as random. But outcomes are not and never will be random. How the world is arranged affects not only the costs and strategies of redistribution but also the redistributional goals that I, at least, want to adopt.

The customary utilitarian approach rests on assumptions about the degree of happiness each individual obtains from some object. Under this approach, identical utility functions and diminishing utility of income are sufficient to make complete equality optimal (efficiency considerations aside). Okun rightly criticizes this approach to equality because of its heavy reliance on interpersonal comparisons—and he might also have criticized it for its reliance on identical utility functions.

But this is not the kind of utilitarianism implicit in economics. In particular, it is not the kind used in the theory of the optimal tax, the topic within which the issues of efficiency and equality are explicitly and simultaneously analyzed. Using this theory, each individual is required to evaluate how much *he* likes alternative income distributions. His welfare function depends on *his* perception of the utility enjoyed by each person, given that person's income, and on his evaluation (or weighting) of that utility. In no objective sense is the practical measurement of utility necessary to this calculation. All that is necessary is that each person be willing to decide for himself how important another dollar is to Okun or Kristol, and be willing to attach his own subjective weight to their gains. He does not need a "utilometer," and even if he had one, and if it showed that some persons were much better pleasure machines than others, he could still consistently be a complete egalitarian, because his welfare weights might disregard or offset these "pleasure-machine" differences.

It is true that he might have to defend or explain his egalitarian preferences. But he could do so by introspection, citing his own diminishing marginal utility (that he takes care of his most pressing wants first, and spends increments of real income on progressively less important items). He could then state that he thinks most people behave in about the same way, though their tastes may differ from his, and that the burden of proof rests on anyone bent on asserting the reverse. He could also state that he sees no reason to attach a greater weight to some people than to others in his welfare function, and that the burden of proof rests on anyone who wishes to convince him that other weights are proper. Finally, he could acknowledge that the way people come to their present endowments does matter, and that he does care about efficiency losses as well as equality gains.

He could then sit back and wait for someone to persuade him to change his mind. He should certainly not be seduced into abandoning what he actually knows about people and their history merely because (like Nozick) he might attach weight to the actual position and how it was arrived at, though (unlike Nozick) not exclusive weight. He might wonder, as I do, why egalitarian principles, based on a lottery in a state of ignorance that never has and never will exist, are more compelling than egalitarian principles based on the kind of introspection I have just described. He might well be dismissed as a *naïf,* unworthy of attention, but he could keep company with the growing band of economists who are productively integrating issues of equality and efficiency within just such a framework. One might even hope to induce this band to take account of rights and prior possessions in this framework. Such a utilitarian framework would be immune, I think, to Okun's criticism and free from the strained and unattractive concept of the original position.

Third, Okun suggests that within the mildly redistributive society he advocates, real incomes are determined in two distinct phases: the receipt of factor incomes and the redistribution through taxes and transfers. I suggest, and I do not think that Okun would disagree, that this distinction is really somewhat artificial. Factor incomes depend on government tax, transfer, and expenditure policies. Indeed, so long as the government provides public services that are not equally valuable to everyone—and, in practice, this means all services—and collects taxes to pay for them, redistribution is pervasive and inevitable. *The government cannot choose not to redistribute income. It can only choose, and it must choose, how to redistribute income.* Thus, Kristol's appeal to a proportional tax system as somehow "natural" for nondefense expenditures is merely an appeal for a different kind of redistribution and every bit as arbitrary as the alternatives he criticizes. Redistribution occurs as much through parks and schools, through the award of licenses and the imposition of zoning ordinances, and through the purchase of particular nondefense goods and services, as through taxes and transfers or defense outlays. Redistribution suffuses the activities of a modern government. There is no way to avoid it. But we must do it consciously, not blindly.

My first comment on Kristol is that he chooses not to discuss practical policies or modest income redistribution, but to tilt with "liberal or neo-socialist ideologues." None is named. He scorns "crisis mongers" though no responsible advocate of reducing inequality uses the word *crisis* in this context. Those who argue for less inequality are in the throes of a "passion" that is equated with a "passion for power," a patently silly equation unless one is prepared to argue that anyone seeking to convince a majority to change the status quo politically is similarly gripped by passion.

My second comment is that I would urge those interested in statistics on poverty not to swallow whole Edgar Browning's provocative—but, I think, misleading—article in the *Public Interest* that Kristol cites.[1] Those interested in the impact of in-kind benefits and transfer payments on the poor should consult the work of Timothy Smeeding and Eugene Smolensky, both of the Institute for Research on Poverty of the University of Wisconsin, who reach much more muted conclusions about the decline of inequality.[2]

My third comment is that Kristol simply does not understand the concept of the marginal utility (not "marginal productivity") of income. All economists, not just liberal ones, reject the distinction between necessities and superfluities (ask Milton Friedman and James Buchanan, for example). They know that one person's luxury is another person's necessity. They also know that the rich, like the poor, would curtail purchases of items of least import to them if their incomes were reduced and that the extra items bought with increasing income would be less pressing than items previously purchased. Habits might be formed and hard to break, of course. The fact is, the rich have satisfied most present needs of their own, and the government subsidizes giving by the rich through tax deductions far more generously than it subsidizes giving by the poor. As Martin Feldstein has amply shown, this subsidy has a major impact on giving.[3]

---

[1] Edgar K. Browning, "How Much More Equality Can We Afford?" *Public Interest*, no. 43 (Spring 1976), pp. 90-110.

[2] See Timothy Smeeding, "The Anti-Poverty Effectiveness of In-Kind Transfers," presented to the annual meetings of the American Economic Association, Dallas, Texas, December 28-30, 1975; "The Economic Well-Being of Low Income Households: Implications for Income Inequality and Poverty," mimeographed; Morgan Reynolds and Eugene Smolensky, "The Post Fisc Distribution: 1961 and 1970 Compared," Institute for Research on Poverty Discussion Paper 191-74, March 1974.

[3] Martin Feldstein, "On the Effects of the Income Tax Treatment of Charitable Contributions: Some Preliminary Results," Harvard Institute of Economic Research Discussion Paper 337,

Kristol then comes close to defending a view not seriously advanced by any reputable economist for a few decades, that the distribution of income generated in the capitalist marketplace enjoys some kind of moral status. In an economy marred by numerous outcroppings of monopoly (much of it due to government action) and rampant inequality of opportunity from accidents of birth and from government policies, this presumption has been abandoned almost universally. Its reappearance here gives Kristol's paper a quaintness that takes us back to the late nineteenth century when social Darwinists proclaimed that the general good would be promoted if the cruelties of natural selection were replicated by cruelties of economic selection. Kristol is right in asserting that there is no objective basis for rejecting this (or any other) distributional rule. The corollary of course is that there is no objective reason for accepting it either. The suggestion that acceptance of the results of the marketplace is necessary for liberal society is contradicted by the examples of the United States, much of Western Europe, and of the richer members of the British commonwealth.

Kristol and others would help, rather than hinder, needed discussions about income distribution if they would talk about the consequences of specific actions and stop talking about oversimplified abstractions that bear little relation to reality.

Robert Nozick

I find myself disagreeing, significantly, with Dr. Okun and also with Professor Kristol. My comments here will be directed to Okun.

It is possible to think that the central question about distribution is: What pattern should holdings take in a society? or To each according to his or her what? This would assume that distribution should be in accordance with some dimension that people value and would ask the question, What should that dimension be— moral merit, contribution to the society, revolutionary fervor, parents' income? Whatever it is, one would face the question, How should things be distributed in the society?

That conception is a very common one, and it is one that I reject. It is important to see that it is a *particular* conception, for it looks, at first blush, as though the whole subject is, How should things be distributed? and What should the pattern be? I want to argue that there is an alternative view that would ask, By what method is it appropriate that things be distributed? Under this alternative view, whatever comes from that mechanism is an acceptable distribution. There is no judgment about the resulting distribution which would introduce the coercive

---

January 1973; Martin Feldstein and Charles Clotfelter, "Tax Incentives and Charitable Contributions in the United States: A Microeconometric Analysis," Harvard Institute of Economic Research Discussion Paper 381, September 1974; and Martin S. Feldstein and Amy Taylor, "The Income Tax and Charitable Contributions: Estimates and Simulations with the Treasury Tax Files," Harvard Institute of Economic Research Discussion Paper 409, April 1974.

arm of the state. Individually, we could make particular judgments about the desirability of whatever the appropriate mechanism produces—and then, if we did not like what it produces, we could choose to transfer some of our own resources to rectify it by philanthropy, or we could try to persuade other people to do this.

Usually, when economists ask what pattern there should be, they assume that the answer will be "that pattern which maximizes the sum of the utility in the society." Since it is not clear that one *can* make interpersonal comparisons of utility (in a theoretically general way), economists investigate rules of thumb whose results they hope will approximate the "sum of utility" principle. The emphasis on the diminishing marginal utility of income is based on an underlying assumption that what we want to do is maximize total utility.

Okun's paper is based on the assumption that people want more equality. He speaks of the preference revealed in society, but there has been some disagreement as to whether society's institutional arrangements do reveal such a preference. I do not want to focus on whether this preference exists, but on what weight it should have if it does exist.

Okun raised the question of why we want equality in the political realm but not in the economic realm. There is an inconsistency here, he says, which has to be explained, and to explain it he introduces costs that occur in one realm and not in the other. But there may be particular reasons—not related to costs—why we insist on equality in the political realm. Given that the political realm deals with the coercive arm of the state—forgive my using that loaded expression—that is, with force and ultimately with guns, there are particular reasons why we want each individual person to cast one vote rather than weighting votes by education or other qualifications.

Okun, I sense, would not like some of those particular reasons. He speaks of certain distinctions he considers pointless. He wonders whether there is really a difference between having a right that one is unable to exercise and not having the right. Is there a point to saying that people have a right—what sometimes is called a bourgeois formal right—as opposed to the opportunity to exercise that right? Are we not as concerned about the opportunity to exercise the right as about having the right itself?

This point about rights connects with the distinction between the state and other institutions in the society. If we do not have the right to do a certain thing, that is, if there are penalties for our doing it, then there is no opportunity at all for us to do it. There is no way to do it even by voluntary arrangement, or by seeking out someone who might enable us to do it. In a society with significant decentralization of resources, having a "formal" right is significant because there are various ways that we could be aided in exercising the right—for example, poor people could approach others and ask them for voluntary contributions in order to be aided in exercising certain rights.

A similar and deep distinction arises when one talks about coercion. It is often asked, "Why must there be an intention to coerce someone else—why must the coercer *intend* to bring something about?" This can be puzzling. From the point of view of the recipient, he is no worse off if his options are limited than if someone intentionally limits them even by using force.

If someone says to me, "If you walk out of your home, I will hit you with a significant charge from my ray gun," that is a threat and involves coercing me. If there is a lightning storm outside which yields the same probability of my getting hit, that is not coercion, even though my options *are* limited by natural forces. Why should there be any difference at all between the two?

There are certain vague things one can say on this subject. When someone else is coercing me, his intentions enter into my actions, and I am acting on his intentions and not on my own. When forces of nature provide the "coercion," the acts are fully my own. Rather than trying to introduce an answer here to what I view as a significant philosophical question, I only want to say that certain sorts of distinctions should not be ignored merely because one does not yet have an adequate account of their rationale. Some distinctions may seem irrational if one has the view that the only thing that matters is the end result. If I am limited in my options, how can it matter how I came to be so?

In the same way, in considering the allocation of medical resources, some believe that the only relevant question to ask is, In which way will we end up saving more lives? When there are two alternative actions, they think we must decide what to do according to the number of lives ultimately saved. If we could give a kidney machine or some rare drug to this group or that, we should compare the number of lives saved by either.

But the view that all that matters is how we end up is not morally acceptable. If there were one person who could be helped by a certain drug and five others (with a milder form of the illness) who could be helped by lesser quantities of that drug, we might choose to give it to the five rather than to the one. Since lives are at stake, the only question might appear to be whether five lives should be saved or one.

But that is not the case if we could save the five lives by sacrificing one life. Perhaps the five could benefit by some serum made out of the protoplasm of one healthy person who is a rare chemical type. However, we are not morally permitted to sacrifice that one life in order to save five. Economists are often attracted to the general view that all that matters is how things end up, which we might call end-state theories, though Okun may not be entirely attracted to it. In any case, it is a view whose intuitive appeal and power we ought to try to dispose of.

Okun also remarked about markets that decree starvation. Markets do not decree anything, though the people involved in those markets may be reduced to straitened economic circumstances. But this "market" result is different from the state's saying, "You may not eat and anyone who gives you food will be punished for doing so." To say that being without food feels the same, regardless of the cause, ignores the significant difference between its being decreed by the state and its being a result nobody intentionally tried to bring about.

Finally, Okun says that there is a social preference for equality. I do not want to discuss whether he is right because even if he were, the social preference would not have the consequences he thinks it does. I admit the notion of social preference is not one I clearly understand, and in a meeting before a group of economists I expected a little more detail about it than we have been given here. I assume Okun does not have in mind unanimous preference, and this is surely not an audience that I must tell about Arrow's impossibility theorem concerning aggregation of individual preferences.

Recent studies, using far stronger apparatus than Arrow's to try to break out of the bounds of such impossibility results, have led (I think it is fair to say) to even stronger impossibility results. To talk about social preference without elaboration seems to me to avoid the serious problems about what that could mean. I will assume that what Okun means is majority preference. Suppose there are two options, one a redistributive scheme and the other not, and that a majority would prefer the redistributive scheme. Is this fact by itself sufficient reason to justify carrying out the majority preference by government means? In his paper, Okun accepts the ruling out of some preferences. Even if a majority had certain sorts of preferences, he would not think the society should follow them. He says, "The legal ban on stealing a loaf of bread does not imply a judgment that the bread stealer would gain less utility than would be lost by the potential victim." This, Okun says, is not a utilitarian judgment about maximizing the total utility. "The relevant social judgment is that he would be violating the rights of others and that his own utility from such activity should be disregarded." [1]

There are two ways to read these sentences. One is that the action violates the rights of others, so it does not matter what the potential violators prefer; the other is that there is a relevant social judgment that there is a violation of rights.

The second way does not start with rights, but with social judgments about rights. We have to ask the question, What does it mean to say there is that social judgment, and if the social judgment went the other way, would Okun really want to follow it? Asking what it is a social judgment *about* might bring us back to the first interpretation.

Let us assume—and it does not matter whether this example is historically accurate—that the relevant social judgment in Germany in 1933 was that it did not violate anyone's rights or go against any social judgment to expropriate Jews and, eventually, exterminate them. The social judgment, let us assume, was in favor of this; a referendum would have supported it.

---

[1] Arthur M. Okun, p. 24 of this volume.

My position, and I assume that it is also Okun's position, is that it would not be morally permissible to do this, whatever the preferences of the (non-Jewish) people in that society. Individual people, in this case Jewish people, have a right not to have certain kinds of things done to them. The other people had no right to do these things even if they wanted to, even if it would maximize total utility.

One might reply, "Who decides what the rights are?" Who is to decide? One has to be serious about this issue, and not ask the question merely to reject the hard subject of ethics. It will not do to reject the position that there really *are* limits and moral constraints on what we can do—whether or not anyone agrees to them and even if a majority says there are no limits.

I assume there are some actions we would forbid even if a majority wanted them. We would say, "No, they may not be done because they violate the rights of other people"—and we would say this even if a utilitarian calculation supported these actions.

Rights stand as barriers to maximizing utility and, indeed, to satisfying the preferences of the people in a society. If everybody preferred that I shut up, I assume it would still be illegitimate for them to stop me from speaking. It is important in looking at majoritarian preferences to look at actual surveys—for example, on the subject of civil liberties. I assume there is no controversy about this here, though Kristol has some views about censoring pornography and obscenity that I would want to argue about in another context.

A book published in 1955 by Samuel Stouffer indicated that strong majorities were against various provisions of the Bill of Rights.[2] If we do not take an unlimited majoritarian position, and if we insist that there are moral limits on what we can do, then we must look at what those limits are. It is legitimate to wonder how to decide questions about moral correctness or natural rights, and, with more time, I would want to talk about Okun's bemused claim that there may be a natural right not to be poor and claims similar to that.

The first step is to realize there is a subject of ethics, and not just to poke fun at the claim that something may be wrong (or right), even if the majority does not think so. A majority preference for equality does not necessarily lead to the conclusion that the government ought to institute more equality, because there is the further question of whether the government, in doing so, will violate moral limits and the rights of individuals. If it will, then morally it may not satisfy the majority preferences. The question is whether property and other rights place limits on further (and existing!) governmental redistributive activities. I claim they do (and very serious limits at that), but I have not attempted to argue for that claim here. Rather, I have argued for the crucial importance of the question, a question left out in Okun's "social preference" approach.

---

[2] Samuel A. Stouffer, *Communism, Conformity, and Civil Liberties: A Cross Section of the Nation Speaks Its Mind* (Garden City, N.Y.: Doubleday, 1955).

Okun also said he would sacrifice some efficiency for equality. One way to do that would be to redistribute voluntarily. There is literature on Pareto-optimal redistribution covering situations in which everyone in a society might want to redistribute, or at least no one would be opposed to it. In *Anarchy, State, and Utopia,* I describe ways redistribution might be carried out voluntarily.[3]

A compulsory government program might involve half the people, each making an individual transfer to an anonymous other individual in the society. The question arises, If the government did not require this, why would they not continue doing it? After all, the person being helped by the redistribution (whom by hypothesis they want to help) still would be helped. The standard answer is the following: An individual might want everybody to be helped and believe it worth the cost of making his contribution; but he would not want to contribute separately because it would not be worth the cost to help only one particular person. Everybody in the society might say that.

This is not terminology that I normally use, but notice that we have here an example of a divergence between private and social costs. By hypothesis, we have *in the voting mechanism* individuals who consider only the private costs to themselves, though they know that other persons required to contribute to the redistribution also might not find it worth their cost to help the one person they are helping. Each individual voter similarly ignores the social cost to the others who contribute, and the voting mechanism aggregates this ignoring.

We can work out the details for ourselves. I would hope that Okun would be equally concerned about this divergence between private and social costs in the mechanism that he describes, as I am sure he is about other divergences.

Finally, Okun says that limitations of property rights are not really limitations of liberty. The view that liberty is the only right—the word libertarian is sometimes thrown around here—is not a view that I would accept. There are rights *other* than liberty, and property rights may well be one of them. Suppose I had a machine that could produce, by my pressing a button, a headache of a certain degree of severity in another person whenever I wanted to, but not a headache severe enough to interfere with any action he was doing. Some of his activities might require more concentration than others, but, by monitoring closely, the machine would not prevent any activity. (Do not say that this would take away his liberty to do certain activities *without* a headache, for similar statements can be made about taking property.) To use the machine would violate another sort of right, the person's right not to have certain things inflicted upon him. Thus, to say the only thing that we should care about is liberty seems to be mistaken. It is still open to discussion whether there is a violation of property rights and whether property rights morally constrain the actions of government.

---

[3] Robert Nozick, *Anarchy, State, and Utopia* (New York: Basic Books, 1974).

Marshall Cohen

My own substantive views are far closer to Arthur Okun's than to Irving Kristol's, but I cannot accept Okun's notion that the fundamental issues are matters of taste. Still less can I accept his view that ethical questions are simply questions about personal or social preferences. He quotes Henry Simons's remark that inequality is unlovely, and says that there is no logical escape from the conclusion that we have equal rights because we like equal rights. But even those who find inequality "lovely" (as Kristol does) had better admit that inequalities are sometimes unjust. And even those who do not "like" acknowledging equal rights may have to admit that people are sometimes possessed of them. These are not questions of aesthetics or of collective preference: they are questions of justice and of moral right. Furthermore, the constitutional protection of "equal" rights as well as statutory attempts to achieve equal opportunity and a decent minimum standard of life for all are more than legal requirements. They are the embodiment and articulation of persuasive moral judgments.

I take it that some such thought stands behind the remark of Ronald Dworkin that Kristol finds so shocking. Kristol quotes Dworkin as saying that a more equal society is a better society, even if its citizens prefer inequality. From this, according to Kristol, it inevitably follows that justice may require a people whose preferences are corrupt "to be coerced into equality." "The passion for equality," Kristol goes on to say, "is always dangerous to liberty because it is a passion for power: the power to impose one's ideal of justice-as-equality on other people." Dworkin was speaking, in context, of the right to equal protection of the laws and of the right to treatment as an equal—not of a right to equal distribution or of equality quite generally. Is Dworkin not right in saying that a society which protects and enforces these rights is a morally better society than one that "prefers" not to acknowledge and enforce them? Is Kristol suggesting that a majority which prefers to infringe these rights should be allowed to do so and that those who believe that the Constitution ought to be enforced reveal a somehow shameful "passion for power"?

A similar set of attitudes is displayed in Robert Nisbet's review of John Rawls's *A Theory of Justice*.[1] Rawls observes that in a just society the basic liberties of citizenship are taken as settled. They are not subject to political bargaining or to the calculus of social interests. But Nisbet regards this fairly standard affirmation of constitutional rights as astonishing. For Nisbet this assertion of equal rights is a repudiation of conventional politics for the politics of virtue. Far from being incompatible with all known forms of democracy, Rawls's remarks simply formulate a fundamental assumption of the kind of constitutional democracy we actually practice. It is astonishing to hear that an acknowledgment of the very rights that protect against tyranny suggests to some minds the sanctity

[1] John Rawls, *A Theory of Justice* (Cambridge, Mass.: Harvard University Press, 1971).

of any form of power that might fulfill social justice—to hear that the best safe-guards against tyranny are in fact an invitation to it. Do Kristol and Nisbet, those embattled defenders of high culture, simply misunderstand the sophisticated theorizing of writers like Dworkin and Rawls? Or is the new antiegalitarianism we find in the pages and purlieus of the *Public Interest* not just a defense of right-of-center conservatism but in fact a radical attack on the constitutional foundations of American democracy?

The relation between equal rights and the just distribution of income is diffi-cult to articulate. And it is by no means obvious that a defender of equal basic rights must defend an egalitarian distribution of income. For Okun, the connec-tion is straightforward. He says that:

> Equality in the distribution of incomes . . . as well as in the distribution of rights would be my *ethical* preference. Abstracting from the costs and the consequences, I would prefer more equality of income to less and would like complete equality best of all. This preference is a simple extension of the humanistic basis for equal rights. To extend the domain of rights and give every citizen an equal share of the national income would give added recognition to the moral worth of every citizen, to the mutual respect of citizens for one another, and to the equivalent value of membership in the society for all.
>
> Nonetheless, my preference for one person, one income, is not nearly so strong as that for one person, one vote. Equality in material welfare has much lower benefits and far higher costs than equality of political and civil entitlements.[2]

The case for an equality of political and civil entitlements is unquestionably stronger than the case for "one person, one income," but the difference probably has little to do with the fact (if it is a fact) that the "costs" of material equality are higher than the costs of political and civil entitlements. Rather, it seems to be related to the connection between these rights and the humanistic values to which Okun alludes, which is more intimate than that which obtains between those humanistic values and a strict equality of income. Is it Okun's view that, if guaran-teeing the basic political and civil entitlements turned out to be more "costly," they might be sacrificed as "impractical"? To think so is to misunderstand the justifica-tion for their special status and for their exemption, as a matter of principle, from sacrifice to considerations of economic "efficiency" or to the "preferences" or "interests" of the majority. Okun seems to understand the possibility that the special status of civil and political rights has a different justification, one that has nothing to do with the terms of the trade-off between equality and efficiency, when he writes, in a different context:

> The legal ban on stealing a loaf of bread does not imply a judgment that the bread stealer would gain less utility than would be lost by the poten-

---

[2] Arthur M. Okun, *Equality and Efficiency: The Big Tradeoff* (Washington, D.C.: The Brook-ings Institution, 1975), p. 47.

tial victim. The relevant social judgment is that he would be violating the rights of others and that his own utility from such activity should be disregarded. Indeed, any system of law involves decisions that certain types of preferences . . . should not be allowed to influence allocation.[3]

Similarly, civil and political entitlements are not negotiable. They are not open to balancing—especially against values of a less fundamental kind (they enjoy a "preferred position")—and they cannot be traded off in favor of other interests or in favor of the preferences of other persons.

In my view, this is the position not only of the equal rights of citizenship but also of a fair equality of opportunity and (in a relatively affluent society) of the just claim to a decent minimum standard of life. These requirements are all exempt from Okun's "big trade-off," which operates only in areas untouched by these strict moral requirements.

We cannot accept Okun's leaky bucket analysis. When he tries to apply it to questions of fundamental justice, we must insist that the bucket stops here. Okun argues that the proper principle is this: "Society will carry the leaky bucket to pursue equality up to the point where the added benefits of more equality are just matched by the added costs of lesser efficiency." [4] The principle is, of course, an empty one until we know the criteria for assessing costs and benefits. But even supposing ourselves in possession of these criteria, it must be clear that we would sometimes (perhaps often) find ourselves obliged to sacrifice a large measure of efficiency to gain only a modest quantum of equality. This would be so, for instance, if this sacrifice were required to meet the minimum standards of justice. We can insure that we will never accept great "costs" in efficiency for small "gains" in equality (an "irrational" trade-off) only by saying that the benefits of meeting minimum standards and of justice always outweigh the costs in inefficiency required to secure them. But to say this is to offer an utterly implausible reading of the terms *cost* and *benefit* and to acknowledge that the foundation of the analysis rests on an indispensable judgment of justice. To admit this is to admit that talk of trade-offs, and costs and benefits, is both misleading and otiose.

If Okun is wrong in thinking that the fundamental issue has to do with the terms of the trade-off between equality and efficiency (the choice of terms being, in his view, like the choice between different kinds of ice cream), he is equally wrong in denying the significant conflict between the interests of liberty and those of equality. As justice sometimes requires efficiency to be sacrificed to equality, it also sometimes requires liberty to be sacrificed to equality (or to other requirements of justice). Conservatives and libertarians may make too much of this, or the wrong thing of it, but there is no reason to deny it. Thus, Okun writes:

> I do not see a general trade-off between equality and liberty, so long as equalization is pursued through the tax-transfer reshuffle and the other

---

[3] Arthur M. Okun, p. 24 of this volume.
[4] Okun, p. 21 of this volume.

mechanisms that I recommend—which do not include extended government control over employment or greater public ownership of the means of production. In insisting that the second-round redistribution need not compromise liberty, I believe that I am making the same distinction that Henry Simons intended in the following passage: "What is important, for libertarians, is that we preserve the basic processes of free exchange and that egalitarian measures be superimposed on those processes, effecting redistribution afterward and not in the immediate course of production and commercial transactions." [5]

But this does not show that liberty is not "compromised" by redistribution. It only suggests that the liberties the libertarian cares most about can be preserved better by achieving redistribution by "taxation" than by "extended government control over employment." This is, unquestionably, a preferable way to achieve egalitarian ends, and the judgment it embodies suggests why we should resist Robert Nozick's assimilation of redistributive taxation to forced labor. For the infringement on the freedom to dispose of one's property as one wishes, though a restriction on liberty, is not so profound as the imposition of forced labor or other control over employment would be. We should, of course, restrict liberties as little as possible and impose restrictions on less important liberties before more important ones. But that liberties must sometimes be restricted cannot be denied. At the least, freedom to associate with whomever one pleases must be sacrificed to the requirement of equal treatment by the state. Freedom to say certain things must be restricted in the interests of a fair trial or to safeguard soldiers in dangerous circumstances. The freedom to enjoy and dispose of one's property as one wishes, I would argue, must be sacrificed to various requirements of justice. The fair value of our equal rights can be guaranteed only if private or corporate wealth cannot be put to certain political uses. Similarly, equality of opportunity can be approached only if wealth is taxed heavily enough to rectify major developmental disparities. (Even among those who believe the market's distributive verdict is "fair," few would claim, as Kristol seems to, that this is so in the absence of at least a rough equality of opportunity.) Finally, justice requires that, in an affluent society, a decent minimum standard of living be achieved by those willing and able to work for it. Meeting this standard may require limits on the ability of some to enjoy, and dispose of, their wealth as they see fit. It must be said, however, that when the fair value of equal rights is achieved, and a rough equality of opportunity established, redistribution for this purpose is likely to be a much more modest affair than it would be in present circumstances. Once equality of opportunity is a fact, far greater equality of wealth is likely to be decreed by the market. There is no reason to deny the inevitable conflicts that arise between some exercises of liberty and some precepts of equality. And there is no reason to believe that a just society always prefers the one to the other. A just society will

---

[5] Okun, p. 30 of this volume.

regard certain liberties as absolutely fundamental. It is remarkable how often professed libertarians fail to appreciate this fact, or that still other freedoms—such as the freedom to make unfettered political use of great concentrations of wealth —threaten them. The defense of our fundamental political freedoms requires a more egalitarian arsenal.

DISCUSSION

DR. OKUN: Once before on a panel of this sort, I made a nonaggression pact with a conservative member of the panel: if he refrained from saying anything about the United Kingdom, I would refrain from mentioning Sweden. I did not, however, have the opportunity to negotiate such a pact with Professor Kristol, and I would like to mention Sweden here. There is some recent evidence that Sweden might usefully reform its Internal Revenue Service much as we might reform our Federal Bureau of Investigation. But the efficiency or the growth of the Swedish economy along with the almost fanatical Swedish redistribution of income in the postwar period has been quite a remarkable phenomenon.

I intended to spend a fair amount of time refuting this voluntary equalization option that Kristol and Nozick discussed, but Professor Nozick covered the point, in my view, completely. The fact that I do not now pay more than my income tax but at the same time would be prepared to support a measure that raised my income tax is not at all inconsistent. I am willing to pay more taxes if everybody pays more taxes and if more redistribution is taking place, because society's potential gain from that same expenditure, on my part, is much greater than its potential gain if I alone make that payment. This is a divergence between private and social costs which is exactly what society and public action are all about. Analogously, if I am a citizen of a western frontier town and everybody in the town lays down his gun, I am ready to lay mine down, but I cannot afford to disarm unilaterally.

I never know when Professor Kristol is quite serious, but I am convinced he is not serious when he says that inequality is lovely. If he were serious, he would be obliged to recommend a regressive tax transfer reshuffle. If inequality is a wonderful thing, we ought to pursue it, and I have not heard him say anything that suggests his advocacy of such a pursuit.

One more point on voluntary equalization. Professor Kristol asks if everybody in a position to do some equalizing wants to equalize, why we do not see them doing it. But there is an asymmetry here. If my income is above the average, I can reduce the variance of income by giving it away, but if I am below the average I cannot merely opt for an average income. That limitation ought to be noted.

61

My point on liberty and minimum coercion is exactly the point Professor Nozick made—liberty is not all that we care about. The most dramatic examples are the property rights created out of thin air by the government—patents, copyrights, broadcasting certificates, taxicab medallions, and so forth. I do not know how these property rights can be interpreted in any way except as extending the range of coercion of the state. Although they are good ideas, they reduce the scope of liberty in the traditional sense that conservatives or libertarians have used —that minimum coercion is maximal liberty.

Just one last point: I read Professor Nozick as saying that the end state has no relevance, and he apparently reads me as saying that the end state is all that counts. I certainly did not intend the latter, but I think he did intend the former. To be sure, starvation that comes through the market is different from starvation decreed by the state. But starvation is bad enough to justify some action by a community that can form a voluntary insurance association as well as a voluntary protective association.

PROFESSOR KRISTOL: I see nothing wrong with the status differentials that Dr. Aaron finds so repugnant. I think status differentials testify to real differentials of character, ability, and talent, that they are deserved, and that we should have as many of them as possible.

Okun argues that if I admire inequality, I should have the government institute a regressive income tax. Now I believe in the people's right to pursue inequality, but I do not think it is our government's job to redistribute income, either progressively or regressively, simply for the purpose of achieving equality or inequality. Moreover, I find it interesting that Okun's first thought was that I should want to make this the job of the state.

Okun suggested that we should have made a deal: I would not mention Britain, and he would not mention Sweden. But it is quite all right with me if he mentions Sweden, because the Swedish experience raises a major question that we should consider here. Sweden is a perfectly decent country, with good economic growth (something economists care more about than I do), but—and this is the question—do we really want America to be like Sweden? In effect, our discussion of income redistribution and inequality is not so much a discussion in economics as it is a discussion in political philosophy. What kind of civilization do we want to live in? What kind of social, political, and economic order do we want? What kind of life do we want? I find Sweden boring and would not want to live there. When I read Swedish literature, I find that Swedes seem to find Sweden boring too: I am not aware of any literature of exultation coming out of Sweden. The only Swede I know who says what a great country Sweden is happens to be Gunnar Myrdal, who spends most of his time elsewhere.

I am not saying there cannot be a decent society with a large state, a bureaucratic state, an intrusive state, a state that imposes a high degree of equality. But that is not the kind of society I want. Nor is it the kind of society that, I think, the majority of the American people want. Nor do I see why they should want it, because, I think, our society is in many respects more interesting, more varied, more lively, and more creative than any such egalitarian society.

ROBERT E. WEINTRAUB, U.S. Treasury Department: I would like to direct two questions to each member of the panel, and both can be answered with a simple yes or no. My questions are designed to try to educate me as to what it is that you are really saying. In a race in New York, a horse named Ruffian, a marvelous filly, tripped, and a lot of money was spent trying to save her life. As it turned out, she had to be destroyed. My first question is whether you think it was worthwhile to spend the money on Ruffian. My second question is whether you think it was worthwhile to spend the money that was spent to repair Michelangelo's *Pietà*.

PROFESSOR KRISTOL: The answer is yes, yes, since both of those works, the horse and the *Pietà*, were works of excellence and were worth saving.

DR. AARON: I would agree. The only question I would have is whether I want a distribution of income in which some people are able to devote resources to horses and others are not able to devote them to their children.

PROFESSOR NUTTER: I think it is irrelevant what I believe. If there were people who wanted to save the horse's life and wanted to repair the *Pietà* and do it voluntarily, I do not believe we should stop them from doing so.

PROFESSOR MARSHALL COHEN: I think it was worthwhile trying to save the horse's life, though it does not seem to me, by any means, the most worthwhile thing that could have been done with the money. It is another question whether the people who had that money to spend on the filly ought to have had it. The *Pietà* should certainly have been restored. I do not take the view that the relief of human (or of animal) suffering gets the highest priority in all circumstances.

PROFESSOR NOZICK: I think the people had a right to spend the money as they wished, given that they had acquired it justly. A lot of money is spent for things that I would not choose to spend it for. But those who tried to save the horse's life had a right to spend their money as they chose.

PROFESSOR KRISTOL: Could I add something? My view is different from the others here. I think it would have been wrong not to spend the money that way.

PROFESSOR BUCHANAN: I want to follow up what Warren Nutter said. I think it is an irrelevant question. The question is not what I believe or what you believe. I would commend the philosophers for bringing in the question of the constitutional level of decision making. Then they respond to this question as if it were meaningful. I can go along completely with Nozick's criticism of patterns and end-state results and with his emphasis on process, but not with his attempts to define individual rights.

Let me bring in a little of Rawls here. The ultimate test is whether we can agree at some sort of basic contractarian level. At the level Okun was considering what we can agree on is irrelevant.

As Professor Marshall Cohen said, there is a feedback. What we predict about the end-state results influences how we think different processes will work. But the ultimate test is the extent of our agreement on the processes that will produce whatever results emerge. Nozick is quite right that observing particular results is completely irrelevant. The question on distribution is what we will allow the state to do in its coercive role. We can talk about that as much as the market, but that seems to have been missing from this discussion.

J. CARTER MURPHY, Southern Methodist University: I am not sure I understand Nozick's position completely, but I was intrigued by his use of analogy in discussing the process and the outcome. He said I would be constrained either if I left my house and were struck by lightning or if someone were standing by to paralyze me with a gun. One might argue that it makes no difference which constraint applies; it is the outcome that is essential. I contend it would make an enormous difference in one's behavior. In the one case, one would not be hostile, and in the other case, one would be. This may be Nozick's position, but I am not certain.

Earlier in the conversation it was said that the reason we are concerned about income distribution is that we are concerned about status. I think that is exactly right. I contend that human beings are, for the most part, concerned about their relationship with other human beings. And, in the matter of income distribution, what is important is the contest. If, in fact, the suicide rate is high in Sweden— or if Sweden is boring—it is, in part, because somebody spoiled the contest, and the contest has a certain utility. In utilitarian theory, it was asked why people gamble, since gambling is obviously irrational. We finally recognized that there is pleasure in the game. I think there is also some pleasure in the game of competing for a higher share in the distribution of income.

PETER GOULD: My understanding of Kristol's analysis is that he would let the market do its work. I take this to imply a rejection of the notion that there is a morally justifiable minimum level of income that everyone should have, regardless of the results of the marketplace. Okun's view is that poverty is, in part, a result of market failure, discrimination, or something similar. My question for Mr. Kristol is whether he can conceive of any market failures that would make some form of income redistribution justifiable within his scheme and, if so, where he draws the line.

PROFESSOR KRISTOL: I said that a certain measure of income redistribution could, in fact, be justified and mentioned the case of the aged, infirm, and disabled, though that is not the only relevant case. My idea of a good society is one that takes proper care of the people who cannot work. I see no objection morally, politically, or economically to being generous to those who cannot work and that generosity must in fact be carried out through income redistribution—though such redistribution is not an end in itself, merely a means to a particular and limited end. I also believe there is a case for income redistribution—or at least a case for the progressive income tax—when national defense takes a very large portion of the national budget. Expenditures for national defense involve and legitimate the principle of "equality of sacrifice," and this is always a redistributive principle. But that is as far as I go. I think market failures in general can be coped with by insurance schemes that do not necessarily involve redistribution of income.

PROFESSOR MARSHALL COHEN: There is one thing about Professor Kristol's position I would like to understand a little better than I do. He says, in discussing the morality of capitalism, that it is "fair" that income should, on the whole, be distributed according to one's productive input into the economy, as this is measured by the marketplace. I take it he thinks that if people have come by their income in this way, they have a right to it. How, then, does he justify even a moderate redistribution?

PROFESSOR KRISTOL: I have no problem in society's occasionally balancing a right, not only against another right, but also against another purpose.

PROFESSOR NUTTER: May I defend Professor Kristol on this question a little more than he has defended himself? It has been said twice that he believes the market determines the best distribution of income. In his paper, he says: "There is no method in political philosophy which permits us to determine, *in the abstract,* which principle of distribution is superior."

PROFESSOR KRISTOL: I can imagine all sorts of ways of distributing income that could lead to a perfectly decent society. We must not be absolutely dogmatic about the superiority of the market. But if we are talking about a highly industrialized, technologically advanced, large, densely populated society, I think that the best principle on the whole is the market principle.

PROFESSOR NOZICK: What is admirable about market distribution is that it takes place through voluntary exchanges. There are other voluntary exchanges in society that do not take place through the market and are not in accordance with productive capacity. There is philanthropy, there is what parents give to children, and there is patronage of the arts. I want it to be clear that I am in no way especially endorsing market distribution as opposed to whatever arises out of other voluntary means.

Professor Kristol mentioned earlier that absolute dependency corrupts absolutely. I would like to see some more detailed social psychological evidence. Would he say that inherited wealth always produces social pathology?

PROFESSOR KRISTOL: I would like to have some studies done on that. As a matter of fact, I think that inherited wealth does produce social pathology. I think it is bad for young people to inherit large sums of money. I think it is bad for their character. But I know of no study that demonstrates this.

HOWARD TUCKMAN, Florida State University: This is a question addressed to Professor Nozick. I am puzzled about the implications of the distinction between what economists take as the traditional form of analysis, namely, the preference function, and the idea of natural rights. I think Arthur Okun spoke to this point earlier but I would like to pursue it further now. If we have a set of abstract natural rights, which are not recognized by some individuals, and then these individuals become subject to certain actions that are justified by these natural rights, there is, presumably by definition, no net benefit increase and no net increase in utility, either for these individuals or the aggregate; yet, Professor Nozick, if I understand him, has asserted that in some sense the stock of social welfare increases.

PROFESSOR NOZICK: I did not say that the stock of social welfare increases if *social welfare* is defined as the sum of individual preferences. I said that people have the right not to have certain things happen. Suppose that the rights of Jews not to have their property seized and not to be exterminated had not been in the preference functions of other people in Nazi Germany. How would we describe that situation within Dr. Tuckman's framework? Should we say that it would have been proper to impose constraints on the Germans, even though it contradicted their preference functions, so that they would not persecute and exterminate the Jews, or should we say that social welfare would not have increased if we had stopped the Germans from doing what they did so it was proper for them to do it? We should not think of all moral questions—though economists tend to—as questions of maximizing social welfare or preference satisfaction. The most fundamental moral questions are not of this sort.

DR. TUCKMAN: I would not presume to define a social welfare function to be imposed on all. I would suggest that perhaps the way such questions are decided currently is by a set of institutional rules and laws. But the laws, as a given, do not enter directly into a person's utility function. The difficulty with entering them directly is that somebody must define the nature of those natural rights. And we must also make a second assumption, namely, that no individual has the right to violate his own natural right. For example, whether I have a natural right to die is a question that has become of some importance in the Quinlan case. Under what circumstances do I have the right to will my own death? And does the state infringe upon me by saying I do not have the right to "pull the plug"? It seems to me that this point is not really considered in Professor Nozick's line of thinking.

PROFESSOR NOZICK: I think it is considered and I would take a strong anti-paternalistic position. We could discuss that.

PROFESSOR KRISTOL: I think Professor Nozick's example of Nazi Germany is important. I would like to propose an answer but I do not know if he will accept it. My answer is that, under the circumstances of Nazi Germany, the people demonstrated that they had no right to any utility function, that they were too corrupt to have a utility function. That is to say, they were incapable of self-government and therefore had no right to it.

PART
TWO

INCOME MAINTENANCE AND
THE ECONOMY

SOCIAL INSURANCE

Martin Feldstein

Social insurance programs have grown at a remarkable rate and now account for more than a third of the federal government budget. In fiscal year 1975, federal spending for social security (OASDI), unemployment compensation, and health insurance (Medicare and Medicaid) exceeded $100 billion. These transfer payments alone accounted for 10 percent of personal income. The list might be extended to private insurance programs that the government either requires (workmen's compensation) or subsidizes (private health insurance).

As recently as 1965, social insurance expenditures for these programs were only $20 billion. Even after adjusting for inflation and the growth of the population, real per capita social insurance expenditures grew at 10 percent per year while real per capita disposable income grew at only 2 percent. Although the economic impact and inefficiency of social insurance might have been neglected with little consequence a decade ago, the greatly expanded programs now require careful analysis and reform.

Despite their size and importance, social insurance programs still receive surprisingly little attention. The economic effects of social insurance are largely unanalyzed. The principles and criteria by which social insurance programs should be designed are largely unexplored. The purpose of the current paper is to begin this analysis of the common issues in social insurance programs.

Although there has been little economic analysis, there has been much argument about the definition of social insurance. The controversy has centered on whether social security and the other programs are consistent with general principles of insurance or are really general income transfer programs. The truth is that social insurance is neither an insurance program nor an income redistribution program. Social insurance payments may be characterized as "event conditioned transfers," not general income redistribution. Social security is paid after retirement, disability, or death. Its payment depends on these events and not on the income or wealth of the beneficiary. Unemployment insurance is paid to those who become unemployed after sufficient work experience and therefore not to everyone

Note: This paper summarizes research that was previously presented in various economic journals. I am grateful to the National Science Foundation for support of that research. This paper also draws on material presented in nontechnical papers in the *Public Interest,* the *Harvard Business Review,* and the *Proceedings of the Industrial Relations Research Association.*

without a job who wants to work. Again the benefits are independent of other family income and assets. But unlike private insurance, in social insurance participation is compulsory; it is this compulsion that distinguishes social insurance from private insurance.

This paper will begin with a general discussion of the principles of social insurance design. I will discuss seven ideas that are relevant to all types of social insurance. The remaining sections of the paper will then discuss individual programs: social security and unemployment insurance.

Seven Principles of Social Insurance Policy

The seven ideas discussed in this section are general principles intended to aid thinking about social insurance policy and not to provide precise rules. Although they may all sound almost trivial, I am convinced that they are violated more often than they are respected.

1. *Designers of social insurance policies should recognize the substantial effect of these programs on the economy.* Most evaluations of social insurance programs focus on the extent to which these programs meet the assumed needs of the beneficiaries for income or for such specific expenditures as the purchase of medical care. It is implicitly assumed that social insurance is a passive transfer system that does not affect the behavior of the beneficiaries or the overall performance of the American economy. I think the opposite is closer to the truth. I believe that our extensive program of social insurance has important effects on the economy, that these effects are generally unintended, that they are often harmful, and that they are almost always not fully perceived by the public, the Congress, or the responsible officials.

To be more specific, there is general agreement among students of the economics of health care that Medicare and Medicaid ignited an explosion of health care costs. Today, patients over age sixty-five pay more out of pocket for medical care than they did a decade ago before the beginning of Medicare. There is also growing evidence that unemployment insurance creates substantial unemployment and that social security, rather than being a passive program that supplements the inadequate savings of those who are forced to retire early, actually depresses saving and induces retirement. I will return to these effects in the next two sections.

Some of this adverse result is a necessary by-product of serving the proper purpose of the social insurance program. But much of it is the unnecessary result of poor program design. The possibility of such adverse effects is too often ignored or denied by those responsible for the program. And when the issue of adverse incentive is faced, the magnitude of the effect is generally underestimated or misinterpreted.

Consider for example the assertion that the taxes that finance social insurance do not alter work effort. This conclusion is based primarily on the econometric studies that show that the labor force participation and average hours per week of adult men do not appear to be affected by differences among them in net wage rates.[1] This evidence does not warrant the interpretation that taxes have little or no effect on labor supply. For adult men, participation in the labor force is generally a necessity, though the length of the workweek is constrained by the available jobs and social convention. The more important dimensions of labor supply include work effort, choice of job, the demand for education and on-the-job training, and the willingness to relocate. On these we have no evidence. In contrast, for women the labor force participation is far from universal, and the length of the workweek varies substantially; econometric evidence shows a very substantial sensitivity to taxes and to net wage rates.[2]

The recent "negative income tax experiment" in New Jersey and elsewhere has given support to the conclusion that there are no adverse work incentives.[3] The use of an experimental method and the great cost of the exercise add further weight to their conclusions. But I believe that the evidence is much weaker than it appears, and the conclusion may be quite wrong. First, this was a short-term experiment; there was little time for a change of individual attitudes and little incentive to continue previous jobs in order to have a good employment record after the experiment. Second, because of the relatively small number of participants, there was no change in the supply of part-time jobs. Individuals in the experiment might prefer a 10 a.m. to 4 p.m. job, and such jobs might be available with a universal program, but there was no scope for such a response in this experiment. Finally, individual behavior is governed in part by peer group pressures, the "brother-in-law effect": What would your brother-in-law say if you took a lower-paying job or were continually quitting work? Only when a program is generally available will its disincentive effects be reinforced rather than countered by social pressures.

In addition to understating the likely impact of taxes on work effort, most discussions misinterpret the evidence in two important ways. There is a significant difference between a tax that is used to finance defense and other general government services and a tax that is used to finance benefits for the taxpayer himself. A general tax has two effects: it makes goods purchased with after-tax dollars more expensive relative to leisure and thus discourages work effort, but it also reduces income and therefore encourages effort to recoup some of the lost net income. The net effect on work effort is indeterminate. But when a tax is used to finance benefits for the taxpayer, as it would with national health insurance, there is no such reduc-

---

[1] See, for example, Robert E. Hall, "Wages, Income, and Hours of Work in the U.S. Labor Force," in E. G. Cain and H. W. Watts, eds., *Income Maintenance and Labor Supply* (Chicago: Rand McNally, 1973), pp. 102-62.

[2] Harvey S. Rosen, "Taxes in a Labor Supply Model with Joint Wage-Hour Determination," *Econometrica,* vol. 44, no. 3 (May 1976), pp. 485-507.

[3] Joseph A. Peckman and P. Michael Timpane, eds., *Work Incentives and Income Guarantees— The New Jersey Negative Income Tax Experiment* (Washington, D.C.: The Brookings Institution, 1975).

tion in real income to stimulate additional work. And a program like Medicaid decreases the work effort of beneficiaries even though they pay no tax, but it has an ambiguous effect on the effort of the taxpayers who support the program but get no benefit.

The second misinterpretation is to assume that a tax with no effect on the supply of work effort (or on other behavior such as saving) has no adverse effect. Every student who has passed the first course in economics should know better. The lack of a change in work effort masks an important distortion caused by the tax. The tax discourages work and increases the consumption of leisure instead of goods. This fact is obscured because the tax reduces net income and thus provides an incentive for more work. This is not a case of two wrongs making a right, or two negatives a positive. The change in the relative price of goods and leisure is a real loss, an "excess burden" or "welfare loss" in the language of economics. Reduced income causes more work but does not offset the loss of welfare because the income that is gained by working is offset by the loss of leisure.

The fact that an income tax causes a loss of welfare vis-à-vis a fixed "lump sum" tax is neither a case for using a regressive lump sum tax nor a case for not raising revenue to finance social insurance programs. But it does imply that this *extra* cost of raising revenue should be borne in mind in deciding on the size of social insurance programs.

Although more research is needed, an illustrative calculation will indicate the importance of this. Suppose that actual work effort (including job choice, effort, and so on) is reduced only 3 percent in response to a 30 percent tax rate—which, in economic terms, gives a 10 percent uncompensated supply elasticity. Suppose also that if a representative individual received an annual gift of $1,000 he would reduce his work effort by enough to reduce his net earnings by $400; he would buy $600 worth of goods and $400 worth of leisure. This implies a "compensated" supply elasticity of 50 percent. From these quite reasonable assumptions it follows that to raise an additional $30 billion involves a total cost of $35 billion of forgone consumption and leisure.

2. *Social insurance policies should reflect a balancing of desired protection and inefficient distortions.* Unemployment insurance should provide adequate protection against earnings loss from unemployment without unduly encouraging unemployment. Medicare should protect the aged against financial hardship of medical expenses without unduly exacerbating the excess use of health resources. Similar goals are relevant to social security, welfare programs, and other transfers. Their application requires information and analysis that are within the state of the art but beyond the scope of this paper.

Note that this issue is rather different from the usual equity-efficiency trade-off that pervades discussions of optimal taxation. The problem of balancing protection and efficiency would arise even if everyone were identical and exposed to the same risks. Payment of insurance benefits during spells of unemployment is not based on equity considerations: no investigation is made of other income and assets. The protection-efficiency trade-off poses a problem in optimal insurance that is mathematically similar to the equity-efficiency trade-off but conceptually very different. A utilitarian approach to the design of optimal insurance will appeal to many who reject a utilitarian approach to income redistribution as inherently unfair.

There is also, of course, an equity-efficiency trade-off in social insurance programs, but this should be viewed as a smaller problem than the protection-efficiency trade-off. Social insurance programs do not distinguish among the risk classes of the insurees in the way that a private program would. Medicare provides the same coverage at the same expense regardless of previous illness or current condition. There is also a tendency to use the financing of social insurance as a form of income redistribution. But these taxes, except insofar as they are used to finance differential and actuarially equivalent benefits, should be regarded as part of the total tax structure (including the personal and corporate income taxes) and not a problem of social insurance as such.

3. *Balancing protection, equity, and efficiency may be less important in practice than trying to get more of all three.* Discussing the hard trade-offs among efficiency, protection, and equity suggests that it is not possible to have more of one without forgoing some of at least one other, but we are still not faced with that necessity. There are still many ways to improve both efficiency and protection by restructuring the individual programs. These restructurings need not result in adverse distributional effects, frustrated expectations, or other inequities.

A more equitable treatment of working wives under the social security program would also increase their protection and reduce the distortion toward early retirement. A restructuring of Medicare benefits would prevent the inequitable and humiliating impoverishment required to qualify for Medicaid when an expensive illness occurs. Such a restructuring would also strengthen the financial protection provided by the program and would reduce the bloated demand for the expensive services of physicians and hospitals for minor conditions.

4. *Social insurance programs should be redesigned periodically to keep pace with changing conditions.* Our social insurance programs today are largely an inheritance from the 1930s. Adverse effects have developed primarily because the economy has changed dramatically since the programs began but the programs themselves have not changed correspondingly. It is unfortunate that the current forms of social insurance have become almost sacrosanct, almost beyond critical examination. Only if loyalty is focused on the purposes of the programs instead of on their forms can their good features be strengthened while some of their harmful effects are eliminated.

In other sections of this paper I will explain how the vast unemployment of the Great Depression and the collapse of financial institutions shaped the social security and unemployment insurance systems. With the economic conditions of the present and the future, quite different systems are appropriate. Even our Medicare and Medicaid programs and many of the proposals for national health insurance rely on ideas about the delivery of medical care that have been inherited from a period of quite different technological and economic conditions.

5. *The morality of redistribution in social insurance is not unconstrained utilitarianism.* It is tempting to look on today's social insurance program and on the progressive income tax as evidence of the public's willingness to redistribute income generally.[4] The current redistribution can be interpreted as a poor approximation of a general negative income tax. I think such a view is wrong.

Redistribution is fundamentally a moral issue and the distributional morality of the United States is not simply unconstrained utilitarianism. An important distinction is made between the progressive tax that emphasizes "fair shares" of the total burden and a redistributive tax system in which some are actually gainers. Progressivity may be viewed as achieving equal sacrifice of utility rather than as maximizing total welfare.

The actual payments by the government are not regarded as general transfers to achieve greater equality. Rather they are benefits initiated by particular events, by catastrophic conditions, or by the inability of the beneficiary to act on his own behalf. Most of the benefits are regarded as insurance benefits to which rights are earned through the payment of compulsory taxes: unemployment insurance, social security, Medicare, and others. Welfare, Medicaid, and food stamps are seen as reserved for those who are catastrophically poor. And methods of awarding educational grants and places in mental hospitals reflect the agreement that the beneficiaries are incapable of making their own decisions.

To appreciate this view of progressive taxation and social welfare payments is to understand why the public rejects confiscatory estate taxes on millionaires and why it opposed McGovern's "demogrant" scheme. It is the public's moral sense of appropriate redistribution that stops a majority from voting to set taxes and transfers to maximize its own well-being. Social insurance policy should regard appropriate redistribution in this limited way.

6. *Social insurance should start by preventing catastrophic losses.* The primary purpose of insurance should be to prevent or compensate for very large financial losses that occur with relatively small probability. Individual savings and other assets should be used to smooth variations in the timing of moderate expenses or losses. These widely accepted principles are almost always violated by social insurance.

Consider first the rationale: While any loss causes some hardship, a very large loss causes hardship which is disproportionately greater. A $500 medical bill may

---

[4] See Arthur Okun, *Equality and Efficiency: The Big Tradeoff* (Washington, D.C.: The Brookings Institution, 1975).

require months of saving to repay but a $5,000 bill may cause the loss of one's house or some other major and permanent dislocation. Two weeks of unemployment without pay could be absorbed by reducing savings balances or by postponing purchases and payments. But the closing of a plant, when that results in a long spell of unemployment and would require expensive relocation or retraining for the plant's employees to achieve their previous level of earnings, may be a financial disaster. And yet unemployment insurance is much more ample for short spells than for long, and the quite comprehensive shallow coverage of Medicare is exhausted by very expensive illness. Similarly, a young worker who is disabled finds that his social security benefits are very low and that they continue to fall relative to the general standard of living.

Social insurance programs would be improved by restructuring them to improve protection against catastrophic losses while reducing protection against small losses that can be financed by the individuals themselves.

7. *Categorical programs are desirable even if a general negative income tax is introduced.* The idea of replacing the multiplicity of categorical programs with a single negative income tax (NIT) has obvious appeal. So too does the argument that, since poverty comes from a lack of sufficient money, it is best cured by giving money to the poor.[5]

The fundamental difficulty with this argument is that it ignores the substantial differences in the likely impact of means-tested transfers and taxes on the behavior of different groups. To be specific, changes in the benefits paid to a seventy-year-old blind woman are likely to have less effect on her work effort than payments to a young woman or to one at age sixty. This has two interrelated sets of implications: those relating to cost and those relating to efficiency.

One of the effective criticisms of a negative income tax is that it is extremely expensive. The real reason for this lies in the likely effect of such a tax on incentives. If there were no incentive effect, a negative income tax could simply supplement the income of every family until the family reached, say, $5,000 and pay nothing to any family above that level. But why would anyone now earning $3,000 not then retire since the loss of earnings would result in no loss of net income? And would not many who now earn $6,000 prefer to retire with $5,000 of income and no work? To avoid these adverse incentive effects, NIT proponents suggest combining a lump-sum payment with a high rate of tax over the low and middle range of income—for example, a $5,000 grant and a 50 percent tax on all income to $10,000. This would assure all families an income of at least $5,000 and would provide even the very poor with some incentive to work. But as a result benefits would be paid to families far above the poverty line with average or above-average

---

[5] See Milton Friedman, *Capitalism and Freedom* (Chicago: University of Chicago Press, 1962), and Edgar K. Browning, *Redistribution and the Welfare System* (Washington, D.C.: American Enterprise Institute, 1975).

wage earnings. And paying benefits over such a wide range would make the NIT very expensive.

Extending the NIT to middle-income families also creates an adverse incentive for them. By taxing away half of any additional income (actually more than half because of the existence of current income tax payments, social security, and state taxes) the NIT would substantially reduce incentives in this range. There is no way to pay a reasonably high minimum without having effective "recapture" tax rates that are quite high or that extend over a very wide range of incomes.

Categorical programs—payments to the blind, the disabled, the aged—have few incentive effects, even if the benefits are much more ample than general income support. The eligible beneficiaries are generally unable to work themselves so there is no direct disincentive effect,[6] and they constitute a relatively well-defined group so that there is no indirect disincentive effect. Payments for mothers with dependent children raise greater problems but still not as many as are raised by general financial aid.

There is a strong argument therefore for relying on categorical programs instead of on a general NIT. But even if a general NIT is introduced, an appropriate mixture of general support and categorical support should be developed, with higher levels of benefit for those with the less sensitive response.[7]

Social Security

The largest component of our social security system is the program of benefits for retirees, the disabled, and surviving dependents. The basic features of social security were designed in the midst of the Great Depression. Features that were valuable then are inappropriate in the very different economic conditions of the present and of the foreseeable future. The time has come to reexamine the purpose of social security and to redesign the form of the program to serve this purpose with the most favorable (or the least adverse) side effects.

Two aspects of the Great Depression had a major effect on the design of social security. The length of the depression and the failure of financial institutions had destroyed the lifetime savings of a great many families. More than 20 percent of the labor force was unemployed. A social security program that paid benefits to retirees would replace lost savings, stimulate consumption, and open the jobs left by the retirees to the younger people who were currently unemployed. Moreover, the new Keynesian economics stressed the belief that the depression would persist as long as the full-employment rate of savings remained greater than the rate of investment. The fear that an excessive savings rate would cause a permanent

---

[6] This conclusion is less applicable to the "younger aged." I think there is a strong case for making their benefits unconditional (abolishing the retirement test).

[7] Economists will recognize here the optimal taxation argument that tax (subsidy) rates should vary inversely with elasticities.

depression remained a firm conviction of many leading economists into the 1940s. By providing a substitute for private saving, social security would reduce the future saving rate and thus help to promote full employment.[8]

Economic conditions are now very different. The past twenty-five years have seen a relatively low average unemployment rate, less than 5 percent. There is a consensus among economists that much of this 5 percent represents adverse incentives rather than inadequate demand. The "forced" early retirement at sixty-five no longer serves a socially useful purpose. The early fear of excessive savings has now changed to a serious concern about a capital shortage. A social security system designed to reduce saving was appropriate forty years ago but is no longer appropriate.

The valid purpose of social security today is to provide annuities that could not or would not be purchased otherwise. There is, of course, a substantial intellectual difference between a "could not" and a "would not," between correcting an imperfect market and imposing a paternalistic policy. Both deserve a more complete discussion.[9]

Not everyone covered by social security could buy equivalent annuities on the private insurance market. Of course, insurance companies do sell retirement and disability annuities, and life insurance can provide an annuity for surviving dependents. Although annuities adjusted for inflation to preserve the same real benefits are not currently available, their lack of availability would be remedied quickly if the government offered to sell price-indexed bonds. Insurance companies can offer annuity policies that are close to being actuarially fair for large- and moderate-sized groups. Sizable employers or unions can make a collective purchase of insurance for their members. It is understandable, however, that insurance companies generally cannot sell actuarially fair policies to individuals or very small groups. Adverse selection—that is, a greater demand for insurance by those with higher expected benefits—forces insurance companies to charge higher premiums for individual coverage than for group coverage. These higher premiums exacerbate the problem of adverse selection, thus causing further premium increases, and so on. Many of those who have no reason to believe that they are high-risk cases find the cost of insurance so high that they choose not to insure. Social security avoids the adverse selection problem by forming one big group. It might reasonably be objected that a compulsory social security system is not necessary to remedy this defect in the market. To permit everyone to buy as much insurance as he currently gets from social security and on the same financial terms, it would be necessary only to offer such insurance on a voluntary basis. Individuals could buy all of their insurance in this way or could supplement group plans they regarded as

---

[8] Seymour Harris developed this argument in his *Economics of Social Security* (New York: McGraw-Hill, 1941).

[9] I regard the next few pages as an attempt to deal with the objections to social security raised by Friedman in *Capitalism and Freedom*.

inadequate. Although the insurance would not be sold at individually actuarially fair rates, the terms would be as good as they are under the current compulsory program. Anyone or any group that found such terms unsatisfactory could either buy commercial insurance or simply remain uninsured.

This brings us to the second purpose of social security, to provide insurance to those who would not otherwise buy it for themselves. Why should the government be so paternalistic as to compel individuals to buy annuity insurance that they would not otherwise choose to buy? I think that there are three distinct reasons. First, if there were no social security it would be necessary to have a welfare program for older people with no other means of support. Such a means-tested program would induce low-income workers to avoid accumulating assets because of the high implicit rate of "tax" implied by such a means-tested grant. When these workers retire, their level of consumption may be lower than it would have been in the absence of a means-tested welfare grant. Social security, by providing retirement benefits without regard to wealth, avoids this distortion of saving. In this respect, the desirability of social security depends on balancing the reduced distortions in the saving of this group against the other distortions introduced by social security.

The second rationale for compulsory annuity insurance is the potentially high cost of private choice. Insurance, annuities, and compound interest are all hard concepts for a large part of the population to understand and use correctly. The government might try to educate the public so that every individual could make a well-informed choice. But this would be expensive both in government spending and in the time that individuals must spend in learning. If everyone would eventually reach the same conclusion (and therefore a conclusion that the government can anticipate), it would obviously be more efficient to avoid the information and decision-making costs than not to avoid them. Of course, such unanimity is most unlikely. But to the extent that there is agreement among individuals with the same social and economic characteristics, a compulsory program will be more efficient than using the extra resources to inform individual choices. Since the workers with higher earnings are likely to want the larger annuities, there is a justification for the income-related character of the benefits provided by social security. Again, the efficient answer is not clear-cut but requires a balancing of opposing considerations. Moreover, libertarians would regard a restriction on individual choice as unjustified by any efficiency gain. And pessimists would regard the variety of individual answers as a safeguard against the imposition of a single answer that is wrong for everyone.

Finally, even if all the objective information about survival and disability probabilities, interest rates, future incomes, and other relevant factors were fully known and fully understood by everyone, some individuals would still make the "mistake" of giving too much weight to current consumption and not enough to future consumption—that is, if left to their own choice, they would eventually look back with the hindsight of old age and regret that they had not saved more. If everyone were so myopic in his individual decision making, a benevolent government could raise everyone's lifetime well-being by compelling additional saving. Unless myopia becomes less important as income rises, the amount of compulsory saving should increase with income. If, as is more likely, only some individuals are myopic, the appropriate policy would be to require additional saving only if the individual's choice was below a given level. If this is not possible, or if the appropriate saving differs among individuals according to characteristics that the government cannot observe, it is necessary to balance the gain from offsetting insufficient saving against the loss of forcing saving that is too high. Again there are some who will reject these criteria and insist that efficiency gains must be subservient to individual liberty or, at least, that the two must be balanced against each other in reaching this decision.

Although these are reasons that may justify requiring individuals to purchase income-related annuities, none of these reasons indicate that the annuities should be provided by the government on a pay-as-you-go basis. I have discussed elsewhere the case for a capital fund if social security remains a purely government program.[10] The choice between public and private programs will be discussed below.

All three of the reasons that I have indicated must be considered along with other effects (that I will discuss below) to determine the best structure of social security benefits and financing. Although we do not yet know enough to predict how individuals will respond to different combinations of social security benefits and financing, we can begin to understand and quantify these effects. I will here discuss the impact of social security on saving decisions and on work behavior as well as the implications of these effects on the welfare of the population. The choice among alternative social security designs will be the subject of a later paper.[11]

Reducing Capital Accumulation. The most serious effect of our social security program is to reduce the nation's rate of savings and therefore our rate of capital accumulation. Recall that with our current pay-as-you-go method, social security tax receipts are paid out as concurrent benefits and are not accumulated. There is no real investment of social security tax payments, and therefore no interest (as such) is earned on these compulsory contributions. When we, the current generation of workers, retire, we will not receive social security benefits by drawing down an accumulated fund. Instead, our benefits will be financed by the tax payments of those who are at work when we retire.

Because of the growing population and rising level of real wages, the taxes collected in the future will allow us as retirees to receive social security benefits

[10] Martin Feldstein, "The Optimal Financing of Social Security," Harvard Institute of Economic Research, Discussion Paper No. 388, 1974.
[11] "Social Security Benefits and Financing," to be written for the *American Economic Review*.

greater in total value than the amount we will have paid in taxes while we were working. Past experience suggests that the level of benefits will be equivalent to receiving a modest real rate of interest on our previous compulsory contributions to social security. If there is no further expansion of coverage or of benefit replacement rates, future social security benefits will on average reflect a real rate of return equal to the rate of growth of total wage income (that is, the rate of growth of the labor force plus the rate of growth of the wage rate). With zero population growth, the implicit real rate of return would be about 2 percent; although this seems low, it should be remembered that this is a real after-tax rate of return and therefore about as much as most low-income and middle-income households have traditionally received from personal savings accounts or government savings bonds.

For most Americans, the social security program is the major form of saving. Consider, for example, an individual, with an income of $10,000, who in the absence of social security would wish to save 10 percent of his total income for his old age. With social security, such an individual would not need any saving at all for the ordinary expenses of his retirement. He need save only to buy consumer durables and to have a cash balance for emergencies. Similarly, an individual, with an income of $20,000, who in the absence of social security would want to save 10 percent of his income (or $2,000), finds that social security now involves compulsory savings of about $1,800. He would therefore need to save only an additional $200 instead of $2,000.

In 1975, total social security contributions were some $70 billion, or 7 percent of total disposable personal income. If individuals think of these contributions as equivalent to savings and reduce their own personal savings accordingly, the effect on total savings would be substantial. In 1975, personal savings were $90 billion, or 9 percent of disposable personal income. If there were an $80 billion reduction in personal savings because of social security, personal savings would have been cut to half what they would otherwise be. Of course, not all private savings are personal savings. Corporate retained earnings account for nearly half of all private capital accumulation. In 1975, those corporate savings were $30 billion, and, when these are added to personal savings, total private savings were $120 billion. If social security reduced savings by $80 billion, the total potential private savings of $200 billion will have been reduced by about 40 percent. In the long run, this implies that U.S. capital stock is at least 40 percent less than it would otherwise be.

Because social security taxes are not actually compulsory savings, but only an exchange of taxes for an implicit promise of future benefits, it is also useful to look in a quite different way at the likely effect of social security on savings. Instead of considering the social security contributions, the individual might focus on his expected benefits. Being covered by social security is like owning an annuity— that is, a claim on future annual payments when the individual reaches sixty-five. Although the individual is not guaranteed these benefits by contract and could in principle be deprived of them by a legislative change, the past experience of the program and the recent legislative proposals suggest not only that benefits will continue to be paid but also that they will increase with the general level of income. These implicit social security annuities are an important part of each family's wealth. An individual with such an annuity could proportionately reduce his own private accumulation of wealth—whether held directly or through private pensions.

It is therefore interesting to use the total value of these social security annuities as an estimate of the likely effect of social security on the total private stock of real wealth. The total value of these annuities reflects the number of workers at each age, their age-specific mortality rates and the mortality rates of their wives, the rate at which per capita income can be expected to grow in the future, and the appropriate rate of interest at which to discount future benefits in evaluating the future annuity benefits. In a recent study, I estimated the 1971 value of this social security "wealth" at $2 trillion.[12] Since the total private wealth of households in that year was about $3 trillion, the calculation suggests that social security may have reduced the stock of private wealth by about 40 percent—that is, from $5 trillion of wealth that would exist without social security to the $3 trillion that currently exists. The 40 percent reduction is remarkably close to the estimate obtained by looking at the reduction in personal savings that would occur if households viewed social security taxes as an alternative to savings.

The relative importance of social security "wealth" has grown rapidly in the past two decades. In 1950, social security "wealth" was 88 percent of gross national product. A decade later it had increased to 133 percent of gross national product. Today it is more than 200 percent of gross national product. The impact of social security "wealth" on capital accumulation is thus likely to be more important now than ever before.

Two caveats must be noted at this point. First, while it is clear that rational men who are fortunate enough to have had a basic course in economics might understand the wealth implied by the social security program, the typical American household might not behave as this theory predicts. The two preceding calculations showed the extent to which the social security program would reduce private capital if households did substitute social security "wealth" for private savings, but the calculations did not show that such substitution actually occurs. Second, even if households are perfectly rational in reducing private wealth accumulation by the value of their social security "wealth," the effect of social security is more complex than the preceding discussion has indicated. Moreover, an important effect of the social security program (and especially of the rule that benefits are paid only to those who effectively retired) is to induce a higher rate of retirement

---

[12] "Social Security, Induced Retirement and Aggregate Capital Accumulation," *Journal of Political Economy,* vol. 82, no. 5 (September-October 1974), pp. 905-26. This social security "wealth" is not real wealth but only an implicit promise that the next generation will tax itself to pay the annuities currently specified in the law. Although there are no tangible assets corresponding to this "wealth," it is perfectly rational for households to regard the value of their future social security benefits as part of their personal wealth.

among older persons. But a higher rate of retirement will in itself increase the rate at which people choose to save. A man who plans to continue working until his death need only accumulate enough wealth to support himself (and any surviving dependents) if he becomes unable to work before he dies. If that same man is induced to plan to retire at sixty-five, he will want to accumulate sufficient wealth to provide for this lengthier retirement period. At age sixty-five a man now has a life expectancy of more than thirteen years. Since social security benefits are generally less than pre-retirement earnings, the induced retirement is likely to lead to some additional private savings before retirement.

The net effect of the social security program will therefore depend on the balance between the extra savings preparatory to induced retirement and the reduced savings resulting from the replacement of private accumulation by social security "wealth." The relative strength of these two effects will, of course, depend on the magnitude of the increase in retirees as a result of the social security program. In 1929, some 45 percent of men over the age of sixty-five were retired. By 1971, the retirement rate had increased to 75 percent. Although the higher rate of retirement also reflects higher income, changing life expectancies, and a changed occupational mix, the social security system is no doubt responsible for some of the increase. Nevertheless, it is clear that even if half the increase in retirement were attributable to social security, the reduction in savings from the replacement of private wealth by social security "wealth" is almost certain to be much greater than the increase in savings prior to induced retirement.

A few years ago I completed an econometric study of savings behavior in the United States since 1929, the study being designed to estimate the net impact of social security on the nation's accumulation of capital.[13] The results confirmed the view that social security does substantially reduce private savings. More specifically, the statistical estimates imply that social security reduced personal savings in 1971 by between $40 billion and $60 billion. The actual level of personal savings in 1971 was $61 billion. The estimated fall in savings therefore implies that social security reduced personal savings by 40 to 50 percent. Total private savings, including corporate savings, were therefore reduced by 32 to 42 percent. I noted earlier that if private wealth were reduced by the full amount of social security "wealth," the decrease in our capital stock would be about 40 percent. The current estimates of a reduction of between 32 and 42 percent in the savings rate therefore imply that households do rationally respond to social security "wealth" by reducing their private savings, and that the positive effect of induced retirement on savings is relatively small.

Some further evidence of a different kind also supports this conclusion. The major developed countries of the world differ quite substantially in the fraction of national income saved. The United States, with postwar private savings equal to

---

[13] Ibid.

about 9 percent of national income, is well below average. Social security programs also differ substantially among these major developed countries. An analysis of this international evidence indicates that the higher the level of social security benefits and the more complete the coverage of the population by the social security program the lower will be a nation's rate of private savings.[14]

How does this substantial reduction in savings affect the U.S. economy? How would our economy be different if the rate of saving were substantially higher? To be specific in my answers, let me use the estimate that social security reduces the nation's rate of saving by about 35 percent. If this asset substitution had not occurred, the long-run capital stock would be some 80 percent higher than it currently is. As a rough approximation, gross national product would increase by about 19 percent. For 1975, then, GNP would have increased by more than $285 billion. To put this number in some perspective, note that $285 billion is nearly 30 percent of total consumer spending, more than twice the total of individual income tax payments, and substantially more than double the national defense expenditures. Viewed somewhat differently, $285 billion is $1,300 per person, or more than $3,500 per family. Let me emphasize that this lower level of GNP reflects the pay-as-you-go nature of our social security system. It is because social security taxes are used to pay concurrent benefits that the capital stock is smaller and income is less than it would otherwise be.

The substantial reduction in our nation's savings implies that there is less capital per worker in the economy. This change in the relative scarcity of labor and capital implies that the current social security program makes wage rates lower and the rate of profit higher than they would otherwise be. If in the absence of the current social security system the capital stock were 80 percent greater, the wage rate would rise by 19 percent and the rate of return on investment would fall by 34 percent. These changes imply a rather significant redistribution of income to less wealthy families, for whom wage income is much more important than capital income.

The current social security program also has a dramatic effect on the distribution of the ownership of capital.[15] In our country, capital is distributed much less equally than income. The top 1 percent of income recipients earn some 5 percent of total household income. In contrast, the top 1 percent of wealth holders own approximately 40 percent of the capital owned by all households. How does this greater inequality of wealth reflect the impact of the social security system? To the great majority of Americans, anticipated social security benefits are an adequate

---

[14] Martin Feldstein, "Social Security and Private Savings: International Evidence in an Extended Life Cycle Model," in M. Feldstein and R. Inman, eds., *The Economics of Public Services,* International Economic Association Conference Volume (New York: Halstead Press, 1976). For a summary of other research on this question, see Feldstein, "Social Security and Saving: The Extended Life Cycle Theory," *American Economic Review, Proceedings,* vol. 66, no. 2 (May 1976), pp. 77-86.

[15] See Martin Feldstein, "Social Security and the Distribution of Wealth," *Journal of the American Statistical Association,* vol. 71, no. 356 (December 1976), pp. 800-807.

substitute for almost all private wealth holdings. Only for those with incomes above the base of the social security tax, now $15,300, is there a need for substantial private wealth. To put it somewhat differently, if the social security "wealth" of more than $2 trillion were instead part of our private wealth, it would be distributed much more equally than income is currently distributed. And the distribution of the larger total wealth of $5 trillion would be much more equal than the distribution of the current wealth. I have estimated that the concentration of the ownership of capital in the top 1 percent would be halved (from 40 percent today to only 20 percent). The political consequences of a widespread ownership of an additional $2 trillion of private capital can only be conjectured.

However, the current degree of inequality is in large part an illusion, based on incorrect measurement of each household's wealth in a way that excludes the value of social security benefits and private pension rights. The problem is thus largely a false one. The true distribution of wealth would not really be altered if individuals held claims to their retirement income directly instead of through a social security system.

But the important implication of the reduction in saving is not the fall in income or wages per se. The reduction in welfare comes from the distortion in saving, the substitution of an asset with a very low implicit rate of return for real capital accumulation with a much higher social rate of return.

Distorting the Labor Supply. The social security system distorts work effort in two distinct ways. For those over sixty-two years old, social security induces partial or complete retirement. For most younger workers, the social security tax substantially changes the reward for additional work. Let me discuss both of these in more detail.

A man who has earned the median wage throughout his life can now retire at age sixty-five with benefits equal to about 46 percent of his preretirement gross earnings. If he has a wife who is not working, he will receive an additional dependent's benefit equal to one-half his own benefit or 23 percent of his preretirement gross earnings. His total benefit is thus 69 percent of his previous gross earnings. Because the social security benefits are completely untaxed, they represent a substantially higher fraction of his preretirement net earnings. The effective average rate of tax on someone with median earnings—including the federal income tax, the individual's social security tax and a state income tax—is at least 15 percent. Thus net earnings for a married man over sixty-five with median earnings are no more than 85 percent of gross earnings. Social security therefore replaces at least 69/85, or 81 percent, of previous peak net earnings. Surely there is very little reason for the recipient to continue working past age sixty-five.

Because of the progressivity of the benefit structure, the incentives for retirement are even greater for lower-income workers. For them, social security benefits can easily exceed previous net income. This is also true for workers whose earnings have recently fallen. In families with two earners, a wife who has worked long enough will often be induced to retire by untaxed benefits because additional earnings would be taxed at a rate at least equal to her husband's marginal tax rate.

Of course, high-income individuals will find the replacement rate relatively low. Similarly, if both husband and wife have worked, their combined replacement rate will be low. Not everyone will face a strong incentive to retire, and even some of those with such incentive will prefer to continue at work. But statistical evidence now accumulating shows that the social security program does have an important effect on retirement. Strong evidence in a cross-section of countries that the labor force participation of men over sixty-five is substantially depressed by an increase in social security benefits and by the presence of a retirement test has been demonstrated in several studies.[16] Much more detailed analyses of microeconomic data for the United States confirm the view that social security benefits and the earnings test have a large effect on the annual retirement decision.[17]

The likely effect of social security on work effort before retirement age is ambiguous and no statistical evidence is yet available. The source of the ambiguity is the fact that paying higher social security taxes raises future benefits. Although the link between taxes and benefits is diluted by the progressivity of the system and the dependent's benefits, an increase in tax payments always raises the basic monthly benefit to which the worker will be entitled. If social security had no redistributive element—that is, if each worker received for his taxes an annuity with the same present value—the social security contributions would be a tax only to the extent that (1) the implicit rate of return paid by social security is less than the rate of return available elsewhere, and (2) the worker is forced to allocate more consumption to his retirement years than he would prefer. If the social security contributions are not a tax but only a requirement to save in a particular form, there should be no effect on labor supply. This condition is probably satisfied for an unmarried worker with below-average earnings. However, if he has a wife who has not worked, each dollar of contribution produces an additional 50 percent in benefits. This married man actually obtains a greater net subsidy for each extra dollar of tax he pays. If work effort is an increasing function of the net wage, social security should actually increase his work effort.

The same principle applies to other situations. Lower-income individuals and those with dependent wives are subsidized while higher-wage workers and two-

[16] Margaret S. Gordon, "Income Security Programs and the Propensity to Retire," in R. H. Williams, C. Tibbitts, W. Donahue, eds., *Processes of Aging* (New York: Atherton, 1963), vol. 2, pp. 436-58. Henry J. Aaron, "Social Security: International Comparison," in O. Eckstein, ed., *Studies in the Economics of Income Maintenance* (Washington, D.C.: The Brookings Institution, 1967), pp. 13-48 and "International Comparisons," Appendix D in J. Pechman, H. Aaron, and M. Taussig, *Social Security: Perspectives for Reform* (Washington, D.C.: The Brookings Institution, 1968), pp. 294-304. Martin Feldstein, "Social Security and Private Savings: International Evidence."

[17] Joseph F. Quinn, "Some Determinants of the Early Retirement Decision: A Cross Sectional View," unpublished manuscript, Boston College, May 19, 1975.

earner families lose. On balance, the system represents a tax because it yields a low return and forces saving. It should be noted, however, that the tax is paid during the working years, but the benefits come only after retirement. To the extent that individuals are forced to save more than they otherwise would, the marginal utility of current consumption is increased, and increased work effort is likely to follow. Finally, for those with earnings above the maximum covered earnings (currently $15,300), social security has no marginal effect on the net wage, but it does reduce current and lifetime income, thus encouraging additional work effort. All of this depends, of course, on individuals' perceiving correctly the link between taxes and benefits and basing their work decisions on this perception.

Although social security has an ambiguous net *aggregate* effect on work effort, it clearly distorts individual labor supply decisions and thus causes an aggregate welfare loss. There are two separate issues here. First, the total welfare loss depends on the absolute size of individual changes in labor supply, not on their net sum. If we tax the earnings of A and subsidize the earnings of B, the decisions of both are distorted. If A reduces work effort and B increases work effort by an equal amount, there are still two welfare losses even though aggregate work effort is unchanged. Second, each individual's welfare cost depends on the "compensated" labor supply response and not the observed response. It is widely believed that there is no observable response of work effort to the net wage rate;[18] if so, the increased income is used to buy just enough extra leisure to offset the substitution effect of the higher wage. The compensated elasticity is thus the marginal propensity to "buy" leisure, unambiguously greater than zero. If the effective rate of net tax and net subsidy is half the gross rate and the compensated supply elasticity is 0.5, the annual welfare loss is now more than $5 billion.

As I mentioned earlier, the important effects of social security on savings and work effort should be carefully considered in reshaping the social security program. I will return to that fact in a subsequent paper. I now turn to a second major social insurance program that has important effects on our economy.

Unemployment Insurance

The structure of the unemployment insurance program is a vestige of the economic conditions during the depression of forty years ago. When the current unemployment insurance system was enacted, the country had been in a severe depression for more than five years. The national unemployment rate was more than 20 percent. The typical unemployed person may not have had steady work for a year or more. The Unemployment Insurance program was shaped by this extreme experience and by the sense that such mass unemployment had occurred as a result

---

[18] I discussed the inadequacy of this evidence above.

of forces beyond the control of the individuals or their employers. And with jobs scarce and wages low, there was little temptation toward voluntary unemployment.

Since the inception of the program, there have been prolonged changes in the nature of unemployment and therefore in the impact of unemployment insurance. Not only are unemployment rates now very much lower, but the causes and nature of unemployment are also very different.

The conventional view of unemployment might be described as follows: the growth of demand for goods and services does not keep pace with the rise in output per man. Companies therefore lay off employees and fail to hire new members of the labor force at a sufficient rate. The result is a pool of potential employees who are unable to find jobs.

This picture of a hard core of unemployed persons unable to find jobs is an inaccurate description of our economy and an unfortunate basis for policy. A more appropriate picture is an active labor market in which almost everyone who is out of work can find his or her usual kind of job in a relatively short time. Since this picture is so contrary to common belief, let me describe in more detail some of the characteristics of U.S. unemployment during the past decade.

First, the duration of unemployment is quite short. In 1974 the overall unemployment rate of 5.6 percent was relatively high for the postwar period. Even so, more than half of the unemployed were out of work for four weeks or less. Similarly, only 7 percent of the unemployed were without jobs for as long as twenty-six weeks.

Second, job losses account for less than half of total unemployment. In 1974 only 44 percent of the unemployed had lost their previous jobs. The others were new entrants to the labor force, reentrants, or individuals who had quit their previous jobs.

Third, the turnover of jobs is extremely high. In manufacturing, total hirings and separations have each exceeded 4 percent of the labor force per month for more than a decade. Even with the high unemployment of 1974, more manufacturing workers quit than were laid off.

Finally, and this is important in understanding the nature and impact of the unemployment insurance program, most layoffs are temporary and brief. In 1974 manufacturing companies were rehiring two-thirds of the people they had laid off. Indeed, over the past five years the average company has rehired about 85 percent of the same people that it had previously laid off.

Under the economic conditions that have prevailed in the post-World War II period, our current system of unemployment compensation is likely to have increased the average rate of unemployment. The common presumption—that unemployment compensation reduces unemployment because it automatically increases government spending when unemployment rises—misses the point. The same fiscal stimulus would now be provided through other expenditure increases or tax cuts by a government committed to maintaining aggregate demand. The primary effect of our current system of unemployment compensation on aggregate unemployment lies not in its contribution to aggregate demand but in its adverse impact on the incentive of employers and employees. As a result, unemployment compensation is likely to increase nearly all sources of unemployment: seasonal and cyclical variations in the demand for labor, weak labor force attachment, and unnecessarily long durations of unemployment.

Our current system of unemployment has two distinct but related bad incentives. First, for those who are already unemployed, it greatly reduces and often almost eliminates the cost of increasing the period of unemployment. Second, and more generally, for all types of unsteady work—seasonal, cyclical, and casual—it raises the net wage to the employee relative to the cost to the employer. The first of these effects provides an incentive to lengthen unemployment inappropriately. The second provides both employers and employees with an incentive to organize production in a way that increases the level of unemployment by favoring casual and temporary jobs and seasonal and cyclical variation in unemployment. Both of these disincentive effects require further explanation. First, however, I will describe how unemployment insurance now replaces a much larger fraction of lost income than is commonly believed.

The High Rate of Wage Replacement. The reform of unemployment insurance is fundamentally impeded by the false notion that unemployment benefits replace only a small fraction of lost wages. The most common assertion is that benefits provide only about one-third of the unemployed individual's usual pay. For example, a *New York Times* editorial cited this figure in praising a proposed increase in unemployment compensation: "The present national average benefit of roughly $55 a week is just a little over one third of usual pay, a gap that causes unfair hardship to many." [19] With this figure of one-third in mind, much of the legislative pressure has been to increase the replacement rate. But a more accurate description is that unemployment insurance currently replaces two-thirds or more of lost net income. In some extreme cases, the individual may receive more net income by being unemployed than by returning to work at his previous wage.

To understand the high replacement rate, it is useful to examine a detailed example. Consider a worker in Massachusetts in 1975 with a wife and two children. His gross earnings are $120 per week or $6,240 per year if he experiences no unemployment. She earns $80 per week or $4,160 per year if she experiences no unemployment. If he is unemployed for ten weeks, he loses $1,200 in gross earnings but only $227 in net income. How does this happen? A reduction of $1,200 in annual earnings reduces his federal income tax by $194, his social security payroll tax by $71, and his Massachusetts income tax by $60. The total reduction in taxes is $325. Thus net after-tax wages fall by only $875.

---

[19] *New York Times*, April 17, 1973.

Unemployment compensation consists of 50 percent of his wage plus dependent's allowances of $6 per week for each child. Total unemployment compensation is therefore $648.[20] These benefits, which are not taxable, therefore replace 74 percent of the net wage loss of $875. Viewed slightly differently, the combination of taxes and unemployment compensation imposes an effective marginal tax rate of 81 percent—that is, the man's net earnings fall by only 19 percent of his gross pay (by $227 out of $1,200) when he is unemployed for ten weeks. Moreover, part of this difference in income would be offset by the cost of transportation to work and other expenses associated with employment.

Because of the original one-week waiting period even these remarkable figures understate the effect of unemployment compensation on the cost to the individual of remaining unemployed longer.[21] If he stays unemployed for eleven weeks instead of ten, he loses an additional $120 in gross earnings but only $15.50 in net income. The reward for working is less than $0.50 per hour. The implied tax rate is 87 percent.

These astounding figures are not especially sensitive to the specific details of the family in the example or to the use of Massachusetts rules. For a wide variety of representative unemployed men in the nation, the compensation benefits replace more than 60 percent of lost net income; for women who are unemployed, the typical replacement rates are substantially higher. In the more generous states, the replacement rate on net earnings is generally over 80 percent.[22]

The common statistic that average benefits are only about one-third of average covered wages is a misleading observation for two reasons. One reason is that the average benefit applies to those who become unemployed, while the average wage refers to all covered workers. Since the lower-paid workers are more likely to become unemployed, the average wage overstates even the gross earnings of these unemployed. The other reason is that the figure of one-third is a ratio of nontaxable benefits to gross wages. The incorrect perception of the relative level of unemployment compensation reflects a failure to recognize the high marginal tax rates currently paid by individuals in the middle- and low-income ranges. The combination of federal and state income taxes and the social security payroll tax generally makes the marginal tax rate of such individuals 30 percent or even higher. The majority of unemployment compensation recipients collect benefits that are at least 50 percent of their previous gross wage. These benefits are not taxed, so that a 30 percent marginal tax rate on earnings (or a 70 percent net income) implies that the ratio of benefits to net earnings is five-sevenths, or that benefits replace more than 70 percent of the net wage.

---

[20] The individual is also entitled to $26 of food stamp subsidy per month of unemployment.

[21] There is typically a one-week waiting period *per benefit year.* An individual with more than one spell in twelve months only has to forgo a week's benefits during the first spell.

[22] For a detailed analysis, see my article, "Unemployment Compensation: Adverse Incentives and Distribution Anomalies," *National Tax Journal,* vol. 27, no. 2 (June 1974), p. 231; these replacement rates are based on typical earnings for men and women in each state.

These high replacement rates are quite unintentional. They reflect the fact that the system of taxation has changed dramatically since the origin of the unemployment insurance program. The federal income tax at the time the program began was very small and restricted to high-income families: in the 1930s only 4 percent of the total population was covered by taxable returns, and the tax rate at the 1938 median taxable income was only 4 percent. State income taxes were virtually nonexistent when unemployment insurance began. By 1974 the percentage of the population covered by taxable returns had increased to over 80 percent, and the federal income tax rate at the median taxable income was over 19 percent. In addition, there are sizable state income tax rates and an 11.7 percent social security payroll tax.

Effect on Temporary Layoffs. Although most discussions of the adverse impact of unemployment insurance focus on the prolonged duration of job search, I believe that the effect on the frequency and duration of temporary layoffs is at least as important. The high level of untaxed benefits and the inadequate system of experience rating used in the financing of unemployment insurance provide very strong incentives for an excessive volume of temporary unemployment.

The temporary layoff is the most neglected form of unemployment in economic analysis. The common picture of the unemployed worker is someone who has lost his job and is looking for new employment. Even economists who should know better are surprised to learn that this description is appropriate for less than one-third of all of those who are officially classified as unemployed. Among men and women aged twenty-five to sixty-four, nearly half of those who have been laid off are not looking for work because they expect to be recalled by their employer.

The official terminology is a source of confusion. First, the Bureau of Labor Statistics defines someone to be unemployed only if he has looked for work within the past four weeks *unless the individual is on temporary or indefinite layoff*.[23] Second, when the unemployed are classified as job losers, job leavers, reentrants, and new entrants, the group of job losers includes many who have not lost their job but have been laid off and are awaiting recall. Because the Department of Labor does not publish any information on temporary layoffs, I recently prepared some special tabulations using the March 1974 Current Population Survey, the official survey used by the Bureau of Labor Statistics to measure unemployment.[24]

During the average survey week in March 1974 there were some 950,000 unemployed men aged twenty-five through sixty-four who were officially classified as job losers. An additional 350,000 were unemployed new entrants, reentrants, and job leavers. Among those officially listed as job losers—that is, the 950,000

---

[23] There is another small group who are classified as unemployed even if they are not looking for work, that is, those who have a *new* job and expect to start work within thirty days.

[24] A full summary of this study is in my "The Importance of Temporary Layoffs: An Empirical Analysis," *Brookings Papers on Economic Activity,* 1975:3, pp. 725-45.

who had been laid off—more than 40 percent considered themselves to "have a job" and were therefore classified as on layoff awaiting recall. Less than 12 percent of this group had actually looked for work during the previous week.

Employees on layoff receive a substantial subsidy from the employment insurance system because of the ineffective method of experience rating. Employers now contribute to their state's unemployment insurance fund on the basis of the unemployment experience of their own previous employees. Within limits, the more benefits that these former employees draw, the higher is the firm's tax rate. The theory of experience rating is clear. If each employer paid the full cost of the benefits that his employees receive and if the benefits were treated as taxable "wages" to the employee, unemployment compensation would provide no incentive to an excessive use of unstable employment. Although it would not reduce the duration of unemployment of a person who was changing jobs, it would reduce the frequency and duration of temporary layoffs.[25] In practice, however, experience rating is a very imperfect check on the substantial subsidy entailed by unemployment compensation. A crucial feature of the unemployment insurance tax is that there is a relatively low maximum rate and a positive minimum rate. As a result, many firms with high layoff rates have "negative balances" in their accounts—that is, have paid less in taxes than their employees have received in benefits. These firms with high unemployment rates face the maximum tax rate; an increase in layoffs causes no increase in tax payments. Similarly, the large number of firms with substantial positive balances face the minimum rate and would continue to do so even if their rate of layoffs increased, as long as that increase was not too great. Joseph Becker, in a detailed study of experience rating,[26] presents extensive evidence of the importance of firms that pay no effective marginal tax. In New York in 1967, for example, some 59 percent of all benefits were related to firms with negative balances while 28 percent of firms paid the minimum tax. In Massachusetts, the corresponding figures were 57 percent and 18 percent.

With effective experience rating, the frequency and duration of temporary layoffs would reflect the employers' attempts to produce at minimum cost and the employees' balancing of higher wages and periods of temporary layoff. In contrast, the current inadequate experience rating and the tax-free status of unemployment compensation induce employers and employees to organize production and work rules in ways that create excessive unemployment. It is not surprising that temporary layoffs are such an important part of unemployment in an economy in which a spell of temporary unemployment is almost costless to both the worker and the firm.

---

[25] A full analytic model of temporary layoffs and experience rating is presented in my "Temporary Layoffs in the Theory of Unemployment," *Journal of Political Economy,* vol. 84, no. 5 (October 1976), pp. 937-57.

[26] Joseph Becker, *Experience Rating in Unemployment Insurance* (Baltimore: Johns Hopkins University Press, 1972).

Unnecessary Job Loss and Excessive Job Search. Unemployment insurance increases the frequency of job loss and the duration of job searches. Consider first the duration of unemployment. As we have seen, a man who normally earns $120 per week will lose only about $16 of additional net income if he remains out of work for eleven weeks instead of ten. The cost is even less than this if there are expenses for traveling to work, union dues, and other outlays connected with employment. The unemployed person who does not anticipate being recalled by his previous employer can expect to find a better job by searching and waiting than by taking a new job immediately. Because the cost of additional waiting time and searching time is very low, the unemployed worker is encouraged to wait until there is almost no chance of a better job. For example, since finding a job that pays as little as 5 percent more means an increase in net income of approximately $200 per year, even an additional ten weeks of unemployment would pay for itself within a year. It is clear that an individual who is actively searching for a better job in this way is neither loafing nor cheating. He is engaged in trying to increase his long-run income. His search is economically rational from his personal point of view but inefficiently long for the economy as a whole. The unemployed individual loses valuable productive time in order to achieve a slight gain in future income because taxpayers provide a $1,000 subsidy during his ten weeks of increased search.

Not all the increased duration of unemployment is due to the search for a better job. When the return to work adds less than $20 to the week's net income, there is certain to be a strong temptation to use some time for doing repairs and other tasks at home or simply taking a short period of additional vacation. Some who are waiting to be recalled to a previous job may also engage in casual work for unreported income. All of these temptations are likely to be even stronger when there is another person in the family who is employed. Glaring evidence of this type of voluntary unemployment is found in the "inverse seniority" provisions that are now part of the employer-employee agreements in several industries; these provisions give workers with more seniority the privilege of being laid off earlier than other workers and rehired later. The more general effect of unemployment compensation is to increase the seasonal and cyclical fluctuations in the demand for labor and the relative number of short-lived casual jobs. It does this by raising the employee's net wage for such unstable jobs relative to the cost to employers. The resulting distortion in the cost of unstable employment influences the patterns of production and consumption in the economy. Because the price of unstable labor has been artificially subsidized, employers organize production in a way that makes too much use of unstable employment. Similarly, the economy as a whole consumes relatively too much of the goods that are produced in this way.

A worker who accepts a seasonal job knows that he will probably be laid off when the season ends. Similarly, a worker in a casual or temporary job or in a highly paid cyclical industry knows that he is much more likely to be laid off than a worker with a regular job in an industry that is not cyclically sensitive. If there were no unemployment compensation, workers could be induced to accept such unstable jobs only if the wage rate were sufficiently higher in those jobs than in the more stable positions in which they could find alternative work. The pay differentials among jobs would reflect the chances of being laid off and the expected duration of unemployment after being laid off. The higher cost of labor in unstable jobs would induce employers to reduce the instability of employment by greater smoothing of production through increased variation in inventories and delivery lags, by additional development of off-season work, by incurring costs to improve scheduling, by less cyclical sensitivity of employment to changes in production, by the introduction of new techniques of production (for example, new methods of outdoor work in bad weather to reduce seasonal layoffs), and so on. The higher wages in unstable employment would also increase the prices of the output produced by firms and industries providing such employment. The higher prices of these goods and services would reduce the demand for them, further reducing the amount of unstable employment in the economy.

In the absence of subsidized unemployment compensation, the amount of unstable employment would reflect the employees' balancing of higher wages and employment stability, the employers' attempts to produce at minimum cost, and the consumers' choice among goods and services at prices that reflect their cost of production. The effect of subsidized unemployment compensation is to offset the market forces that would otherwise prevent an excessive amount of unstable employment. Because unemployment compensation provides a subsidy to workers in unstable employment, it reduces the wage differential required to attract workers to seasonal, cyclical, and temporary jobs. Because employers pay a relatively small premium for their unstable employment, there is little incentive to reduce this instability. Finally, the prices of these goods and services do not reflect the higher social cost of production with unstable employment. The taxpayers subsidize the consumption of those goods whose production creates the unstable employment.

Unemployment insurance can also increase an employee's willingness to quit a job. In twenty states, with nearly half the U.S. labor force, unemployment insurance benefits are available to those who quit their jobs as well as to those who are laid off.

The Magnitude of the Problem. There is little room for doubt about the qualitative conclusion that our current system of unemployment compensation increases the rate and duration of unemployment. Although the magnitude of this effect is unknown, it should be emphasized that fairly small changes in the duration of unemployment, the cyclical and seasonal fluctuation in labor demand, and the frequency of temporary jobs can have a very important impact on the overall rate of unemployment.

In my 1973 study of this question for the Joint Economic Committee of the U.S. Congress,[27] I hazarded the guess that the present form of unemployment insurance may contribute 1.25 percent to the permanent rate of unemployment. Although the statistical basis for estimating this effect is still extremely weak, the evidence presented in the past few years tends to confirm my view about this order of magnitude.

Of the recent work on this subject, Stephen Marston's study for the Brookings Institution has received the most attention.[28] Marston estimated that the average duration of completed spells of unemployment is 31 percent greater for the insured unemployed than for the uninsured unemployed. Since approximately 50 percent of the unemployed are covered by unemployment insurance, Marston's estimate implies that eliminating the adverse effect of unemployment insurance would reduce the mean duration of unemployment for all the unemployed by 12 percent. If the present "full employment" rate of unemployment is 5 percent,[29] a 12 percent reduction would lower it by 0.6 percentage points. For the current labor force of approximately 90 million, the adverse effect thus entails additional unemployment of 540,000 man-years annually.

Although the statistical basis for Marston's estimate is very weak,[30] this 540,000 man-year increase in unemployment indicates the effect of what he and others regard to be a "small" increase in average duration. Moreover, Marston's method is likely to understate the effect of unemployment insurance on duration because he ignores its effect on temporary layoffs. Since those who are temporarily laid off have shorter spells of unemployment than those who must find a new job,[31] an increase in temporary layoffs would tend to lower the duration of unemployment by the insured relative to that of the uninsured. The comparison of actual average duration therefore understates the effect of unemployment compensation on the duration of those who would have been unemployed even in the absence of unemployment insurance.

There has been no statistical analysis of the effect of unemployment insurance on the volume of temporary layoffs. If half of the unemployed who are on layoff awaiting recall are unemployed as a result of the substantial subsidy provided by unemployment compensation, this contributes 0.46 percent to the "full employment" rate of unemployment. There are also workers in industries like construction who have technically lost their jobs but, because of union seniority, are effectively on temporary layoff.

---

[27] U.S. Congress, Joint Economic Committee, *Lowering the Permanent Rate of Unemployment*, 93rd Congress, 1st session, 1973, p. 48.

[28] Stephen Marston, "The Impact of Unemployment Insurance on Job Search," *Brookings Papers on Economic Activity*, 1975:1, pp. 13-60.

[29] Recall that the average unemployment rate has been 4.8 percent from the end of World War II to the beginning of the current recession.

[30] See my comment in *Brookings Papers on Economic Activity*, 1975:1, pp. 52-58.

[31] Evidence of this is reported in my "The Importance of Temporary Layoffs: An Empirical Analysis."

Finally, there are those who are unemployed and looking for a job because the current unemployment compensation system induced them to quit or to prefer unstable employment. Since 30 percent of the laid-off unemployed are without a job, if even a small fraction are the result of unemployment insurance, the total contribution to unemployment is large. For example, if one-sixth of job seekers would not have been unemployed—that is, would previously have chosen jobs with a lower probability of layoff—this would contribute 0.25 percent to a permanent rate of unemployment of 5 percent.

It seems likely, though it is far from proved, that the current adverse incentives in unemployment insurance add more than 1 million people to the permanent number of unemployed. The problem for the future is to revise unemployment insurance to protect those who lose their jobs and to reduce the distortions that lead to unnecessarily frequent job loss and unnecessarily long duration of unemployment.[32]

Conclusion

The current analysis could be extended to health insurance (Medicaid, Medicare, the tax subsidy of private insurance, the design of national health insurance), to welfare (AFDC, food stamps, and so on), and to smaller programs of flood insurance, workmen's compensation, and others. The basic ideas would remain the same: that social insurance has a profound impact on behavior, that programs designed for a different economy and technology should be revised, that our current programs could be revised to yield greater protection and greater efficiency.

We know enough now to redesign our social insurance programs in ways that would achieve greater equity and protection with a less adverse effect on productivity and economic efficiency. There is now more interest, more concern, and more searching than at any time in the past two decades. I hope that the opportunity will not be wasted.

---

[32] For a brief discussion of possible changes in unemployment insurance that will reduce these adverse incentives, see my "Unemployment Insurance: Time for Reform," *Harvard Business Review*, vol. 53, no. 2 (March-April 1975), pp. 51-61.

COMMENTARIES

James M. Buchanan

Like most of those at this conference, I receive perhaps hundreds of papers in the course of a year, in the form of early drafts, working papers, preprints, reprints, offprints, or whatever. I read relatively few of these on receipt. Most of them accumulate on the floor of my office until, one day every few months, I get a burst of enthusiasm to clean up, at which point I glance hurriedly at the papers, perhaps as many as ten or fifteen in an hour. But anything I receive from Martin Feldstein is a clear exception to this rule; anything I receive from him I open immediately and read, and I almost always learn something. I make this exception because I know that a Feldstein paper will, first of all, be readable—that it will not require the wholly wasted effort of translation from esoteric mathematics into straightforward economics. Secondly, I know that a Feldstein paper will be relevant—it will address an issue or issues of current policy interest and importance.

At this point I am tempted to say that a Feldstein paper also reflects a basic intellectual honesty or integrity. This is, of course, a true statement, but it does not convey precisely the meaning I want to convey here, and to make a categorical distinction in this respect would be unfair to the others. But I do want to take a shot at the question Feldstein poses, why modern economists seem to have been so reluctant to apply straightforward economic theory to the central policy issues he notes. Why have so many of our intellectual peers chosen, instead, to launch off into the never-never land of abstruse mathematics on the one hand and the tedious detail of empirical rigor on the other?

The most plausible hypothesis suggests that many modern economists do not really want to face up to the rather direct policy implications that emerge from a straightforward application of their logic. They are essentially escapist; they maximize personal utilities by divorcing their subject matter and method from reality. They can, in this way, join their fellow intellectuals in quasi-serious policy dialogue without jeopardizing their "progressive" role. It is to members of this group, who surely dominate our profession today, that Feldstein's work must appear most disturbing. They can reject neither his analysis nor his empirical results, and he challenges them to earn their keep as economists.

Feldstein's strictures do not apply so directly, or at least in the same way, to those of us in the minority of economists who have worked within the classical paradigm, who have incorporated the spontaneous coordination of markets into our thinking about economic policy at all levels. Members of this minority do not really need empirical proof that "water runs downhill"—to borrow one of Frank Knight's phrases. We do not need convincing by numbers that compensation payments increase unemployment rates, that graduated income taxes affect work incentives (the more so the more progressive the rate structure), that transfers reduce work effort, that social security induces early retirement, that an unfunded public pension system reduces private saving. When I see sophisticated efforts by professional economists to disprove such elementary verities, my own reaction is one of cynical amusement, based on a long-held suspicion that truth is not really the motive force behind the fanciful facades. In a sense it is a mark of the disintegration of the economics profession that the considerable talents of Professor Feldstein must be concentrated on convincing his fellows that the elementary principles are, in fact, valid ones.

But let me shift quickly away from my general comments on the efforts of my fellow economists. I have only one minor technical criticism of Feldstein's paper. He notes that when a person is taxed directly for the payment of benefits he expects to receive, the income effect washes out, leaving the directionally predictable substitution effect. This is, of course, correct, but Feldstein seems here to imply that there is no comparable washing out of the income effect when such a fiscal quid pro quo is absent. However, so long as income effects are roughly symmetrical over all persons and groups in the community, there will always be a netting out over the whole group, provided only that the governmental transfers or provision of services are valued by those who receive them.

My main criticism is a general one and reflects my public-choice perspective, as opposed to the perspective of an orthodox price-theory economist. Throughout his discussion in this paper, Feldstein seems to imply that the institutional reforms in social insurance that he calls for can be made if only our political decision makers will get their ideas straight, if only they will recognize the inconsistencies in existing programs, if only they will, indeed, act in the "public interest." I recognize the need for a division of labor here, and it is perhaps desirable that Feldstein should concentrate his energies on the strict economics of policy. But neither he nor anyone else should be so naive as to expect that policy reform will follow directly upon an understanding and appreciation of the economics of the matters at issue.

The politics are also important. The political setting within which policy decisions are made can influence the outcomes that emerge, no matter what their economic content. To illustrate this, let me take a single example, admittedly the one that allows me to make the strongest case. Consider the development of the unfunded public pension system, along with Feldstein's suggestion for a needed shift toward fund accumulation. Even if we fully recognize the peculiar historical circumstances of the 1930s, the collapse of the financial structure in the Great Depression, and the subsequently influential ideas of Keynes and the Keynesians, should we not also recognize the institutional biases that democratic politics itself might have exerted and might have been expected to exert on observed results? Elected politicians like to spend and they do not like to impose taxes. Is this not enough to suggest that we should hardly have expected democratic decision making to produce a funded system which would, of course, have required the collection of current taxes in excess of current outpayments? Congress acted consistently with the most elementary public-choice model when projected tax increases were postponed until these seemed necessary to keep the system on a pay-as-we-go basis. The system that we now observe is "explainable" at least in part by public-choice theory, quite apart from economic ignorance or economic error.

The conflict that seems likely to emerge over ensuing decades is not, however, so amenable to elementary public-choice analysis. As Daniel Orr has suggested, it seems likely that the whole social security issue will dramatically shift from one that has embodied apparent political consensus to one characterized by sharpened conflict when legislators recognize that commitments coming due require additional current financing.[1] The choice between reducing the rates of return on the intergenerational investments made by workers who have legitimate expectations and increasing rates of tax on currently productive workers will have important economic effects. But the political interplay of alternative coalitions will do as much toward determining the final outcome as the underlying economic analysis.

We can rely on elementary public-choice theory to predict that a modern Congress will not go beyond minimal pay-as-we-go requirements. It is not likely to change its stripes suddenly and commence to accumulate a positive fund balance in the OASI account, as Feldstein urges, and despite evidence to the effect that the economic results might be beneficial. Even the most sophisticated and effective congressman could scarcely return to his constituents with the news that he supports an increased payroll or income tax in order to benefit future pension recipients, with spillover benefits for the economy as a whole. In a wisdom that we have almost lost, James Madison and the other founding fathers knew that democracy can effectively make only a limited number of nonsophisticated decisions. Until economists relearn this lesson, they will continue to seem quixotic in their discussions of policy.

My criticism in this respect is not, of course, directed at Feldstein in particular. It becomes, finally, a plea for more research and more analysis of the institutional processes through which economic policy is made—research and analysis which will necessarily draw attention to the potential for reform of these processes, as such, rather than in the particular pattern of outcomes generated.

Nancy H. Teeters

I find it rather difficult to comment on a paper whose point of view regarding social security and even whose interpretation of history is so radically different from

---

[1] Daniel Orr, "Social Security and Social Values," University of California, San Diego, April 1, 1976.

mine. In the discussion of the impact of social security on savings, capital formation, and, in fact, throughout, Feldstein overlooks one important fact. Before the social security system was started, we did not shove our elderly, disabled, and other dependent members of our population into a gas chamber. We supported them. The lucky ones were supported by their families; the unlucky ones in poor farms and orphanages.

Probably very few saved enough to be completely self-sufficient when they were disabled or aged. The support of the dependent population was not costless. They were clothed, fed, and housed, and the clothing, feeding, and housing were paid for by either the family, the local government, or charity. While the savings rate without social security might be somewhat higher, the levels estimated by Feldstein, I think, are unrealistic. Without social security, I would be contributing to the support of my mother, my mother-in-law, and, quite possibly, my aunt, and that would depress my savings rate.

I consider social security a partial transfer to the public domain of what had been a family function, support of the dependent population. The transfer has been only partial, because most children are still supported by their parents. Under this view of social security, the only insurance-like aspect of the system is to spread the risk. Under the older system, older people faced the risk that their children might die or behave irresponsibly, and the younger people faced the risk that they might end up supporting a large number of the elderly.

Social security is a public tax and transfer system that replaced the system of private support, local taxes and charity. This meeting should be discussing the problems remaining within the current system of income maintenance and how to integrate the various systems—it should not be discussing the savings rate.

Before turning to that, there is one part of Professor Feldstein's paper I cannot ignore. His account of the history of the social security system can only be attributed to his youth. He has obviously not read the reports or the debate about the program in Congress in the mid-1930s. The idea that the U.S. Congress was dominated by Keynesian economists in 1935 is unrealistic. Even by 1939, I do not think Keynes had a major influence in the halls of Congress. In 1936, a tax was levied on workers in commerce and industry. Almost nothing else in this line happened until 1950, not even the payment of very much in benefits. Benefits totaled $1 million in 1937, $10 million in 1938, and $14 million in 1939. As late as 1949, benefits totaled only $146 million, and receipts were $1,816 million. If Feldstein is worried about savings, he should realize that the system actually provided savings. It had accumulated $11.8 billion in assets by 1949. The creation of the system as we know it today was carried out essentially between 1950 and 1967, when coverage was extended to include not only the people in commerce and industry but also the self-employed, the military, medical workers, and others. At the present time, about 90 percent of all employed persons are covered by social security.

Since 1967, there has been a major expansion in real benefits under the cloak of cost-of-living increases. The cost-of-living increases were generally about twice the size of the actual cost of living. At the present time, it seems to me, the further expansion of real benefits is not called for.

Given my view of the world, then, what are the major problems that remain in the system? First of all, the benefit system has to be decoupled. The automatic cost-of-living benefits adopted in 1972 adjust future benefits for price increases twice. Workers retiring in the future receive benefits based on their past wage record. That past wage record reflects past increases in prices. By decoupling, I mean creating a system similar to the one for military and civil service retirement, in which the cost-of-living increases in benefits would go only to the people who are already retired. Under the current social security system, cost-of-living increases in benefits not only go to the people who are retired but also are fed down through the retirement schedules for all future retirees. Correcting this is fairly simple, and it is necessary to keep the cost down in the future.

The second needed correction lies in the grossly unequal treatment accorded women, particularly working women. As the system now works, there is double taxation of a two-worker family. To the extent that the family's combined income exceeds the current social security wage limit, that family is paying more social security taxes than a family that has only one earned income. In addition, since the average salary of women is much below that of men, when it comes time to receive benefits, the woman is frequently better off taking 50 percent of her husband's benefit than 100 percent of her own benefit.

This, too, could be easily rectified. A simple solution is to make social security payments a tax on family wages by crediting half of the family wages to the wife and half to the husband, regardless of whether the wife or the husband happens to be working. This would solve many problems. It would make it possible for a woman to be divorced and to carry her entitlement to benefits with her. We would not get into the ridiculous situation where a divorced wife is eligible for benefits only if she has been married for twenty years. Such a change would end some of the discrimination that results from the higher average wage levels of men.

The major problem I cannot quite solve is the inequity that has been in the system from the beginning: that of the 150 percent of benefits that is given to a married couple. One possibility is to credit 75 percent of the primary insurance amount (PIA) to each member of the primary family.

Another major problem area is the program for the disabled. The number of people receiving disability payments has recently been growing at an average annual rate of at least 10 percent a year. Fortunately, it started from a small base and is not as big as the retirement program. But it is rapidly increasing, and I am sure the Social Security Administration is concerned. It should find out what is happening rather than simply asking for an increase in the tax rate to cover the increased cost of the program for the disabled.

Another major reform I see needed in the system lies in the very nature of the payroll tax. Not only are two-worker families taxed twice, but the tax itself is regressive. There had been no relief even at the lowest income levels until we were given the earned income credit this year. At the present time, it looks as if some of the people eligible for the earned income credit are not actually claiming it. The problem appears to be that low-income people are unaccustomed to the complexity of the income tax.

The amount of income redistribution accomplished by the tax system is relatively small. We pride ourselves on our progressive income tax, but we pretty much offset it with the regressive payroll tax. When we look at the distribution of income after taxes, we find that it is almost unchanged from what it was before taxes. If we look at the distribution of income after taxes and transfers, we find there is a shift, but it is a shift primarily toward the elderly. If we look at the distribution of income over, say, the twenty-five-year period since 1950 and make the distinction by age, we find that there has been a distinct redistribution of income from the working-age population to the elderly population.

Finally, I find myself somewhat in sympathy with Feldstein on the retirement test. Every time I talk about the retirement test, the Social Security Administration tells me that it would be too expensive to abolish it. I translate this to mean that abolishing it would mean an increased tax, and I think the payroll tax is too high already. On the other hand, I think older Americans should be allowed to work— in fact, encouraged to work if they feel like it, if they are capable, and if they can find a decent job. Moreover, the distinction between earned and nonearned income in the application of the retirement test strikes me as irrelevant. Moreover, the retirement test does not apply after age seventy-two.

If a means test is built into the system, it should have some meaning other than how one's income is obtained. My ad hoc suggestion would be to abolish the retirement test and finance the increased cost of abolition by taxing social security benefits. But that suggestion does not get far in Congress.

Surprisingly enough, I almost find myself in agreement with Feldstein's comments on unemployment insurance. I find it hard to believe that we experienced a year with the unemployment rate at 8.5 percent without major public demonstrations. I think the experience rating for the tax rate should be greatly expanded. There should be a larger range for the tax rate, and it could be adjusted, not just once a year, but perhaps two or three times a year to reflect the employer's experience.

Moreover, unemployment insurance should be made more flexible than it is. In Europe, and particularly in West Germany over the past year and a half, the work has been shared. Employees have sometimes worked four days a week and received unemployment insurance benefits for the fifth day. Our unemployment insurance will not permit the payment of unemployment for one day a week. There are a number of reforms that should be made. This might be a good time to investigate unemployment insurance and find out why we did not have protests in the street last year. Our unemployment rate is still high by post-World War II standards. Now would be a good time to find out what is going on in that program.

Robert J. Lampman

My remarks are directed not specifically at the Feldstein paper. They are rather wide-sweeping.

Income maintenance is a title or slogan or phrase whose specific meaning is hard to nail down. I think this recently adopted term is already becoming obsolete in the expert literature and in the political arena. The reason for this is that income maintenance programs are only part of an overlapping set of institutions directed at five distributional goals, which are becoming more and more closely interlocked.

These goals are (1) the attainment of high employment, (2) the offsetting of income losses arising out of such stated contingencies as unemployment, old age, disability, and family dissolution, (3) the reduction and eventual elimination of income poverty, (4) helping people buy such essentials as food, health care, housing, and education, and (5) achieving a fair distribution of the burden of taxes. All five of these have a distributional content and reflect interest (albeit a diffused and inchoate interest) in wider sharing of opportunities and income.

Income maintenance is sometimes used interchangeably with the term *cash transfers,* which are addressed to the replacement of income loss and reduction of income poverty. Cash transfers currently are paid out in an amount equal to 9 percent of gross national product. About two-thirds of cash transfers go to the aged and the disabled. About one-fourth goes to broken families, and only 6 percent to all others.

Expenditures equal to another 10 percent of GNP are designed to help people buy essentials. By far the largest part is for education and health. Relatively small amounts go for welfare services, nutrition programs, housing, and employment and manpower services.

Two of our distributional goals are being attained to an important degree by existing cash transfer programs. The social insurances replace about one-fourth of the total income loss from unemployment and about a third of the loss from retirement, disability, and premature death. Public assistance also serves to offset income lost as a result of these hazards and from the break-up of a family for reasons other than death. Over 50 million people now receive a cash income maintenance benefit in a typical year. However, many who suffer an income loss do not receive a benefit. For example, only about half of those counted as unemployed draw unemployment insurance benefits. Also, certain risks are quite uncovered—for example, temporary disability and permanent but partial disability are generally ignored.

These cash transfers also serve to reduce income poverty. Over half the $80 billion of cash benefits in 1972 went to the pretransfer poor—that is, to people whose pretransfer income was below the poverty line for their family size. This lifted almost half of those who would have been poor in the absence of transfers over the poverty line. But it left 12 percent of the population, or 24 million people, still in income poverty. This cash transfer system did well for the aged but it did relatively little for the intact family headed by a nonaged, able-bodied male. Some of our cash transfer programs are quite helpful to the poor. The old age and survivors program is particularly helpful to the poor. Unemployment insurance, however, directs only 21 percent of its benefits to the poor.

The purpose of helping people buy essentials is met according to a rather different pattern; only a third of these noncash benefits go to the poor, as far as we can estimate it. But it is worth noting that if the food, housing, and health benefits could be counted as being as good as cash, they would exceed the $12 billion counted as the poverty income deficit. So one could say with some reason that the war on poverty was pretty nearly won as of 1972.

We mentioned another goal, that of having a fair distribution of taxes. It is probably not necessary to point out that provisions of tax law in the form of exclusions, deductions, and exemptions bear on the other goals referred to above. Taxes—whatever their merits as a system—are not particularly redistributive; they change the Gini coefficient of income distribution relatively little.

It is not an explicit goal, as I read public documents, to redistribute income toward less inequality, but many academics (as opposed to people in public office) have asserted that this has been an implicit goal of all this spending and taxing. And so it is worth reviewing how the income redistribution is changed.

My colleagues Eugene Smolensky and Morgan Reynolds have a forthcoming book on prefisc-postfisc distributions. For any one year, the share of the low fifth in prefisc income is much smaller than it is in the postfisc income. That is, after we are done with all the taxing and transferring, both in money and in kind, the lowest fifth goes from something like 3 percent or so of prefisc income up to 10 percent or more of postfisc income.

Interestingly, they do not find any trend over the last twenty years in the actual share of postfisc income held by the lowest fifth of the spending units. Professor Browning, of the University of Virginia, has recently published estimates which do show a trend toward a larger share, postfisc, for the lowest fifth of the population.[1] There is likely to be some controversy about these two conflicting estimates.

I would like to make a brief cautionary remark, however, about how easy it is to be misunderstood on the subject of redistribution. It is possible to set up many

---

[1] Edgar K. Browning, "How Much More Equality Can We Afford?" *Public Interest*, no. 43 (Spring 1976), p. 93.

different definitions and measurements of redistribution. The authors that I cite are talking about redistribution within a single year. On the other hand, one might want to consider redistribution across a lifetime. And of course our conclusions on redistribution will change as our definition of the family unit changes.

A few comments on the future. If we simply project the recent rate of growth of social welfare expenditures, we are led to the conclusion that such expenditures could equal half of gross national product by the end of this century. They are now about 20 percent, having increased from 12 percent in 1950.

It is certainly true that the goals of social welfare are potentially expansive in several directions. Thus, income maintenance could be aimed at offsetting still larger parts of income loss from the designated hazards. For example, replacement rates at time of retirement could be raised and, indeed, retirement age could be lowered; eligibility for disability income benefits could be further liberalized. A major expansion of income maintenance would follow adoption of widely supported job creation proposals that would make government the employer of last resort.

The goal of eliminating income poverty is a relatively modest and finite goal and could be attained promptly by a major overhaul of the income maintenance system. The introduction of supplemental security income, in 1974, should virtually eliminate income poverty for the aged and disabled. What remains to be done to achieve the elimination of income poverty, assuming no great recession in the near future, is a similar revision of the aid program for dependent children and an extension of benefits to the "noncategorical" or so-called working poor. The revision and extension could take the form of a negative income tax with a guarantee at the poverty line and a 50 percent rate of benefit reduction as earnings rise. This would cost, assuming no great reduction in work effort on the part of the recipients, something on the order of $25 billion over and above what we are now spending.

It is noteworthy, in this connection, that Congress has taken up a new line of thinking on categorization. The food stamp program, which is a negative income tax in-kind, extends its benefits to the working poor, to the intact family, and to persons without children. Also, we now have an earned income credit which pays benefits out to intact, as well as to broken, families with children.

The goal of helping people buy essentials is, of course, open-ended. In education, in housing allowances, in child day care, and mental health care—just to name a few—the possibilities for budget expansion are quite remarkable.

However, there are some reasons to believe that the rate of growth of social welfare expenditures will slow down. First, social security has "matured" in the sense that virtually all the aged are now eligible for benefits. Second, the demands for education, health care, income maintenance, and welfare services all tend to be age-related and changes to come in the age composition ahead should slow the rate of increase in benefits.

Perhaps the recent decisions to expand social welfare spending were made in the belief that society as a whole would be better off because extra social welfare benefits would exceed the additional private costs. The external benefits are alleged to include better citizenship, higher productivity, a more stable economy, and a healthier and more integrated community.

In the same vein, we can believe that voters will turn against further expansion of social welfare expenditures if they see undesirable side effects as outweighing the external benefits. Professor Feldstein is a leading contributor to the literature on these undesirable side effects. He has argued that unemployment insurance increases unemployment, that health insurance increases unnecessary utilization and cost of health care, and that retirement insurance, when financed on a pay-as-you-go basis, inhibits growth of the nation's capital stock. Other critics have alleged that social welfare spending weakens family responsibility and solidarity and contributes to the elevation of a remote and unresponsive bureaucracy which threatens the existence of democratic government.

Scholars can help voters to appraise these undesirable side effects and to compare them with the external benefits that may flow from alternative ways of pursuing the five distributional goals enumerated at the outset of my brief remarks.

Rita Ricardo Campbell

Because of the many comments already made and because I have been involved with social security for a number of years, both as an economist with the House Ways and Means Committee in 1953 and 1954 and as a member of the Quadrennial Advisory Council on Social Security in 1974–1975, there are many things I would like to say here.

First, I would like to thank Martin Feldstein not only for what he said today, on behalf of married working women, but also for his testimony of May 15, 1975, to the House Subcommittee on Social Security. He supported the recommendation of the Subcommittee on the Treatment of Men and Women of the Quadrennial Advisory Council, which subcommittee I chaired. The subcommittee had recommended to the advisory council, as a whole, that the two-worker family be permitted to add its combined earnings up to the current annual limit of the earnings tax base, now $15,300, and count its combined earnings for its benefits. The advisory council, however, rejected our recommendation.

This recommendation would help low-income two-worker families. It has some similarities to what Mrs. Teeters suggested. Those interested in the general problem should read the report of the Subcommittee on the Treatment of Men and Women in Appendix B of the 1974 Quadrennial Advisory Council's report.[1] In my

---

[1] U.S. Congress, House of Representatives, *Reports of the Quadrennial Advisory Council on Social Security,* House Document no. 94-75, 94th Congress, 1st session, March 10, 1975, pp. 133-53.

dissent, I tied this recommendation to the long-run actuarial imbalance in such a way as to present an option to diminish the long-run imbalance.

The long-run imbalance is basic. It is no secret that the social security fund is in short-run actuarial imbalance. It appears, however, to be somewhat of a secret that it is also in long-run actuarial imbalance. Two-thirds of the imbalance will be demographic. Thirty years from now, the OASDI trust funds will have run out of money, barring future changes by Congress, primarily because the World War II baby boom will be entering the sixty-two to sixty-five age bracket and retiring at the same time the working population will be determined by the lower birth rate of the last few years. The birth rate during the first quarter of 1976 was 14.4 live births per 1,000 population, an all-time low in the United States. The Quadrennial Advisory Council's long-run estimate of the total fertility rate was 2.1 births for each woman over a lifetime compared with a rate of 1.8 in 1974 and a slightly lower rate in 1975. The estimate seems to me to be even less defensible now than when I, as a member of the council, registered my dissent to it. The ratio of OASDI beneficiaries to workers will change, roughly from 30 to 50 or more for every 100 workers. In 1950 this ratio was 6 beneficiaries for every 100 workers. I do not see a long-run future for the social security program as it now exists in the United States.

I would like to point out that over half the families in the United States are now two-worker families, and this fact affects both savings decisions and employment rates; it affects the intensity with which persons who are unemployed look for work. There is some self-selection by people who take seasonal jobs and then take unemployment compensation. Mrs. Teeters wondered why, with a high unemployment rate, we do not have riots in the street, or did not have. We do have unemployment compensation, and some of those who are unemployed want to be unemployed. They are not intensely looking for work, and actually they planned it that way. Let me return back to the days of Professor Sumner Slichter, for whom I worked as a research assistant when I was at Harvard, who liked to tell stories about the men in the lumbering industry in the Northwest or in Minnesota, who took low-paying jobs in preference to the more stable jobs, because they dovetailed work with the hunting and fishing season.

I watched on television the other night a young golfing pro who had a good job in Michigan, which paid him high wages, and who unabashedly admitted that he was collecting unemployment compensation of $125 a week in the state of Florida under reciprocal state agreements. He admitted he was not really looking for a job. He met the requirement by going to the poshest club he could find in Florida and saying, "I'd like to be your golf pro." What he did was self-select a seasonal job, which he dovetailed with a winter vacation in Florida, practicing his game.

Let me take up again my major point on married women who work and on the effect of the increase in two-worker (husband and wife) families on the economy. Over the past thirty-five years, the peacetime supply of labor in the United States has varied from 57 percent of the noninstitutional civilian population in 1940 to 62 percent in 1975—and only the wartime year of 1944 (when it was 63 percent) exceeded this 1975 figure.

Feldstein is correct in stressing the point that in recent years there has been a considerable decrease in the percentage of males in the labor force. Men are staying in school longer, and they are retiring earlier. What has kept the labor force at 62 percent of the civilian noninstitutional population has been the offsetting increase in the number of women, primarily older married women, who are working. In 1974, 45 percent of all married women with husbands present in the home were in the labor force; their earnings affect such private savings decisions as whether to buy a home, corporate stock, or whatever.

The peak labor-force participation rate of women fifty-five years to sixty-four years was 43 percent in 1970; it fell to 41 percent in 1974, showing that women, like men, are beginning to retire earlier because of the more liberal social security benefits, civil service benefits, and other pensions available at earlier ages. However, some women sixty-five years and older still work for wages—in 1961, 11 percent were working, and in 1974, 8 percent.

In analyzing the effect on private savings of the social security program it is important to determine what percent of married women whose husbands are in the home are working just prior to their or their spouse's retirement. In March 1974, 81 percent of married men fifty-five to sixty-four years of age, with wife at home, were in the labor force.[2] Only 35 percent of women in that age group, with husband at home, were working. What is missing in the data—and I am sure it is in the data bank for those who want to get at it—is a cross-tabulation, preferably by frequency distribution, by the age of the husband for women fifty-five years and older who are married, with husband in household, and working.

It is generally believed that men on the average are older than their wives. It would be interesting to know what the actual difference is at age of retirement. The necessary data for this calculation are probably available, also. It is known, for example, that for first marriages for each sex the male, on the average, is only two years older than the female. However, with the rising divorce rate, multiple marriages, and sizable differences in life expectancy of men and women, it is plausible that by the time a male considers retiring at age sixty-two on a reduced benefit from social security—as 44 percent of all male retirees were in 1974—his wife may be five or more years younger and working. In 1972, 52 percent of married women with husband present, whose husbands were forty-five to sixty-four years old, had work experience, and 74 percent of these women were working full time. In addition, 21 percent of women, whose husbands were sixty-five years and over, were working, and 61 percent of them full time. These figures

---

[2] U.S. Department of Labor, *Manpower Report of the President* (Washington, D.C., April 1975), p. 252.

suggest that many women are married to husbands older than themselves. If they create a surplus over personal outlays, their incomes tend to increase private savings. If their incomes are absorbed by daily living costs that do not include such investment as purchasing a home, they could decrease savings over time.

As a member of the Quadrennial Advisory Council on Social Security, I became aware of what professional people who like their jobs—and I assume this category includes most of the people in this audience—too often forget—men who work for thirty-five years at jobs they do not like, and look forward to retirement at fifty-five years of age. The economy, however, needs labor, and, though the demand for manual labor may have been falling, the demand for service workers, whose jobs are filled by proportionately more women, is increasing. Men who dislike their jobs—manual workers and men on assembly lines—tend to retire early, and their wives tend to take a job after their children have grown. Social security benefits are not taxed, and the income of a man retiring at age sixty-two may, if his wife's salary after taxes is included, be higher than he could have earned if he did work. Data are needed to explore whether this may be one of the major reasons why older women are returning to the labor force. A noneconomic reason may be summed up in the sentiment, "I love you, but not enough to prepare week-day lunches at home."

I will end with one other major point. In my mind, it is necessary to have universal compulsory coverage of social security. More than 8.5 million jobs are still not covered by social security. Of the 8.5 million exempt jobs, 2.5 million are in federal employment. The Civil Service Retirement Plan, which until October 1974 was an equity plan, pays full benefits at age fifty-five after thirty years of service. Moreover, there are over 3.5 million noncovered jobs out of 12 million state and local government positions. Employees in these can, after seven years of coverage, opt out of social security, if they wish, upon giving a two-year notice. The newspapers in recent months have related accounts of more such groups opting out or giving, as required, the two-year notice. I think that you may have read about New York City, the state of Alaska, a number of different groups in the state of California (as, for example, the city of San Jose, which has a population of over 1 million persons).

A group opts out when the majority gain more by leaving and buying an annuity in the private market. Once a person has forty quarters of coverage, a social security benefit is assured that person by law. Members of the Quadrennial Advisory Council on Social Security noted that during the past forty years, a most inequitable situation has developed. Federal employees who are knowledgeable about the system legally obtain a windfall benefit by meeting the minimal forty quarters of $50 a quarter of earnings in covered employment in some secondary part-time job, and then collect the weighted minimum benefit, which was intended to help those whose primary jobs yield very low income. In 1969, 40 percent of

111

all federal civil service retirees were also drawing social security retirement benefits. The social security system does not seem to have any more recent data.

Civil servants argue that they have a good retirement plan and therefore do not need social security. This argument could be made by millions of other workers in private industry who also have good retirement plans. They also do not want to pay taxes that (in part) support the social adequacy or welfare aspects of the program—that is, to redistribute income to some degree to low-income earners and their dependents.

Although in the case of state and local employees, there may be a constitutional question involved, this is not so for federal workers. The actuaries of the Social Security Administration estimate that if all government employees were covered, "there would be a long-term reduction in the cost of the system of 0.25 percent of covered wages and a short-term reduction of 0.70 percent." [3] The estimated financial deficit of the OASDI system from 1974 to 2045 is about 3 percent of covered payroll.[4] These are significant amounts. The Quadrennial Advisory Council urged that all government employees be brought under social security. Congressmen do not like to discuss this, I suppose because they are government employees. One-hundred percent coverage would ensure that every worker—and not primarily the married women who work—would contribute to the social adequacy aspects. As was noted by Mrs. Teeters, rather indirectly, the married woman who works may collect *either* her own primary benefit *or* a dependency benefit, one-half or, if she becomes a widow, 100 percent of her husband's primary benefit. There are therefore millions of women today who contribute to the system and get very little, if anything, out of it beyond—and even this was disputed until the Weinberger v. Wiesenfeld Supreme Court decision—dependency benefits.[5]

---

[3] *Reports of the Quadrennial Advisory Council on Social Security*, p. 54.
[4] Ibid., p. 48.
[5] Weinberger v. Wiesenfeld, 420 U.S. 636 (1975).

DISCUSSION

PROFESSOR FELDSTEIN: Of course I was flattered by what Professor Buchanan had to say. I would make one defense of my activities in "proving eternal verities." The problem is not so much to convince people that there is "some effect," that the demand curve slopes downward, but to investigate whether effects are large, whether the trade-offs are important, and whether the distortions are significant. And it is important to estimate where it is large and where it is small. While no single body of evidence can succeed in doing that, it is worth trying to encourage others to go along with the research that can produce the necessary evidence.

On the substantive point about the funding, I was very interested in Buchanan's political doubts that congressmen would ever vote to raise taxes not to pay more benefits but simply to increase the size of the fund. I sometimes find myself moving in that pessimistic direction. I doubt that arguments in favor of a fund, about the high rate of return, and about intergenerational equity are going to be persuasive enough.

Let me therefore commend an alternative that may have some of the same desirable effects. If the problem is that high social security benefits offset private saving, and that this offset cannot be remedied by developing public saving at the same time, I think we must look at the benefit side and ask what the future course of benefits should be. A retiree with median earnings now gets approximately 70 percent of his maximum earnings if he has a dependent spouse. If we allow benefits to increase in the future in such a way that the replacement rates at any given real income remain what they are in the current law, then, as incomes rise, benefits will rise, but not nearly as fast. And, to be specific, in some future day when everyone's income exceeds $15,300 per year (in 1974 prices), he would get a replacement rate of 45 percent rather than 70 percent, including dependents' benefits. That is, people should be allowed to move into lower and lower replacement rate brackets as their *real* incomes rise, rather than fixing replacement rates in terms of *relative* income.

This method of "decoupling" has recently been suggested by a panel of economists and actuaries appointed jointly by the House Ways and Means Committee and the Senate Finance Committee. This panel, chaired by William Hsaio, has recommended to the Congress that it act as if the benefits will increase over time in such a way that, as everyone moves to what is currently the highest bracket,

113

the replacement rate for the entire population moves to 30 percent for a primary earner and 50 percent of that for a dependent beneficiary. This recommendation represents important change from the current philosophy that, regardless of the way incomes move through time, the median earner should get 45 percent, plus half again as much for a dependent spouse. Even given the pessimistic demographic projection, this method of decoupling is expected to allow the tax rate to rise once and for all to 10.2 percent and stay there for at least fifty years. The change in the average replacement rate, falling from about 45 percent to 30 percent, would just offset the increasing ratio of dependents to working population—a ratio that will increase from 30 percent to a projected 45 percent in the first quarter of the next century.

PROFESSOR BUCHANAN: What rate of return would they get in that time?

PROFESSOR FELDSTEIN: The rate of return is still very low. Once the expansion of the program stops (as it effectively has stopped) the rate is limited by the growth of the wage base. If we are moving into a century of zero population growth, the rate of return will perhaps be about 2 percent—which is the rate of growth of per capita wages—perhaps a little higher as more women enter the labor force, but not much higher.

This is therefore an inefficient program in the sense that we give up the opportunities for real investment in order to have the other advantages of social security that I alluded to in my paper. However, the program limits the degree of that inefficiency by driving down the average replacement rate as people move into higher and higher incomes. If people are responsive to the replacement rate, a 30 percent replacement rate will not discourage as much saving as is discouraged by the current higher replacement rate. And the program holds out some hope as a politically viable alternative to developing a fund.

Let me turn to Nancy Teeters's remarks, and first to the substantive issue whether social security provides benefits that replace saving or simply replaces previous welfare and transfers within families. It is important to bear one thing in mind: the nature of retirement has changed dramatically. At the beginning of the century almost every man over age sixty-five was working. By 1929, 55 percent of men over sixty-five were still working. Now the figure is less than 25 percent.

The whole notion of supporting retirees had a different flavor when there were very few retirees. To be sure, there were then, and to a smaller extent there are now, retired parents being supported by their children. But, as more and more people have moved into white-collar jobs and high-paying blue-collar jobs, they are in a position to save for their own retirement and, indeed, even to contemplate having enough income during their working lives to retire. Thirty years ago a variety of people predicted a growth in the savings rate—this, in fact, has not materialized, to a large extent because of the impact of social security.

It is important, however, that we not treat this as a black and white issue. Some would have saved, others would have become dependent upon their children. What really matters is the relative magnitude of the two groups. To go back to the comment I made in response to Professor Buchanan's point: the evidence is beginning to accumulate—not just my evidence but also that of others, including international and microeconomic data—that social security has a powerful effect on private saving. If anything, that effect is likely to be more important in the future when almost the entire working population, or their dependents, are being covered under some type of private pension. Something like 60 percent of the working population is now covered by private pensions. Women are less likely to be covered than men, but their husbands may be. The lowest income groups are least likely to be covered, but these groups are really not in social security but are protected by the Supplemental Security Income program.

Once we recognize that private pension programs are providing benefits for a great majority of current workers, and that these programs are typically integrated (as the tax law calls it) in the sense that the companies are permitted to offset their social security contributions against their required private pension contributions, we can see that any change in social security is likely to produce a corresponding change in private pensions.

Let us turn to the "history of thought" question. Wilbur Cohen and I have compared notes and I stick by my statement that the new Keynesian economics stressed that the depression would persist as long as the full employment rate of savings remained greater than the rate of investment, and that social security would offset that problem. Wilbur Cohen confirmed what I had heard from my colleague Richard Musgrave that when Keynes came to the United States in the late 1930s and talked to a group at the Federal Reserve Board, he argued that the problem of permanent underconsumption would go away because of social security.

And it was in the late 1930s that Alvin Hansen was converted both from a non-Keynesian to a Keynesian and from a social security funder to a nonfunder. It was in the early 1940s that Seymour Harris wrote a book about the virtues of social security. One of social security's great virtues, to this protégé of Hansen, was that it would depress private savings which would help to overcome a problem that was concerning all of them at that time.

I am glad Nancy Teeters and I are agreed on the retirement test. I am glad we are agreed on unemployment insurance as well. She said that she was worried why there were no riots in the streets and decided that it because of unemployment insurance. That line of reasoning makes her want to revise unemployment insurance. I go along with that goal also, not because I want riots, but because I believe that unemployment insurance does have substantial distorting effects. The important thing is not to increase the tax base of the unemployment insurance system, as seems to be the drift—not only of Congress but also of individual states —but to increase the maximum rate. To increase the base is to make "good employers" (those who are already paying the minimum) pay more taxes to subsidize "bad employers" (that is, employers with considerable unemployment who are already paying the maximum rate and for whom there is no marginal cost of additional unemployment).

At the same time, I believe we should tax unemployment insurance benefits as though they were wages. This would have no adverse effect on the poor or those who pay no taxes. But it would put an end to anomalous situations in which unemployment insurance replaces more than 100 percent of lost benefits when the social security tax, state tax, federal tax, and other kinds of costs are taken into account.

I am not particularly concerned with the issue of general revenue financing. We now have a mechanism, the earned income credit, by which we can undo with general revenue anything we can do with the social security tax. If we do not like the total package, we can make a direct change through the personal income tax. I would prefer that because I think the closer we come to making a reality of the story that social security contributions are simply forced saving that are given back with a rate of return, the more we can offset the adverse effects on work effort that come if that contribution is perceived as a tax.

It is now neither a tax nor forced saving, but a hybrid. We should make it much more clearly a quid pro quo, a money purchase plan, an individualized account where individuals see that they are paying into the fund an amount they will eventually get back with the pseudo rate of interest that comes from the growth of the program. Then we should use the Supplemental Security Income program to redistribute benefits at the bottom, and we should use the earned income credit to redistribute the cost of that.

Essentially this appears to represent a process of fooling the people, but in fact it does not. Rather it helps them understand that a significant portion of the social security tax—and remember in the majority of households that tax is now greater than the income tax—is on a quid pro quo basis, that the more they pay in, the more they will receive. And this will only come home to the people if we split the two very clearly, which means that we should not use social security as an income redistribution program and should instead use general revenue, both through the Supplemental Security Income program and through the earned income credit, for that purpose.

Robert Lampman had a number of very interesting things to say, but they were not really about my paper. At one point, after cataloging a variety of programs, he came to unemployment insurance and said it was doing well. Unemployment insurance was replacing about a fourth of the income loss resulting from unemployment. It was, however, a pity that only half the people got benefits.

But, why should he say it was doing well? Why not say it was doing poorly, both because there may be some severe cases of unmet needs (support for the long-term unemployed and for those who have severe problems requiring support if they are ever to find reasonable jobs again) and because as many as a million people are unemployed at any time, thereby wasting as much as $5 or even $7 billion of production.

Moreover, I think that term *one-fourth* tends to be misunderstood because the benefits are available only to half of the unemployed and because taxes are not levied on unemployment insurance benefits. The average rate of replacement is more like two-thirds than one-fourth, or a third, or a half. As a result, the potential disincentive effects are very powerful.

When Professor Lampman said that the lowest fifth's prefisc share went from 3 percent to a postfisc lowest fifth share of 10 percent, I worried about two distinctions he did not make.

One was the distinction between the aged and the other poor. The fact that the aged have low incomes is not a surprise or even necessarily a bad thing, if the aged have assets they are dissaving. What we would expect is that they would not have substantial "income" per se, although for this group as a whole the definition of *income* is fuzzy. Is a pension check income, but not withdrawing money from one's bank account? More important, because the vast majority of the aged have little in assets, is the question what they would have had in the absence of social security?

Mrs. Jones has a prefisc income of zero in a given year if she has no assets and no income other than social security. But, as Professor Lampman suggests, we must keep it in mind that the savings that Mrs. Jones made reflected the fact that social security would be provided. The savings that her company made on her behalf under an integrated pension program also reflected the fact that her earnings were below the maximum and that the company had a fully integrated plan recognizing the existence of social security.

Rita Ricardo Campbell's introductory remark made me think that if Ricardo were alive today he would share my concern about the effect of social security on capital accumulation inasmuch as he had the right answer to the question about the impact of national debt on private savings. We generally agree about two-earner families but I would do more than the Quadrennial Advisory Council on Social Security. I would not place a limit on pooling income up to the wage ceiling in 1976 of $15,300. The reasons for that, I think, are important.

There is an equity issue for women whose husbands already make more than $15,300 and get nothing back for what they pay in and have a justifiable sense of outrage. But they are also paying a very high tax. They are paying a combined employer/employee tax of nearly 12 percent—which is likely to increase—and getting back nothing for it, since they can usually claim more as a dependent than they can claim as a retired worker. The effects of that tax must be substantially adverse. Harvey Rosen's estimates of the labor supply of women show high sensitivity to net wage rates, and I would think that the welfare loss—the excess burden as economists would call it—is so substantial that we must take it seriously.[1] This would be the case even though extending the benefits to married women, increasing the potential benefits of two-earner families, will have the unfortunate effect of further reducing their saving.

Discussion about unemployment insurance may get off on the wrong foot if we focus on "cheaters." While I was pleased to see the "60 Minutes" program dramatize the nature of the unemployment insurance system, I think that cheaters must represent a very small part of the total number of people collecting unemployment insurance.

In general, unemployment insurance recipients are people who have lost their jobs and expect to return to work very soon. They are not cheating. They do not look at themselves as getting an especially good deal. They are responding to the natural incentives of the system in which employers and employees organize production in ways that lead to excessive unemployment of a seasonal, cyclical, or temporary type.

Our focus ought to be on understanding the nature of unemployment and, particularly, on the nature of the incentives associated with temporary layoffs (which make up about half of all so-called job loss). And we ought to see to what extent we can rectify the adverse incentives and, at the same time, help those who are really hard hit by unemployment.

DR. RITA RICARDO CAMPBELL: I would like to reply, first, that the mild proposal I suggested was not what I believe to be equitable for two-worker families. It was the best that I could get through a subcommittee of males. One of them was the former executive vice president of the American Telephone and Telegraph Company which had just paid out a huge sum in back payments to women, and another was a union buildings trade man who could not envision women doing anything but carrying bricks. I managed to get this mild proposal through the subcommittee, but the Quadrennial Advisory Council on Social Security, all male except for one other woman, just would not accept it at all.

PROFESSOR FELDSTEIN: Part of the problem which ought to be mentioned is the argument that the proposal to eliminate the retirement test would be expensive. People say it would be expensive because they do not take into account the increase in general income taxes that would come if eliminating the retirement test caused more people to work. They do not take this into account because the tax funds would not accrue to the social security system. In terms of cost to social security, the cost is high; in terms of cost even to the public sector, let alone the nation, it is much lower.

DR. RITA RICARDO CAMPBELL: On the other point about seasonal unemployment, I do not think that we are talking about "cheaters." But I do think

---

[1] Harvey S. Rosen, "Taxes in a Labor Supply Model with Joint Wage-Hour Determination," *Econometrica,* vol. 44, no. 3 (May 1976), pp. 485-507.

a change in moral values has taken place. When I was teaching at Harvard, for example, chocolate candy factories would hire women in the fall as soon as school started and the women's children went back to school. Women took these jobs so that they could work full time for Christmas money, knowing that about a month before Christmas they would be laid off.

When the Unemployment Compensation Act was passed, one major issue in Massachusetts was whether seasonal workers should come under the act and, if so, whether they would "milk" the fund. It was an important issue because one did not have to prove that one was looking for work. I don't think collectors of such benefits are cheating—they are just taking advantage of the law.

DR. AARON: I was glad to hear that Professor Feldstein agreed with Buchanan that the prospects for building up a substantial Social Security Trust Fund no longer look good. But, harking back to his previous, more optimistic stage, I would like to ask him whether he would be willing to marry two independent pieces of his research. One is his argument that we should build up a trust fund, on the ground that the capital stock in the United States is too small. The other is the research in which he has advocated a consumption tax. If one's objective is to build up additional capital, and if one advances an egalitarian case for it—that an increase in the capital stock would drive down the rate of return and increase wage rates— why not kill two birds with one stone and build up that trust fund or build up that capital reserve through a consumption tax? It would not only provide these income effects but also directly affect savings decisions by households.

PROFESSOR FELDSTEIN: On a technical level, I have no objection to that. On a political level, it seems to me that using a surplus to buy back government debt or to provide a government capital fund would be rejected out of hand. There is some glimmer of hope in the argument claiming it is unfair for us to expect the next generation to pay a 20 percent tax to support the same level of benefits we are supporting with a 10 percent tax. It might be politically salable because people might think they were protecting their own or their children's future benefits with such a fund. Putting such a tax in the context of social security seemed more natural than putting it in general taxation.

But I still, as you say, favor both of those measures, and I have no technical objection to using the consumption tax (which I think is better than an income tax) to accumulate a fund or to pay off government debt (which I think is a good thing to do). In fact, I am amazed that I lasted this long up here without making a plug for the consumption tax.

DR. OKUN: I have about half a dozen questions. Let me begin by saying, like Professor Buchanan, I take Professor Feldstein's work very seriously; I think he is dealing with the right questions, and he is dealing with them in a professional way. But I guess my view of the history of doctrine before Feldstein is a little different. It seems to me that the examination of these effects was being left primarily to people who were sympathetic to the objectives of the program, such as those at the Brookings Institution and the Institute of Poverty of Wisconsin. Perhaps some people who were critical of the programs hoped that they would go away or collapse under their own weight rather than be made more efficient.

The question Aaron asked seems to me to make the general point that if one does not like the effects of the social security system on saving, one can correct it somewhere else—one does not have to correct it within the framework of the social security system.

PROFESSOR FELDSTEIN: Are you in agreement with me that it would be easier to do in the social security system than in the Department of Commerce or the Treasury?

DR. OKUN: We are really talking about getting the government to run a surplus, and that is the hard task.

PROFESSOR FELDSTEIN: "Protecting our retirement" may be a rationale for a surplus that is not available if a surplus is simply called a surplus.

DR. OKUN: I am less convinced than Professor Feldstein that I want a higher national saving rate. I think it is important to point out what the facts are as he interpreted them—that social security prevented a large rise in the personal saving rate rather than causing an actual decline over time. This does raise questions, first of all, on whether we really wanted a rise in the saving rate. Second, it raises some question about the interpretation of the results and the confidence with which one should view them. Professor Feldstein says that between 1929 and 1971, we would have experienced a large rise in the saving rate in the absence of social security. Goldsmith, Kuznets, and Denison have told us that for periods going back to 1870, we have had a very steady national saving and personal saving rate.

It seems to me that Professor Feldstein is obliged to explain what prevented the national saving rate from rising prior to 1929. I think that if he back-casts his equation, he would certainly estimate negative personal saving throughout the nineteenth century. I am not saying he ought to have an equation which fits 1843 or even 1897, but there is an implication of a discontinuity in the world that, in the absence of social security, would have produced this rise in the saving rate. Somehow social security came along and just neutralized this incipient rise and extended the continuity of previous years—essentially a steady saving rate at full employment.

The other issue I want to raise is that Professor Feldstein accepts the principle that we should have some kind of an income maintenance program for old people, that we should not let them starve. If we start with that principle, we can add the principle that society really likes transfer payments with a smile better than transfer payments with a frown. Where we can, we want to give people a sense of paying for themselves, of entitlement rather than hand-out. I wonder whether those principles do not amount to something close to the social security system we have now, even including a retirement test.

I also want to raise a number of questions about unemployment insurance. First, I find examples of the replacement of income by unemployment insurance quite impressive. And then I remind myself that in 1973 there were 1.8 million people drawing unemployment insurance, or about 2 percent of the labor force. Why is it that unemployment insurance was no more attractive than this?

Second, I remind myself that two-thirds of the drop in output during a recession takes the form of employers' cushioning layoffs by cutting hours and accepting lower productivity. The drop in hours in the past recession accounted for nearly as large a decline in payrolls as the number of people laid off. There must be something that explains why we use layoffs so little and why unemployment insurance benefits in prosperity are so low; perhaps it is the work ethic. Perhaps experience rating is more effective in some sense than some of the fragmentary evidence suggests.

A few other small points on unemployment insurance: there is a sentence in Professor Feldstein's paper which I believe is the most remarkable testimonial to discretionary, fine-tuning, fiscal policy anywhere in the literature. This passage categorizes as irrelevant the automatic stabilization of unemployment insurance. From the fourth quarter of 1973 to the first quarter of 1975, unemployment insurance benefits under regular programs grew from $4.1 billion to $16.2 billion at a time when the government had taken about $2 billion worth of discretionary action against recession. That is a $12 billion swing at a time when multipliers and accelerators seemed indeed high. The built-in stabilizing benefit in holding down unemployment during that period far exceeded any cost from disincentives in the system.

The last point is that if we take fully actuarially taxed unemployment insurance as a benchmark, that benchmark is not neutral. Rather it is like a tie-in sale. In that situation, the employer is forced to pay unemployment insurance in order to make a layoff. The benefit to the worker is worth something to the employer, but it is presumably worth less than the extra tax rate that the firm has to pay. It cannot be worth 100 cents on a dollar of wages any more than any other tie-in sale is worth 100 cents on a dollar. If it were worth 100 cents on a dollar, we would have had a high incidence of voluntary unemployment insurance back in 1930-32 when layoffs exploded without compulsory unemployment insurance.

I do not know whether the benefit would be worth 80 cents on the dollar or 60 cents on the dollar, but the introduction of an unemployment insurance system which is fully actuarial must reduce layoffs. And it is not clear how far we would have to go in experience rating to come back to where we started. I am not suggesting that we are neutral now, by any means, but it is important to recognize that a full-actuarial benchmark is not neutral; it is a tie-in sale.

PROFESSOR FELDSTEIN: Thank you for the careful questions. Let me speak to each of them in turn.

The issue of whether we save too little or too much is not an issue of whether social security reduces savings or whether what we have observed over the past period is a reduction from what might have been or from what had been in the past. The question that we must ask ourselves is: What do we get in return for more savings? As I read the evidence, smoothing out the cycle, we roughly double our money in about six years; that is, we receive about 12 percent. This is not an option open to individuals, but it is an option open to society. It is not open to individuals because of a combination of factors ranging from the corporate income tax to Regulation Q. The result is that individuals get the wrong signal from the market and they make the wrong decision. Most individuals, given the choice of trading a dollar in 1976 for two constant purchasing power dollars five or six years from now, would make the trade. That would be my guess about the public's taste, in this matter, reflecting my view that people are now facing the wrong prices.

Let me return to the second and more substantial question—what happened between 1929 and 1971 and what other evidence is there of the effect of social security on savings behavior? I think there was something fundamental that happened between 1929 and 1971 and, indeed, between the period before 1929 and the period since. Incomes rose in previously unknown proportions as people moved to a new middle-class standard. The working class was no longer as poor as it had been previously. With these changes came an increase in retirement. In 1900 there was very little retirement. As I mentioned before, there was a substantial increase in retirement by 1929, and then again a very substantial increase between 1929 and the present.

If one is not going to retire, if retirement is not part of one's future, then saving is for liquidity purposes, for emergency purposes, and is not on the scale of retirement saving and social security. Maybe that is what Simon Kuznets had in mind when, looking at his own data, he speculated that the savings rate would increase substantially from 1950.[2] Whether he said this because he believed that there was a pure income effect (that is, that once one was sufficiently wealthy one could think about putting something aside) or whether he foresaw the effect of increasing retirement, I do not recall.

---

[2] Simon Kuznets, "Economic Growth and Income Inequality," *American Economic Review*, vol. 45, no. 1 (March 1955), pp. 1-28, or Simon Kuznets, "Proportion of Capital Formation to National Product," *American Economic Review, Proceedings*, vol. 42, no. 2 (May 1952), pp. 507-26.

I know from the international evidence though that higher income begets higher saving because it increases retirement. If we look simply at the relation of the savings rate to income in various countries, we find that the savings rate is an increasing function of income. When we look at the mechanism, that is when we account for retirement (which differs substantially among developed countries), we see that the income effect is really masking a retirement effect. Higher income means higher retirement probabilities, and higher retirement, in turn, means higher savings.

I do not think that a time series adding one more variable to an equation that begins by explaining almost everything can be given much weight. It is one piece of evidence. The equation is consistent with the international evidence. It is consistent with some micro evidence now. It is consistent with expectations. It is consistent with data on wealth distributions. As evidence accumulates, people will have to judge for themselves what it is worth. But there is not as much of a puzzle now as the question suggests. I think the growth of income and the growth of retirement do make possible, or would have made possible, an independence, a retirement planning, that had not existed before.

Coming to the third question, the issue of welfare for the aged, let me say that what I called necessary, I meant as so probable as to be equivalent to necessary. Yes, we would do it. It was asked whether we could not skip all these arguments about disincentives to saving and add the argument that we like to do it with a smile rather than a frown. I will add that argument.

Finally, one more of Okun's questions. I think his five good questions deserve five attempts at answering them. Unemployment insurance: Why were there not more than 1.7 million people collecting unemployment insurance, on average, in 1973? That year was, as I am sure most observers know, the low point for the 1970s: the number was 2.2 million the year before that, 2.6 million the year after. I do not say that unemployment insurance leads everyone to take up a seasonal job, so that he can cash in on unemployment. I see it having several very small effects that add up. In a year like 1974, when there were 2.6 million people drawing unemployment compensation, I can well believe that, if not half, then 40 percent or a third—some number close to a million people at any time—were unemployed either because they had taken a casual job or a temporary job because of unemployment insurance, or because they had been laid off when the incentive structure favored a temporary layoff rather than production at a lower rate of productivity, or because they were searching for another week, as Kathleen Classen's numbers suggest.[3] All of this adds up to a large amount.

Perhaps I spoke too quickly about discretionary fiscal policy, though I would be surprised if Dr. Okun should advocate nondiscretion and I should advocate

[3] Kathleen Classen, "The Effect of Unemployment Insurance on the Duration of Unemployment and Subsequent Earnings" (Arlington, Va.: Public Research Institute of the Center for Naval Analysis, September 1975).

discretion. Perhaps there is some virtue to the fact that unemployment insurance benefits come during periods of high unemployment. That fact would not be offset by experience rating, and perhaps that fact should be emphasized. Once we get past that period, and the Congress starts considering a tax cut, it asks what the total deficit is. The issue of the extra contribution, then, is not worth much discussion. Perhaps the point to emphasize is that experience rating would not change this at all.

PART THREE

THE CASE FOR THE PROGRESSIVE INCOME TAX: EASY OR UNEASY?

CONSIDERATIONS REGARDING TAXATION AND INEQUALITY

James Tobin

Introduction

The case for a progressive income tax is still as uneasy as it was when Blum and Kalven examined it in 1953.[1] So, for that matter, are the cases for a proportional tax, a regressive tax, a "degressive"[2] tax, or for any proposed schedule of tax rates. The "proper" or "optimal" tax schedule cannot be ascertained either by rational argument or by empirical inquiry. Although reason and information can help, the question is in the last analysis ethical and political. Any individual's answer, any citizen's vote, will depend on his personal interests and values, and society's answer will be the outcome of the political process of choice among conflicting interests and values.

In saying this, I am consciously giving short shrift to attempts, whether as ancient as Plato or as recent as Rawls,[3] to deduce rules of economic justice from first principles. Rawls's criterion, for example, has (at least to me) no compelling intuitive appeal. I doubt that the "haves" of contemporary society would find convincing the contention that they voted for redistribution in a constitutional convention held before that random drawing of endowments of human capital and other wealth in which they were so fortunate as to become "haves." "There but for the grace of God . . ." is a reflection that has evoked more verbal humility than material charity over the years. Blum and Kalven traced many other principles of just taxation and always found arbitrary assumptions at the end of the path. Henry Simons said, "The case for drastic progression in taxation must be rested on the case against inequality—on the ethical or aesthetic judgment that the prevailing distribution of wealth and income reveals a degree (and/or kind) of inequality which is distinctly evil or unlovely."[4] I do not think we can do better.

Let us, however, be careful not to prejudice cases by implicit but arbitrary assignments of the burden of proof. The very title of the Blum-Kalven classic and

---

[1] Walter J. Blum and Harry Kalven, Jr. *The Uneasy Case for Progressive Taxation* (Chicago: University of Chicago Press, 1953).

[2] The Blum-Kalven label for a single-rate tax on income less a subsistence exemption, apparently their preferred schedule.

[3] John Rawls, *A Theory of Justice* (Cambridge: Harvard University Press, 1972).

[4] Henry Simons, *Personal Income Taxation* (Chicago: University of Chicago Press, 1938), pp. 18-19.

of this part of the conference suggests that proportional taxation gets the nod unless someone can advance a convincing case for progressive deviation from it. I do not see any obvious presumption in favor of proportional taxation. One could as well say that the burden of proof is on those who would depart from a quadratic schedule, or from the Revenue Act of 1975. A confidence interval may include zero, but the fact that it includes zero does not validate the null hypothesis against any other parameter value in the interval. Why should tax schedules *not* be progressive?

And why should I continue? I am only going to express my views as one citizen of a democratic society and advance considerations that I think and hope other citizens might find relevant to their views and votes. In such a discussion, what is really going on is an appeal to shared—perhaps widely shared—tastes and values, and there is no way that the appeal will convince listeners who do not share them. Last fall I joined a group of undergraduates discussing economic inequality and redistribution. One of them asked me whether I did not believe in the Tenth Commandment—Thou shalt not covet anything that is thy neighbor's—a query whose point, for him, clinched the matter. For others it was just as obvious that strict equality of income must be favored.

I fail to see how the issue of progressivity is essentially different from the issue of equality. Progressive taxation may not be the only way for government to mitigate economic inequality, but certainly it is one way, and an important one. The overriding purpose of progressive taxation is surely to achieve a distribution of income and wealth less unequal than would occur under proportional taxation. This is what principles like "ability to pay" and even "benefit assessment" come down to. For any given program of government purchases of goods and services and the net revenues required to pay for them, progressive taxation will leave after-tax income and consumption less unequally distributed than proportional taxation.

Note that I said *net* revenues. Let us not be constrained by the arbitrary assumption that taxation is a one-way street: the government can and does pay out transfers—negative taxes—to some citizens, and these payments can be an important source of progressivity. Utilizing transfers, a small government (small as measured by its substantive or exhaustive expenditures) can be as redistributive as a large government. We need not assume, as so many earlier writers on public finance assumed, that pro-egalitarian taxation is limited by the net revenue requirements of the government. There is no significant difference between taxing a citizen nothing rather than taxing him a dollar, and transferring a dollar to him rather than transferring nothing to him. (The Blum-Kalven book is vitiated by failure to treat transfers and positive taxes symmetrically. The "degressive" system the authors apparently favor—a flat-rate tax on income above an exemption—is flawed by their failure to take into account the possibility of paying low-income citizens the implicit tax value of their unused exemptions.)

It would be agreed here, I suppose, that the inequality with which we are concerned is that of *lifetime* income *within* a cohort, not of annual or monthly or daily income. Differences of lifetime income between cohorts of different vintages do not transgress egalitarian standards. There are indeed difficult issues of inter-generational equity, but it is best to keep them separate from our present topic.

Purely age-related differences of income do not call for correction by taxation. However, in applying this principle we should remember that real-world capital markets are by no means perfect: they do not always afford all those who are temporarily poor the opportunity to sustain consumption by borrowing against future wages. Sometimes the young (and others) are liquidity-constrained. Some-times they can borrow only at penalty rates. Consequently the present value of their lifetime incomes should be calculated with higher discount rates than the present value of the incomes of their wealthier and more liquid fellow citizens. This condition can be ameliorated by various measures to provide credit and income insurance. It is also a rough justification for the tax code practice of using tax time units much shorter than a lifetime.

Redistribution of Endowments

In theoretical models of general economic equilibrium, individuals have exogenous "endowments" of commodities, including factors of production. These are genetic or inherited or ascribed. They are the basic sources of inequality, even in an ideal competitive economy which meets all the conditions for efficiency and Pareto-optimality. If it were feasible to tax and redistribute these original endowments, without affecting their allocation among different uses, would anyone be opposed to that?

I can imagine some grounds for opposition, though not (in my view) attractive ones. One argument is the claim that some people are better utility machines than others. Even if interpersonal utility comparisons were meaningful, we have no reason to believe that the capacity for utility is correlated with initial endowments. The propensity of some of the rich to support arts and sciences and their applica-tions is often advanced as a reason to tolerate inequality. It does not matter who these rich are, the argument goes, but it takes concentrations of wealth to divert resources from more prosaic and transient items of consumption.

The argument is not convincing. Modern governments are perfectly capable of mobilizing the necessary resources or of encouraging their private mobilization by tax concessions and subsidies. We do not have to pay huge costs of inequality for the chance that, without any tax incentive, some fractions of some accumula-tions of wealth will be devoted to purposes of enduring social value. Moreover, the argument that the rich spend well is countered by the distaste many observers feel and express for their consumption habits. Blum and Kalven and many other defenders of inequality tell us that the vulgarity and frivolity and arrogance of some

129

life styles are irrelevant to the issues of inequality and progressive taxation. We should neither complain of personal tastes nor infer from them anything about the marginal utility of consumption and income. Perhaps this is true, but then let us not hear about art collections, architecture, and ballet either. And let us apply the same principle to welfare recipients and other consumers at the low end of the income spectrum.

I think Abba Lerner is right.[5] Human beings are human beings—at least that is the faith underlying our modern democratic societies. We do not ascribe social and economic status by caste or class or race. Lacking any other basis for assessing capacity to enjoy life, we must assume the capacity to be randomly distributed, independent of endowments. This provides a probabilistic presumption for equality. Any other assumption would founder not only on the uncertainty of measurement but also on the obvious self-interest of every individual who would have to display more utility potential than his neighbor.

Can Endowments Be Taxed?

If we agree with what has been said so far, then we agree that the failure to equalize resource endowments, by taxation or otherwise, is only instrumentally justified. We do not know how to equalize without inducing tax-reducing or tax-avoiding behavior which deprives both society and tax collector of some of the potential productivity of the resources. If we could assess the value of every individual's native talent in its most productive use and tax him on that basis, he could not escape by loafing instead of working, taking comfortable jobs instead of responsible ones, consuming instead of saving, hoarding instead of taking risks, imitating instead of innovating. Like land, human endowments would be assessed and taxed at the value of their highest use. For better or worse, this cannot be done. The assessment procedure would have to rely on observations obtained with the cooperation of the taxpayers themselves, and the incentive structure would be like that of intelligence and medical tests for the military draft during the Vietnam War.

Society necessarily taxes the individual outcomes of endowments-*cum*-behavior, not of endowments alone. It is fairly clear that the controversies arise from differences in the emphasis placed on the two components. Advocates of equalization usually attribute observed inequality mainly to endowments, and opponents emphasize the role of behavior. These differences affect judgments both about "justice" and about "social efficiency."

We can, I suppose, imagine an economy of disjoint, individual economies, peopled with Robinson Crusoes of equal endowments of physical and human nature, each satisfying all his needs from his own effort and ingenuity, without specialization or trade or cooperation. It will then seem unjust and inefficient to tax the industrious and ingenious in favor of the lazy and improvident. Indeed, even

---

[5] Abba Lerner, *The Economics of Control* (New York: Macmillan, 1946), pp. 29-32.

proportional taxation of measurable income or wealth would not seem to fit the case. However, even these Crusoes may be subject to chance fortunes and misfortunes—for example, the vagaries of weather and health and technology. They may wish to join each other in an insurance scheme, even though the inevitable moral hazard imposes some deadweight loss and injustice.

But endowments are not equal, and individual economies are not independent. Even if endowments were initially equal, they would not remain so from one generation to the next. The children of successful, industrious, fortunate, wealthy parents have a head start. There seems no way to avoid this fact so long as the family is the child-rearing institution of the society, and there does not seem to be an alternative at hand. Indeed, provision of a good environment for children and family is a principal motivation of economic performance. In this sense, as Marshall pointed out, the most ardent and ruthless profit-seeking businessmen are generally altruistic.

Here is a great dilemma. One of the slogans of our casteless democratic society is equality of opportunity, and this equality is our excuse and consolation for inequality of wealth. After all, the unequal prizes are won in a fair race. But if the starting advantages in the next race are correlated with the order of finish of the last one, is opportunity equal? Is the race really fair? As we know, the same problem arises in Socialist societies. Mao Tse-tung had a drastic solution for it, periodic leveling by "cultural revolution." How costly this may be we do not yet know. In our own society we can only hope to mitigate the problem, by a progressive tax-transfer system and by public education.

A work ethic is essential to a society. We have a great stake in maintaining the view that performance pays off, that indolence and inefficiency do not. Since we cannot disentangle the elements of endowment and effort in performance, we must tolerate considerable reward for endowment, in large measure undeserved and redundant. But those of us who benefit from this circumstance should not delude ourselves. When I as chairman of my department tell the dean and the provost and the president that economists' salaries should be raised so that we can attract a better department than we have now, I am making a self-serving argument. When the National Association of Manufacturers tells us that we need to tax high incomes less in order to sustain the supply of capital and management, the NAM is making a self-serving argument.

The interdependence of modern economic life is another consideration to be taken into account. After all, this is not a society of isolated subsistence farmers. Anyone's earning capacity is dependent on a complex web of interdependence—on economic, locational, and professional specialization and trade; on a highly developed legal and governmental system that enforces contracts, protects life and property, fosters markets; on a shared accumulation of culture, learning, science, and technology. Market prices are probably a good way of allocating resources, even when the competitive conditions that would justify identifying factor prices with marginal productivities do not obtain. What is not justified is the presumption that these prices or marginal productivities are just deserts. It is not unreasonable to attribute part of the national product to the general social overhead capital and to allocate it as a social dividend for equal division.

How much inequality can a society stand before the legal, social, and political foundations of its economic productivity are undermined? These foundations depend on consent, expressed not only in formal collective political action but also in the informal daily actions of individuals and groups. A complex interdependent market economy is extremely vulnerable to disaffection. It is a great illusion to believe that one can rely on legal compulsion to sustain the rules of the economic game—to protect every property, enforce every contract. As Weber, Schumpeter, and other thoughtful analysts of the sociology of capitalism long ago pointed out, the framework must be sustained by a widely shared and internalized ethic, an ethic which differs from feudal explanations of inequality precisely in *not* ascribing differences of income and power to differential birthrights. It is too much to expect that loyal consent to the rules of the game will be forthcoming regardless of the outcomes of the game. We do not know the extent to which the disquieting problems of crime, corruption, demoralization, and antisocial behavior which beset our cities are due to highly visible—probably more so now than ever before, thanks to TV—and dramatic differences of opportunity and consumption. It would be imprudent, to say the least, to ignore the possible connection and to rely wholly on police and prison to cope with the problem of antisocial behavior.

Egalitarianism and Disincentives

I return now to the trade-off between the egalitarian gains of progressive taxation and the losses due to the disincentives of such taxation. This is a matter on which utilitarian calculus can conceivably shed some light, though for the reasons I gave at the beginning it can never be conclusive. Unfortunately our empirical knowledge of the strength of the disincentives is notably thin.

Even a voter who places no social value on the utility of those above him in the income scale (or—more accurately—in the endowment scale) will not as a rule—if he is rational and economically literate—favor taxation to bring them all the way down to his level. There is a point beyond which higher surtax rates collect less—not more—revenue. If the voter-taxpayer pushed the surtax on wealthier citizens beyond this point, he would have to impose more taxes on himself, inasmuch as the surtax would induce the wealthier citizens to divert resources to leisure or other untaxed employments. It is also possible that the diversion of resources would reduce the marginal productivities and values of the majority-voter's labor and other resources. This, however, is not certain: the withdrawn resources might be substitutes for, not complements of, the voter's resources.

On the other hand, there is no necessary presumption that proportional taxation is the way to minimize deadweight loss. Consider, for the moment, a system which includes no per capita tax or transfer (negative or positive demogrant). If revenues must be raised for public purposes, there are bound to be some distortions. Roughly speaking, the average of marginal tax rates, weighted by the total incomes in the brackets to which the marginal rates apply, must equal the ratio of the revenue requirement to the tax base. The higher the marginal rate for any bracket, the less effort and taxable income are generated by the taxpayers of the bracket, but the more revenue (up to a point) is obtained from that bracket and higher brackets. The same tax schedule must apply to everyone; we cannot, even if we thought it equitable, practice price discrimination and tailor tax schedules individually to endowments and preferences, because these are unobservable.

Given these constraints, there is an advantage in assigning high marginal tax rates, on the one hand, to those brackets whose labor supply is relatively inelastic and, on the other hand, to increase the average take from brackets with relatively low marginal utilities of consumption. Finding the proper way to tax is a complicated problem, and there is no reason at all to believe that the solution is proportional taxation. There is no such presumption even if all individual utilities are equally weighted, and *a fortiori* there is none if the median voter-taxpayer consults only his own utility.

Furthermore, as I stated earlier, we should not confine ourselves to the assumption of zero demogrant. A flat-rate tax coupled with a positive per capita demogrant—the guaranteed minimum disposable income for anyone with zero taxable earnings—is a progressive system in the sense that the ratio of tax (negative or positive) to income rises algebraically with income. If there are some individuals with zero or near-zero endowments, and if the marginal utility of consumption approaches zero, then any utilitarian calculation which counts their utility will dictate a positive demogrant. To pay this, and to credit it against the gross tax liabilities of more fortunate citizens, will increase the rate of a flat-tax schedule or the average marginal rate of a variable-rate schedule. But the utility losses on this account will be balanced by the utility gains at the bottom.

In this country we have been struggling to dodge this problem for many years, hoping to avoid the costs of a universal demogrant by restricting the payments to citizens who can be observed or reasonably inferred to have zero or minimal endowments. The categorical systems themselves ran into formidable problems of inequity and disincentive. I have discussed them on several occasions, including a previous "rational debate" with Mr. Wallis under the same sponsorship as today's session.[6] I will only repeat here my conviction that the opportunities for innocuous and fair categorical discrimination are quite limited.

---

[6] James Tobin and W. Allen Wallis, *Welfare Programs: An Economic Appraisal* (Washington, D.C.: American Enterprise Institute, 1968).

How Much Progressivity Is Desirable?

On what characteristics of endowments and utility functions does the desirable degree of progressivity depend? It it always hazardous to propose generalizations, since so many formulations of the problem and so many sets of parameter values are conceivable. But the following seem reasonable. First, the utilitarian case for progressivity clearly depends on declining marginal utility of total consumption, and becomes stronger as the assumed decline becomes steeper. Of course, declining marginal utility across individuals may be imposed by the valuations of the observer or voter, whatever the shapes of individual functions may be. Second, the case becomes stronger as the substitutability of leisure for work becomes weaker—or, in general, as the substitutability of untaxed utility-producing activity for taxed activity becomes weaker. Weak substitutability makes it easier to obtain surtax revenues from high-endowment taxpayers and to transfer them to low-endowment citizens in the form either of demogrants or of low marginal rates. Third, the case is the stronger the smaller the nonredistributive revenue requirement. The reason is that a high net revenue requirement already means a high marginal rate in a proportional tax system. If the marginal rate is high there is less room than there would otherwise be to raise rates for any bracket without inducing substitution that actually lowers revenue or gains little revenue for the utility loss imposed.

The utilitarian approach to optimal taxation implies that, contrary to the premise of the Blum-Kalven book, ethical principles and interpersonal valuations, although necessary, are not sufficient to determine even the general shape of the optimal tax schedule. The answer will differ as between economies, and for the same economy at different times. It will depend on a number of circumstances and parameters of behavior, some of which could be empirically derived. Following this line of inquiry, economists may yet contribute to this subject.[7]

---

[7] There is a flourishing literature. See, for example, J. A. Mirrlees, "An Exploration in the Theory of Optimum Income Taxation," *Review of Economic Studies,* vol. 38, no. 2 (April 1971), pp. 175-208; A. B. Atkinson, "How Progressive Should Income Tax Be?" in M. Parkin and A. R. Nobay, eds., *Essays in Modern Economics,* the Proceedings of the Association of University Teachers of Economics (New York: Barnes & Noble, 1973), pp. 90-109.

THE CASE FOR
PROGRESSIVE TAXATION:
EASY OR UNEASY?

W. Allen Wallis

It was twenty-three years ago that Walter J. Blum and the late Harry Kalven, Jr., of the University of Chicago Law School, published their 100-page classic, *The Uneasy Case for Progressive Taxation*.[1] The uneasiness, for which the authors thanked their colleague Aaron Director, startled most of us when the book was published. In fact, the uneasiness startled the authors themselves, for they had set out simply to elucidate systematically the case for progressive taxation.

In 1953 almost everyone—economists, lawyers, politicians, and laymen—took it for granted that progressive taxes reduce inequality and are therefore good. As Blum and Kalven said in their opening sentence, "Progressive taxation is now regarded as one of the central ideas of modern democratic capitalism and is widely accepted as a secure policy commitment which does not require serious examination." The case against inequality was examined occasionally, and rested ultimately on what Henry Simons referred to as aesthetic considerations: inequality is "unlovely."

As to whether progressive taxation does in fact reduce inequality, no one had seriously investigated that; indeed, as far as I know, there is no conclusive evidence on that question even today. Inequality had been diminishing long before progressive taxation was introduced, and what the effect of progressive taxation has been in sustaining, strengthening, or weakening this trend is an extraordinarily complex question. Quite possibly that question is not yet susceptible to a definitive answer; progressive income taxation began in the United States only two or three generations ago (1913), and for at least one of those generations the rates were neither high nor notably progressive. To measure the effects of progressive taxation the unit of time must be a generation. So while **Blum** and Kalven by no means told us that the emperor had no clothes, they did raise a question as to what he was wearing.

My greatest chance of performing a useful function here is to review the principal points in Blum and Kalven's essay and to comment on some of their points in the light of the last twenty-three years. In all probability there have been many findings in the field of public finance of which I am unaware, and some of

---

[1] Walter J. Blum and Harry Kalven, Jr., *The Uneasy Case for Progressive Taxation* (Chicago: University of Chicago Press, 1953).

these may illuminate issues raised by Blum and Kalven; if so, I hope to learn of some of them from others at this conference.

The Uneasy Case Summarized

Blum and Kalven present, and examine critically, four principal arguments in support of progressivity and three principal arguments against it. They also discuss two supplementary topics which, while neither pro nor con, are closely related to the principal arguments both pro and con.

There are four main arguments *for* progressivity:

(1) Such a tax can make a contribution "to maintaining a high and stable level of economic activity." [2]

(2) Progressivity would tend to distribute the burden of taxes according to the benefits received "if it can be shown that benefits increase as income increases, and that at some levels of income benefits increase more rapidly than income." [3]

(3) Progressivity tends to equalize among taxpayers "the sacrifices which the payment of taxes entails," since "it seems likely that a dollar has less 'value' for a person with a million dollars of income than for a person with only a thousand dollars of income." [4]

(4) "A progressive tax on income necessarily operates to lessen the inequalities in the distribution of income" and "may well have some distinct advantages" over all other methods of redistributing income because "by using the tax system for redistribution, the market, at least within large limits, can be left to determine relative values and allocate resources through the price mechanism, with the freedom of individuals left relatively unimpaired, with no significant addition to government manpower, and with no increase in difficult discretionary judgments which government personnel need make." [5]

This fourth argument for progression, that it redistributes income, leads Blum and Kalven to probe the basic objections to inequality and, indeed, the very meaning of equality and of equality of opportunity. They suggest three possible reasons for favoring equality:

(1) There remains "an ultimate doubt about the rationality of any scheme of differential rewards," [6] because of the role of inborn endowment, opportunity, and environment—in short, the rejection of notions of personal responsibility.

(2) Since "any man's production requires the cooperation of many others . . . it has seemed to some not possible to differentiate, except arbitrarily, between the contributions of each to the final result . . . [so] any differential pricing of

---

[2] Ibid., p. 29.

[3] Ibid., p. 35.

[4] Ibid., pp. 39 and 40.

[5] Ibid., pp. 71-72.

[6] Ibid., p. 82.

services should be subject to substantial reduction in recognition of the contribution made by the team itself." [7]

(3) Economic rewards are based on economic achievements, but "there is more to a man than that which the market can appraise or reward. . . . Consequently we are tempted to second-guess the market either by giving recognition to some qualities which the market ignores or by discounting some qualities which it almost inadvertently seems to overrate." [8]

Three principal arguments *against* progressivity are examined:

(1) A price is "paid for progression in terms of complicating the structure of the income tax, expanding the opportunity for taxpayer ingenuity directed to lawfully avoiding taxes, creating very difficult questions of equity among taxpayers, and obscuring the implications of any given provision in the tax law." [9]

(2) Progressivity is conducive to political irresponsibility and thereby "places strains on the majority rule principle which perhaps need not otherwise arise." [10]

(3) "Progression . . . lessens the economic productivity of society . . . either by reducing the amount or quality of work put forth or by impeding the creation or maintenance of capital. . . ." [11]

In analyzing the arguments for and against progressivity, Blum and Kalven examine (1) the effects of government expenditures on redistribution of income and (2) the special case of a tax whose progressivity consists only in exempting some income entirely and taxing the rest at a uniform rate, which they call a "degressive" tax.

In thus briefly summarizing the contents of the Blum and Kalven book, I should remind you that each of the nine points I have referred to—four arguments for progression, three arguments against progression, and two supplementary issues—is examined thoroughly by the authors and none is accepted without serious uneasiness. Their two-paragraph conclusion is worth quoting in full:

> The case for progression, after a long critical look, thus turns out to be stubborn but uneasy. The most distinctive and technical arguments advanced in its behalf are the weakest. It is hard to gain much comfort from the special arguments, however intricate their formulations, constructed on notions of benefit, sacrifice, ability to pay, or economic stability. The case has stronger appeal when progressive taxation is viewed as a means of reducing economic inequalities. But the case for more economic equality, when examined directly, is itself perplexing. And the perplexity is greatly magnified for those who in the quest for greater equality are unwilling to argue for radical changes in the fundamental institutions of the society.

---

[7] Ibid., p. 83.

[8] Ibid., p. 84.

[9] Ibid., pp. 14-15.

[10] Ibid., p. 21.

[11] Ibid.

These implications apart, the theory of progression is a matter of major importance for taxation. The adoption of progression necessarily influences the positive law of taxation more than any other factor. But in the end it is the implications about economic inequality which impart significance and permanence to the issue and institution of progression. Ultimately a serious interest in progression stems from the fact that a progressive tax is perhaps the cardinal instance of the democratic community struggling with its hardest problem.[12]

Although the Blum-Kalven classic remains as enlightening today as it was twenty-three years ago, developments of the past two decades may give us a perspective on some of the considerations expounded in the book different from the perspective of 1953.

Blum and Kalven point out that "in this essay it is assumed that the burden of a tax on the incomes of persons is not shifted"; they also point out that "most of the arguments for progressive taxation of income have been . . . in terms of distributional effects . . . [and] assume that by and large . . . [a tax] on income . . . is not shifted. . . ."[13] But few would argue seriously that, at today's tax levels, personal income taxes are not shifted. Indeed, Blum and Kalven implicitly recognize the existence of shifting when, for example, they discuss the complications in tax laws that result from progression and when they discuss the dampening of incentives. The general effect of shifting is to diminish the redistribution effects that are adduced as the principal justification of progressivity, to lead to complications in the tax law when efforts are made to impede shifting, and to diminish the national product by reducing the quantities of resources used and altering their allocations.

Another major development that changes greatly the perspective with which we now view the Blum and Kalven analysis is the development of massive welfare programs which aim to reduce inequality by direct gifts to the poor: Supplemental Security Income, Basic Educational Opportunity Grants, Medicaid, Medicare, food stamps, housing subsidies, Aid to Dependent Children, Social Security, and so on. According to Edgar K. Browning, "social welfare expenditures by all levels of government rose from $77 billion in 1965 to $215 billion in 1973 " and federal transfers to the poor in cash or kind grew from $8 billion in 1964 to $26 billion in 1976, or from $219 per poor person to $1,139 per poor person.[14]

These direct measures to relieve poverty presumably make it possible to reduce the redistributional burden on the personal income tax and to put more emphasis on the effects of taxes on the national income and on garnering that income for the government. Indeed, the massive growth in government expenditures, which now approximate 40 percent of national income, necessitates a shift

---

[12] Ibid., pp. 103-104.

[13] Ibid., pp. 28-29.

[14] Edgar K. Browning, "How Much More Equality Can We Afford?" *Public Interest,* no. 43 (Spring 1976), pp. 90-91.

in emphasis from the redistributional effects of taxation to the revenue effects, both short and long run.

Welfare grants have greatly complicated the question of progressivity in taxation. Grants are generally diminished as cash income rises, and such ordinary taxes as social security and income taxes rise with income. Browning estimates the effective marginal rate of taxation for a typical poor family to be 65 percent —almost as much as the highest marginal rate of the federal income tax (70 percent) or as the highest joint effect of federal and state taxes together (74.6 percent in New York, unless the minimum federal tax makes it higher).[15] Thus, the disincentive effects that formerly were significant only at high income levels are now significant also at low and lower-middle income levels. Welfare programs have succeeded in introducing the strong disincentive effects of progressive income taxes even at income levels where taxes are negligible.

Complexity

Another matter that is far more significant today than in 1953 is the complexity of the tax laws. Simple though the tax laws of 1953 were in comparison with those of 1976, Blum and Kalven nevertheless observed, "It is remarkable how much of the day to day work of the lawyer in the income tax field derives from the simple fact that the tax is progressive. Perhaps the majority of his problems are either caused or aggravated by that fact." [16] Under a flat rate, for example, it would be immaterial to the government whether an item of income were credited to one person or another, so that such income-splitting devices as the short-term trust, the family partnership, the gift of bond coupons and dividends on stock, the assignment of anticipated earnings, and community property legislation would not have arisen. Difficulties in the proper timing of income and expenses are aggravated by progression. Considerations such as these have led to many intricate provisions in the tax laws, some to block avoidance, others to alleviate hardship. But special provisions affect different taxpayers differently when there is progression and, indeed, may make it virtually impossible for a taxpayer to anticipate the tax consequences of decisions he makes.

In March 1976, in testimony before the Senate Finance Committee, Peter L. Faber, chairman of the New York State Bar Association's Tax Section (which, by the way, has nearly 2,000 members), gave a striking illustration of the complexities of the present tax system.[17] He began with a few miscellaneous tidbits: there are 15,000 words of instructions to Form 1040; "a recent survey showed that

---

[15] Ibid., p. 97.

[16] Blum and Kalven, *Uneasy Case*, p. 15.

[17] See Peter L. Faber, Testimony presented before Senate Finance Committee, March 19, 1976. Reprinted in Bureau of National Affairs, Inc., *Daily Report for Executives*, no. 55 (March 19, 1976), p. 5.

advice given to taxpayers by the taxpayer assistance personnel of the [Internal Revenue] Service was wrong 25 percent of the time"; "some of the most complicated provisions . . . apply primarily to small businesses and individuals"; the provisions allowing an individual covered by a qualified retirement plan to deduct contributions to an individual retirement plan are as long as the Constitution of the United States; "the Internal Revenue Code already contains a single sentence that is almost twice as long as Lincoln's Gettysburg Address"; and the proposed tax reform bill now before Congress introduces a tax saving of up to $7 for the purchase of home garden tools.[18] Faber went on to present a sketch of a lawyer confronting a question relating to two sections of the tax reform bill that limit deductions for artificial losses. The following section of this essay presents Faber's testimony *in extenso*.

The Faber Scenario

Let us assume that we are in the office of a lawyer in general practice who receives a telephone call from a client asking what the new rules are respecting the extent to which losses from a proposed investment in rental real estate can be used to offset his other income. The lawyer, being conscientious and disdainful of secondary sources, tells his client that he will look the answer up and call him right back.

Knowing that the principal component of the tax losses will be depreciation deductions, he turns first to §167 and is somewhat put out to find that there is no reference whatsoever to any limitation on the use of depreciation deductions to shelter other income. He then thumbs through the index of his copy of the Internal Revenue Code and comes across a reference to "limitation on artificial losses" in subpart D of Part II of chapter 1 of the Code. The titles of the sections under that subpart seem vaguely related to depreciation deductions and, taking a chance, he turns to §466, which he is delighted to find is indeed the applicable provision. Section 466(a)(1) seems to have the answer, providing:

> Except as otherwise provided in this subpart, in the case of any taxpayer subject to this subpart, accelerated deductions which are attributable to a class of LAL property and which (but for this section) would be allowable for the taxable year shall not be allowed for such year to the extent that such deductions exceed the net related income for such year from such class of property.

A few of the terms used in this sentence are not entirely clear but our lawyer friend is confident that explanations will be offered. Before moving on, however, he notes a reference in §466(a)(3) to an exception "for certain accrual taxpayers engaged in farming." He knows that his client has a few farm properties and decides he had better check this out. The exception refers to "property described

---

18 Tax Reform Act of 1976, Public Law 94-455, enacted October 4, 1976.

in section 467(a)(3) if the taxpayer "uses an accrual method of accounting with respect to such property and capitalizes preproductive period expenses described in section 468(c)(1)." He dutifully turns to §467(a)(3) which describes the property in question as being property used in farming or property "described in section 1221(1) and held in connection with the trade or business of farming." He turns to §1221(1) which seems simple enough and he concludes that this particular provision may apply. Turning back to §468(c)(1), he wonders why the language from §1221(1) couldn't have been put directly into §467(a)(3).

Section 468(c)(1) indicates that the expenses in question are those used with respect to a "class of property described in section 467(a)(3)." He turns back to that section, remembers he has just looked at it, and returns to §468(c)(1) which, mercifully, seems clearly not to apply.

Concluding that the exception for farming operations in §466(a)(3) does not affect his client, the lawyer turns back to §466(a)(1).

The provision applies only to taxpayers "subject to this subpart" and fortunately those taxpayers are described immediately below in §466(a)(2). Subparagraph (a) clearly seems to apply to his client, who is an individual. Noting the cross references to §1371(b) and §447(a) in the case of corporate taxpayers, the lawyer congratulates himself on his foresight in talking his client out of forming a personal holding company for his investments the year before.

The next expression used is "accelerated deductions" and, turning ahead in the Code, he finds a definition in §468(a). Although the definition seems simple enough, he notes that it applies only to "a class of property described in section 467(a)(1)" so he turns back to that provision. Property in that section is described as property which is "or will be" property "described in section 1221(1)" or property held for rental. Fortunately, he remembers from an earlier stage in his research what §1221(1) is all about. Unfortunately, the definition goes on to say that §467(a)(1) property does not include "any section 1245 property (as defined in section 1245(a)(3)) which is leased or held for leasing." Turning wearily ahead to §1245(a)(3), he finds that it applies generally to property which is or has been "of a character subject to the allowance for depreciation provided in section 167 (or subject to the allowance of amortization provided in section 185)." Fortunately, he remembers that the property is in fact depreciable and that §167 is the section authorizing the depreciation deduction, so he need not turn to that provision. Since his client has indicated that the proposed investment is in real estate, he concludes that subsections (A), (B), and (C) do not apply. Subsection (D) looks disturbing, however, because it applies to real property "which has an adjusted basis in which there are reflected adjustments for amortization under section 169, 185, or 188." Turning to these sections, he finds that they deal with the amortization of pollution control facilities, railroad grading and tunnel bores, and expenditures for on-the-job training and child care facilities. Common sense tells him that none of these sections apply to his client's situation and, without read-

141

ing them carefully, he turns back to the definition of "accelerated deduction" in §468(a)(1). The definition of "accelerated depreciation" in §468(a)(2) refers to deductions "allowable under this chapter" and he checks the table of contents of the Code to make sure that the coverage of the word "chapter" is sufficiently broad. Then, he notices a few pages ahead that §470 seems to have definitions of terms used in subpart D and, sure enough, he sees definitions for "construct" and "construction period." He reviews these to make sure how they apply to his client's situation.

Feeling confident that he has established the meaning of the expression "accelerated deductions," he turns back to §466(a)(1) and sees that it applies only to deductions attributable to a "class of LAL property." This strikes him as an expression that could not possibly have a useful meaning outside the Internal Revenue Code and he turns the page, hoping to find a definition. He almost does. Although there is no definition of "class of LAL property," §467(a) defined "LAL property," and the word "class" as applied to different types of LAL property is explained in subsections (b)-(g). With some trepidation, he decides to apply logic and common sense and concludes that, for purposes of his client's problem, the definition of "classes of LAL real property" in §467(b) is the one he must deal with.

Turning back to §466(a)(1), our attorney finds that his client's accelerated deductions will not be allowed to the extent that they exceed the "net related income" for the year from the class of property. This, too, looks like an expression that must be defined somewhere, and he turns ahead to §468, which includes the phrase in its title. Sure enough, it is defined in §468(g). He shakes his head, wondering why Congress could not have put all these definitions in one place instead of spreading them throughout subpart D. He decides that, like Li'l Abner, he loves and respects the U.S. Congress and if they did it this way they must have had a reason.

The basic definition in §468(g)(1) seems simple enough, but unfortunately subsection (2) is entitled "special rules" and our friend knows that this means trouble. He is right. The special rules indicate that net operating loss deductions under section 172 shall not be taken into account. This is a phrase that he has not run across in his practice and he turns to the section to see what it means. It seems to be concerned primarily with active business and, after looking at it carefully for a while, he decides that it does not apply to his client's case. Another special rule relates to capital gain deductions under §1202 and capital loss carry-backs or carryovers under §1212. Knowing that his client has from time to time bought and sold real estate, he checks these out as well. Section 1202 seems familiar and he does not dwell on it. Section 1212, unfortunately, refers to § 172 again. Not wanting to reenter that particular thicket, he decides to take his chances that this provision does not apply.

Our attorney has now concluded that the deferral of accelerated deductions will indeed be a problem for his client. The next step is to find out exactly how it will work and whether he will ever get some tax benefit from them. Unfortunately, it is late in the day and all hopes of getting in a set of tennis before dinner have vanished. He calls his client and tells him that the research is taking more time than he had hoped and that he will call him tomorrow. He then goes home and has two martinis with his wife before dinner.

The next day, suitably refreshed, he arrives at the office a bit early and gets back to §466. He finds, in subsection (b), that the deferred deductions are placed in a "deferred deduction account." Subsection (c) indicates that these deferred deductions will be allowed in later years if the income from the same class of property exceeds the accelerated deductions attributable to the class of property for the later year. It seems simple enough.

A thought then strikes him. He knows that depreciation deductions reduce the basis of property for purposes of determining gain on later sales. He wonders whether the basis will not be reduced if deductions are not allowed under §466. Knowing that the basis adjustment provisions appear in §1016 of the Code, he turns to that section and finds that it reads the same way it always did. This seems to indicate that there is no basis reduction since the deferred deductions are neither allowed nor allowable. Turning back to subpart D, however, he finds in §470(d)(1) that a deduction not allowed under §466(a) will be treated as "allowed" for purposes of §1016.

Our lawyer notices that §469 deals with the consequences of "dispositions" of property. Section 469(a) indicates that, if any LAL disposition class is sold during the year, any amount remaining in the deferred deduction account is deductible in that year. This seems to say that all of the client's investment real estate must be sold in order to get this deduction. Reading on, however, he finds in §469(b)(2) that in the case of property described in §467(a)(1) this rule applies where any item of property is transferred. Turning back to §467(a)(1), he finds that he has already reviewed this definition and, looking at his research notes from the day before, he satisfies himself that it does in fact apply. It occurs to him that it might not be illogical (although it certainly would be confusing) to provide that the deduction under §469(a) might be limited by the property's depreciation recapture potential (or the depreciation recapture potential the property would have had if accelerated deductions had been claimed). He can find no reference to this in §1250 and decides that he may or may not mention it to his client, depending on how confused the client seems to be when he tells him everything else.

Finally, he remembers that accelerated depreciation is subject to the minimum tax on tax preferences and decides that he had better review the application of the minimum tax in years in which amounts are placed in the deferred deduction account and the year in which the property is sold. He finds in §57(e) that an amount placed in a deferred deduction account under §466(b) is not a tax preference. The law does not indicate, however, whether the deduction resulting under §469(a) when he sells the property is a tax preference item in the year of sale.

Having (he hopes) completed his research, he calls up his client and tells him that he is not absolutely sure but that he thinks there may be a problem. He discusses some of the principles involved, including additional record keeping expenses, at which point his client cuts in with an exasperated tone and says, "Look, I don't care about all these fancy rules, should I buy that property or shouldn't I?" At this, the lawyer shouts into the telephone, "How should I know, ask your Congressman!" and hangs up in disgust.

Why This Complexity?

To one who was familiar with college students during the 1960s, it is clear that this is the generation now on the congressional staffs writing tax laws—and, for that matter, other laws too. (If you will visit Capitol Hill you can confirm this by visual inspection.) This was the generation that sought, and at most colleges obtained, participation in governance: its members proved to have the most bureaucratic mentality of any group since the Byzantine Empire. (I refer to the well-intentioned, good-hearted, intelligent, responsible people who were the great majority of that generation, not to hippies, or to the new left, Walter-Mitty revolutionaries, or spoiled brats who got so much television and newspaper coverage.) They could, and often did, spend six months preparing the by-laws of a minor committee. They attempted to anticipate every possible circumstance, action, and purpose and every permutation of circumstances, actions, and purposes, and to prescribe precisely how everyone should behave in all eventualities. Their guiding precept was that no situation should ever arise in which each possible action of each individual had not been anticipated and either prohibited or compelled by law. Infinite malice and ingenuity in circumventing the laws they attributed to all who might come under them, and efforts were made to defeat every possible manifestation of this anticipated malice and ingenuity. This came to be the meaning of "The Rule of Law" for that generation, and now they are writing the national laws in that same spirit.

This spirit of Byzantine bureaucracy that infects the generation now writing our laws is not, of course, the only explanation for their increasing complexity. It may explain the sudden spurt in complexity, but growing complexity is an inherent characteristic of taxes, especially of progressive income taxes. As one or another hardship situation or worthy candidate for special favors comes to the attention of Congress, changes are made in the tax laws. But under a Supreme Court that will not generally tolerate explicitly naming the recipients of privileges or penalties, it is difficult to define general classes which do not turn out to include some whose inclusion was not intended. Further complexities then arise in the attempt to refine the circumstances under which the privileges and penalties apply, and the process is endless—as is the discovery of new targets for special privileges or penalties.

Degressive Taxes

Developments since Blum and Kalven wrote make what they called degression seem far more attractive today than they found it in 1953. A degressive tax, as they define it, is one in which a certain amount of income is exempt and all income above that is taxed at a uniform rate. Such a tax is, of course, progressive in the sense that the taxable portion of income rises as income rises, but it is only slightly progressive. It avoids most of the complications of the present income tax laws and regulations, since these arise mainly from the progressivity of marginal rates above the personal exemptions.

Blum and Kalven point out that a degressive tax divides the population into two classes, those who pay and those who do not pay, and that uncertainty about where to draw the line will almost certainly lead to compromises that graduate the marginal rate, at least in the range where the line might be drawn. There also would be great incentives for politicians to raise the exemptions.

Recently Milton Friedman has urged again, as he has for many years, a form of degressive tax.[19] His latest proposal is that the present schedule of exemptions and marginal rates and all other provisions of present tax laws be retained, except that all marginal rates above 25 percent be reduced to 25 percent. Friedman argues that even better would be a fully degressive tax having a uniform rate of at most 16 percent "on all income above present personal exemptions less only strictly occupational expenses." He argues (convincingly in my view) that either of these proposals would be an important simplification of the present system, would yield more revenue to the government, and would leave taxpayers better off than they are now.

From tax returns for 1929, when the maximum rate actually was 25 percent, and from the subsequent growth of average income and of population, Friedman estimates that if the maximum rate had been 25 percent in 1972 (instead of 70 percent) the number of 1972 returns reporting incomes of $500,000 or more would have been about six times as large as it was, and the amount of income shown on these returns would have been about twelve times as large as the amount in fact reported in 1972. The government would have collected in tax revenue more than twice the amount that would appear to be lost by cutting the maximum rate to 25 percent if the distribution of returns were as actually reported in 1972. The extra taxable income reported would come not only from the reduced attractiveness of tax shelters, converting income to capital gains, shifting income from one year to another or from one person to another, and so on, but also from

---

[19] Milton Friedman, "Tax Reform: An Impossible Dream," *Newsweek,* April 12, 1976, p. 93.

extra income earned in response to higher marginal incentives. Taxpayers would be better off, even though they paid the government more, because they would save substantial parts of the costs for lawyers, accountants, and personal arrangements that they incur now in attempts to reduce their taxes.

Two developments since Blum and Kalven wrote make Friedman's proposals especially attractive. On the one hand, the enormous growth in the complexity of the tax law has magnified one of the major objections to progression. On the other hand, direct redistribution of income through welfare transfers has diminished the need to rely on progression in tax rates for redistribution of income, and redistribution was the prime merit of progression that survived the scrutiny of Blum and Kalven.

In general, the net result of developments since *The Uneasy Case for Progressive Taxation* was published has been, it seems to me, an increase in the uneasiness of the case for progression and a decrease in the uneasiness of the case against progression. The tax laws have grown infinitely more complicated, political irresponsibility has surely grown, and incentives to production have been seriously attenuated. On the other side, the importance of progression for income redistribution has diminished, and there is less confidence than there was that fluctuations in the yield of personal income taxes contribute to economic stability. In my judgment, the case for progressive taxation is as stubborn today as Blum and Kalven found it in 1953, but considerably uneasier.

THE UNEASY CASE FOR PROGRESSIVE TAXATION IN 1976

Walter J. Blum

In turning again to a consideration of the case for progressive taxation in our society, we must note that the most important development since publication of *The Uneasy Case for Progressive Taxation* [1] in 1953 has been the emergence of what is more or less a consensus that the state is to assure nearly everyone the resources for some minimum standard of life. The question now to be explored is whether achieving this aspect of the welfare state serves to strengthen the argument for distributing the tax burden on a progressive basis.

"Progressive" Taxation

At the outset it is important to clarify the usage of the term *progressive taxation*. The reference in this discussion is to the total system and not to any particular tax. Progressivity in essence concerns the relationship between the distribution of the aggregate burden among taxpayers and the distribution of what might be thought of as their taxable capacity. The relative capacities of taxpayers can plausibly be derived by comparing incomes or expenditures or wealth. In our society, progressivity usually is described and measured against income. For the discussion ahead it is sufficient to label as "progressive" any system that takes in taxes a share of income from the more affluent relatively larger than the share it takes from the less affluent.

Admittedly this is said very quickly. Wide differences exist as to the most appropriate definition of income according to which taxpayers are to be compared. There are, in addition, troublesome questions as to whether the proper unit of comparison is the individual, the marital union, the household, or something else; whether the proper period of income measurement is a single year or a longer time; and whether all taxes in fact can be adequately weighed against an income base. It is particularly difficult to translate wealth transfer taxes (such as those imposed on gifts and estates) into levies scaled against income. Finally, the definition of progressivity must take account of the likelihood that the incidence of a

Note: This article was published in *Occasional Papers from The Law School, The University of Chicago,* no. 11 (November 19, 1976), and was not delivered as a paper at the conference.
[1] Walter J. Blum and Harry Kalven, Jr., *The Uneasy Case for Progressive Taxation* (Chicago: University of Chicago Press, 1953).

particular tax differs significantly from one taxpayer to another through the operation of market forces. Despite these difficulties, it is useful and convenient to talk about the whole system as though it comprised only an income tax not shifted from those who bear the burden directly or through attribution.

An additional oversimplification must be introduced in order to make the inquiry more manageable. There are many possible patterns for a progressive tax on income. One polar pattern consists of levying no tax on the poor—meaning those whose incomes are below a minimum level fixed by legislation—and assessing all other taxpayers at a flat rate on any income in excess of that level. In essence this arrangement, known technically as a degressive tax, utilizes two rates. The exempted income—that below the minimum level—is taxed at a zero rate, while all income over and above the exempted amount is taxed at a uniform positive rate. The zero rate for exempted income results in a progressive tax among those whose incomes exceed the exemption. The larger one's total income, the greater the fraction of it that is subject to the positive rate of tax and the smaller the fraction that is subject to the zero rate. As income increases, the effective rate of tax on that income approaches (but never quite reaches) the uniform positive rate of tax.

The other polar pattern is a very high tax on the incomes of the affluent, a substantial (but not heavy) tax on the middle class, and no tax on the poor. This may be called steep progression. A middle pattern can be loosely described as consisting of a high (but not very high) tax on the affluent, a heavy (but not high) tax on the middle class, and no tax on the poor. This may be called moderate progression. For purposes of analysis the arguments over progressive taxation to a large degree can be reduced to arguments over versions of these three arrangements.

All three of the basic patterns are, of course, in contrast to proportionate taxation. Under proportionate taxation every taxpayer, regardless of total income, pays in tax the same percentage of that income. In an earlier era, before there was general agreement that the government should underwrite a minimum standard of living for nearly everyone, it was quite common to argue in favor of the principle of proportionality. But after the new welfare consensus had been reached, the strict proportion principle became hard to defend. The combination of a commitment to a minimum standard of living and of strict proportionality in taxation would put the state in the awkward position of simultaneously taxing the poor and providing them with greater support benefits to offset the collection of those taxes. In a welfare state, the realistic version of proportionate taxation is the degressive pattern of progressivity—that pattern which calls for exempting the poor and taxing all income above the minimum level at one rate. The relevant question, then, concerns the choice to be made among the three basic patterns of progressivity.

The question can be probed by focusing on the minimum support commitment to the poor. It might be asked: Should the resources made available to the poor be obtained by resorting to steep progressivity that imposes the taxes on high incomes, or by spreading the burden proportionately on all incomes in excess of the minimum level, or by adopting moderate progressivity—a position that lies near the middle of these two poles? Conferring support benefits on the poor by itself acts to reduce the economic inequality between those who are below the minimum line and all other persons in the society. The narrower question for tax policy concerns the extent to which the financing of these benefits should be used for altering the distribution of incomes over and above the minimum level.

This statement of the tax issue has the virtue of confronting a recent proposal that has attracted considerable attention.[2] The suggested program calls (1) for putting a floor under support benefits so that virtually everyone will have an income (in kind or in dollars) not less than half the median income in the society and (2) for covering the full cost of all these incremental benefits solely by increasing the taxes payable on high incomes. The plan would accomplish two things. It would transfer resources from the group above to the group below the "poverty line" as legislatively defined—a matter of gross redistribution policy which is outside the scope of this inquiry. And it would reduce the economic position of the affluent vis-à-vis everyone lower on the economic ladder, making the tax system more steeply progressive. This latter aspect of the plan highlights the central question to be explored: How should the cost of all support benefits to the poor be distributed among the nonpoor?

In addressing the issue, it is useful and not wholly unrealistic to assume that the total tax burden in society is increased by the cost of these support benefits. It is also instructive to assume that such costs can be separated from the cost of all other functions undertaken by government.

The Affluent and the Poor

There are several arguments for concentrating on the affluent the burden of underwriting the economic position of the poor. Some have been put forward explicitly; others can only be surmised from general statements. A considerable degree of overlap in the presentation of these arguments seems inevitable. What follows is an effort to capture and then examine the various points that can be offered in behalf of the steep progression position.

(1) General agreement on a proper criterion for setting a minimum standard of living to be underwritten by the government can never be reached. Of necessity the line must reflect a wide-ranging political compromise. It is therefore unseemly for the government to force the transfer of a dollar from a taxpayer not far above the line to persons somewhere below the line. Such an undesirable consequence can be avoided, it is contended, by placing the tax burden squarely on the affluent

---

[2] Arthur M. Okun, *Equality and Efficiency: The Big Tradeoff* (Washington, D.C.: The Brookings Institution, 1975).

instead of spreading it more nearly in proportion to income among all those who are not in poverty.

Although arresting, this argument is hardly peculiar to support for the poor: every category of government spending reflects a political compromise, and no area is or can be controlled by an external standard. In this respect the case for steeply progressive taxation is not advanced by emphasizing the welfare nature of the expenditures whose funds the taxes provide.

(2) Adequate support benefits for the poor will not be legislated if a pro-portionate part or substantial part of the corresponding tax burden is put upon the middle class, particularly the lower end of the middle class. This contention is the "political realism" counterpart of the previous point. The reality, so the argument runs, is that there will be adequate support for the poor only if the cost is placed in a notably disproportionate manner on the affluent.

This relationship cannot be established by reference to history. But even if it were well grounded in experience, it would not help in formulating a sound tax policy. Suppose that the middle class did resist raising the support level for the poor because of objections to paying higher taxes for this purpose. The existence of such a situation would instruct us more on the subject of designing the welfare program than on the question of a proper tax policy. It would in effect ask what kind of consensus in our society is best for deciding on the contours of the basic support program. Any bearing on tax policy is of a negative sort: the notion seems to be that in focusing on tax policy, our vision should be intentionally blurred in order to escape facing the hard problem of drawing the critical support line in dealing with the poor.

(3) A causal connection exists between the fact that there are both poor and affluent in our society. Affluence, according to the most simplistic form of the argument, somehow rests on impoverishing others who are less skillful or fortunate. It is, therefore, only right that the affluent should be charged with the cost of maintaining the poor at a minimum standard of living.

Such an argument is not easily answered because it lacks specificity and logic. Perhaps it is intended to touch sensitive emotions, to play on the guilt of the non-poor. But both economic analysis and common observation indicate that in our society (at least since the abolition of slavery) the affluent do not have the economic power or means or motivation to prevent individuals from rising above poverty. A satisfactory explanation of the survival of poverty is bound to be complicated, taking account of factors as diverse as natural disadvantages, family attitudes and composition, personal misfortune, and misguided laws. Understanding of the situation is not helped by blaming poverty on an economic conspiracy among the affluent. Indeed, the relationship between poverty and riches generally runs in the other direction: most affluence is based on economic activity that raises the economic level of the society and tends to benefit its members.

(4) The affluent, by using their wealth to exercise a disproportionate share of political power, prevent the passage of legislation that would reduce (if not eradicate) poverty. The crux of the contention is that the affluent "corrupt" the democratic political process and exert too much influence over the course of government. It is impractical to police their activities directly because the "misuse" of wealth is not easily detected. Reducing the resources available to the affluent, reformers urge, will tend to redress the political "imbalance" and improve the position of those at the bottom of the economic scale.

This point in some respects parallels the notion that affluence rests on economic repression of the poor. The poor under this account are impoverished because the affluent turn their wealth into political force that works against programs for uplifting those who are handicapped in the economic race. Thus it is said that the political reach of the affluent holds down public spending on such matters as general education, health maintenance, and job training—all of which presumably would tend to alleviate poverty.

It is by no means clear that the affluent in fact have predominated in opposing increased public spending in these areas. There is considerable evidence suggesting that on balance the middle class has been the most cautious about moves to initiate or expand programs requiring new government expenditures. While the cynic might attribute this reaction to propaganda engineered by the affluent, an explanation that does not denigrate the intelligence of a broad spectrum of society would be more plausible. Government programs often start small and then grow vastly in size. As expenditures by government increase, the resources possessed by the affluent are simply not large enough to offset the increased costs. Members of the middle class can readily recognize that over the long run they will have to bear a large share of the taxes needed to cover the cost of programs being proposed.

Moreover, the chances that affluence will "distort" the distribution of political power is not strengthened if we undertake to provide nearly everyone with a minimum level of resources. Whatever force the point may carry (and it seems to have relatively little thrust in a broadly open society in which political power can be traced to sources as diverse as personal charisma, intelligence, skill at organizing people, and sheer energy), the political position of the affluent would seem to be smaller rather than greater once a commitment to the poor has been instituted. Of course, it is possible to argue that without a support floor the presence of the poor would constitute a greater threat of revolution and that a support program, by diminishing that threat, must augment the political power of the affluent. But such reasoning borders on the perverse. Is it reasonable to think that the relative tax burden placed on the affluent should be increased *because* the economic condition of the poor has improved?

These various arguments, taken singly or in combination, fall far short of showing that the use of public funds to undergird the position of the poor improves the case for steep progression.

151

Progressivity and Welfare

It is time to turn the inquiry around. Are there grounds for believing that the case for steep progressivity is weaker in the context of financing a welfare program than it is in the context of raising revenue for all other government expenditures? Several lines of thought merit exploration here.

(1) Economic disincentives are likely to be greater in the aggregate if taxes are levied to finance redistribution of resources to the poor rather than other types of government programs. This observation should not be taken to imply that the purpose for which a given number of dollars are taken from a taxpayer will have a bearing on his economic conduct. The point, more precisely, rests on the inevitability that any broad transfer of resources to the poor will result in penalizing (or "taxing") the economic activity of the recipients. Such a tax is not imposed by choice: rather, it will be embodied in any feasible transfer program because, as the unsubsidized income of one who qualifies for support increases, the amount to be furnished him by the government under the plan will decrease. Moreover, the penalty ("tax") will affect some who are above the legislatively defined poverty line insofar as support payments are made to them in order to avoid imposing a prohibitively high negative tax on marginal income as the dividing line is approached. This disincentive effect becomes more pronounced as the poverty line is set at a higher level, largely because the penalty will be felt over a larger range of incomes and by more persons. In any event, the total economic disincentive involved in a redistributional measure is composed of the negative impact of the actual levy on those taxpayers who pay for the transfer of resources and the negative impact of the penalty ("tax") on those who are the beneficiaries of the program. It is this dual effect that suggests special caution in relying on steeply progressive taxes to cover the cost of resource transfers to the poor.

(2) Apart from the disincentive effect of any feasible minimum support program, there may well be another undesirable economic consequence to be considered in levying taxes on the affluent to finance the transfer of resources. The recipients of support are not likely to be savers; indeed, the minimum income level reasonably should be fixed on the assumption that the beneficiaries will need to spend all their income on goods and services. The nonpoor, of course, on balance do save, and in general the affluent save proportionately more than the middle class. This suggests that a massive redistribution of income from the affluent to the poor will reduce the aggregate amount of private saving in the economy. In adjusting to higher rates of tax, some of the wealthy are likely to respond by spending less, but on the whole they are most likely to respond (in part at least) by saving less. While any large-scale redistribution from the nonpoor to the poor will tend to have an adverse impact on total private saving, this effect is likely to be intensified if the transfer is from the affluent to the poor.

The importance of saving is well understood and need not be elaborated here. One observation, however, is particularly pertinent in this discussion. The capital base, over time, depends upon the level of saving. Income in the society—including the income of the poor—is closely related to the size of that capital base. A fall in private saving can in theory be offset by a comparable increase in saving by government, but there is good reason to be skeptical about this prospect. Saving by government calls for a budgetary surplus. Most of the pressures in modern times, it should be obvious, push in the direction of operating the public sector at a deficit. The decline in the purchasing power of the dollar bears forceful witness to this conclusion.

(3) An inherent ambiguity in the concept of a minimum standard of living might lead (unintentionally) to intensifying the bite of steeply progressive taxation. It is tempting to define the minimum standard in terms of the existing profile of income distribution; indeed, the recent proposal noted earlier calls for bringing everyone up to half the existing median income. If our economy continues to develop, the median income, and hence the proposed support level, will accordingly rise. It is probable that the total amount of support payments will also rise if the support level is defined with reference to median income or any comparable standard. And if the support payments are to be covered by taxes on the affluent, as urged in the proposal, the total tax taken from that group will likewise move up.

When the impact that such an increase might have on the steepness of progressivity is projected, account must also be taken of any increase in the incomes of the affluent derived from improvement in economic conditions. But it seems most unlikely that incomes at the top will rise relatively more rapidly than payments required under a transfer program in which the support level is defined in comparative terms. There is thus a strong probability that, in the course of time, the disincentive and redistributional effects of the arrangement would tend automatically to expand as the productivity of the economy improved.

(4) A program to provide minimum support for the poor is almost certain to augment the role of government in our society. One can conceive of an income support system that is designed to function more or less mechanically, with payments being based upon factors of an objective nature. In practice, however, the operation is apt to be of a different character. Even if all benefits were in the form of cash payments—a most unlikely arrangement—the plan would require a great deal of administrative implementation. We know enough about welfare measures to be confident that a large bureaucracy goes along with the best of programs.

What, it might be asked, does this fact have to do with financing welfare benefits through taxes that are steeply progressive? From one viewpoint the relationship is close and important. For those who fear that an enlargement of the role and power of government might endanger the vitality of a libertarian or decentralized society, recourse to steep progressivity in the welfare setting appears to pose a special threat. Many private or quasi-public organizations outside of

153

government depend significantly on financial support from the affluent. Steep progressivity would undermine that support, unless the high rates of taxation continued to be powerfully offset by tax deductions and credits for contributions. Loss of support very likely would lead to a contraction or termination of these institutions; it might even lead to a takeover of their functions by the government or to their dependence on appropriations enacted and controlled through the political process.

In short, a program to transfer resources from the affluent to the poor can be expected to strengthen the power of government and weaken the power of potential counterbalancing or moderating forces in the society. The danger is that a crossover point will be reached at which the "outside" (nongovernment) forces will not remain viable.

(5) A plan that taxes the affluent in order to transfer resources to the poor may subtly serve to alter the character of society by markedly changing the accepted meaning of private property. The nature of the justification that is perceived to underlie the tax pattern might in this respect turn out to have a significance that transcends the pattern itself.

Until relatively recent times, almost all the accepted justifications for progressivity avoided embracing redistribution of economic things; and even the few commentators who supported progressivity on redistributive grounds invariably stopped short of proposing that the government explicitly increase taxes on the affluent in order to bestow more resources on the poor. The earlier justifications were predicated on a broad meaning of private property that was strongly and generally held: a person is entitled to his property but the government may take from him an amount that is thought to be a fair sharing of the cost of discharging public functions. Against that backdrop, consider the proposition that the affluent are to be taxed as part of a plan to raise the poor to a higher economic level. This basis for progressivity can readily be read in a broader manner—one that would give a quite radically different meaning to the notion of private property. The larger message in essence seems to be that an individual is entitled to keep only that portion of his resources which the government decides not to take for redistributional purposes.

A shift of this kind would have wide ramifications. The very nature of the dialogue concerning income and wealth could be expected to change. As the legitimacy of property rights and claims to income were subjected to repeated questioning, the politics of envy would increase and might well come to predominate.

Proper Tax Composition for Transfers

Discussions of progressive taxation are invariably impeded by the difficulty of specifying a criterion for arriving at the appropriate degree of progressivity. One is at sea without a rudder, all the more so when dealing with taxation to cover provision for the poor in that the potential governmental expenditures are notably open-ended. For that reason there may well be special attraction in a tax policy formulated along the following line: whatever degree of progressivity is built into the structure of taxes required to finance all other operations of government, all revenues associated with transfer of resources to the poor are to be collected through application of a degressive pattern of rates. It perhaps may not be too visionary to think that the entire welfare program will be more soundly conceived and more deeply accepted if, in the voting to compel such transfers, all taxpayers having income above the minimum level should be required to bear the burden in proportion to that income. By following this principle there might well emerge a better formed consensus—or a kind of "super consensus"—regarding the proper composition of an overall program for support of the poor.

It is interesting to speculate on the reasons that the middle class (everyone between the poor and the affluent) has not embraced with enthusiasm the proposal to place very heavy taxes on the affluent so as to fund a transfer of greater resources to the poor. Various explanations might be offered: the middle class does not understand the proposal, or it has been misled by the affluent and their spokesmen, or it is simply apathetic. The most perceptive explanation may well be that the middle class, adhering to many of the values traditionally associated with private property, is making its own realistic assessment of the situation. It may well perceive, however vaguely, that a plan of this sort is likely to make serious inroads upon a system that over the years has greatly improved the conditions of life for the middle class. To put it bluntly, members of the middle class may believe that their own self-interests will be served better by a system which assumes that individuals are entitled to what they own rather than by a system which assumes that individuals are entitled only to what the government decrees they can keep.

Numerous commentators have elaborated on the theme that there may be little correlation between the income of an individual and the value of his contributions to society. Surely these observers are right in highlighting the deficiencies in the operation of the pricing process and limitations of the market mechanism. They are likewise right in noting that the marginal value of one person's input will depend on the input of many others. They are right also in reminding us of the extent to which incomes depend on luck, family conditions, inheritance, educational opportunities, and a host of other factors. These observations, however, need to be placed in proper perspective. The view that persons are "entitled" to what they own is obviously a view about justice. Of equal or perhaps greater significance, it is also a view about organizing economic relationships among persons. Material well-being or standing is to a large degree perceived in terms of resources available to the individual free and clear of taxes. A dollar spent by government is not equivalent to a dollar that the taxpayer is free to spend. Perhaps the entitlement principle of organization is not the best one imaginable. But until a clearly better alternative is developed and gains acceptability, actions that undermine it deserve to be met with skepticism.

Conclusion

There is no escaping the conclusion that a pattern of steep progressivity at high levels of taxation does not blend comfortably into a society that relies heavily on traditional notions of private property and private initiative as energizing forces. The tension emerges most sharply when very high taxes are levied on the affluent in order to redistribute resources to the poor. Even if the relationship between taxation and benefit payment is kept obscure, the tension will nevertheless be felt as economic incentives are dampened and rights of ownership in property come to be defined in more restrictive terms.

The case for steeply progressive taxation, particularly to finance the transfer of resources to the poor, may seem easy if one considers only the current end-state of the process that produced the prevailing distribution of income and wealth in our society. But in the not-too-long run the more essential qualities of the society are determined by the processes and institutions by which the distribution of the moment came about. For those who look beyond the short run, the case for progressive taxation is still likely to seem uneasy.

COMMENTARIES

Oswald H. Brownlee

I think the basic positions taken by Tobin and Wallis are correct. There is not much we can say about this topic today that has not already been said. There are no sacred tablets we can consult that will tell us how to write the tax code. To be sure, we know what some of the consequences of the various tax structures are, and we know something about the kinds of substitutions that can be caused by taxes at various rates. But the relevant knowledge is far from complete. As Allen Wallis has noted, we do not really know how much progression contributes to equality. Furthermore, as Tobin has pointed out, even if we knew the outcomes of the various tax structures, we probably would not be able to agree as to how they should be ordered. This was brought out in Okun's paper in the first part of the conference.

Some of the difficulties of progressivity, although attributed to progressivity in the personal income tax structure, apply to progressivity with respect to any kind of tax—to an expenditure tax as well as an income tax. For example, Wallis pointed out that if the marginal rate were constant and equal to the average rate—that is, if the tax were proportional—tax collections would be independent of the time distribution of income and its distribution among persons. Consequently, a number of the administrative problems that occur with the present income tax, and would occur with an expenditure tax that was progressive, would be eliminated. Moreover, a constant marginal rate with an exemption would provide the demogrant that Tobin mentioned if we permitted negative as well as positive tax levies. Milton Friedman's proposal is to have a negative tax rate higher than the positive tax rate. This could provide an approximation to the grants now being provided through categorical welfare programs.

It seems to me that some of the distorting effects of the tax structure are not necessarily the result of progressivity, but are more a consequence of high marginal rates. Distortions would occur with a high single constant marginal rate or with high marginal rates that apply only to some high- or low-income people, as is characteristic of the present system. Other distortions result from nonoptimal relative tax rates rather than from a high average rate. The importance of this source of loss of economic welfare has increased as tax rates have risen. Although the complexity of the tax code and the consequent cost of collecting and complying with the tax laws may be greater for a progressive tax system than for a proportional one, there will always be political pressures to exclude or to tax at a lower rate specific categories of income, expenditure, or capital. These pressures will exist whether the tax is progressive, proportional, or regressive. Some groups will want to use the tax system to change relative effective prices—to make relative prices reflect what they believe the terms facing buyers and sellers ought to be.

There will always be someone who suggests deductions or tax credits for home insulation and storm windows—and, as Wallis mentioned, garden tools. There always will be much support for deductions for such items as charitable contributions, interest from state and local securities, state and local taxes, and the imputed income from durable consumer goods. The deductibility of charitable contributions is an interesting example. This feature of the tax system—which most university presidents and heads of orchestral associations and museums find it easy to defend—will be particularly difficult to remove. I find this deduction objectionable for many reasons, one of the most important being the extremely arbitrary criteria used to decide whether an organization is one for which taxpayers may claim deductions for the contributions they make. For example, if a lewd dance were given in Carnegie Hall in support of the New York Philharmonic, contributions to this would be tax deductible. But if the New York Philharmonic played in a whorehouse, contributions to this performance would be considered consumption.

I do not think the pressures to use the tax system for specific allocative purposes would be diminished if we switched from progressive taxation to proportional taxation. It is true that the pressures for special treatment will be greater when tax rates are high than when tax rates are low. One cannot get much effect from a deduction if the tax rate is only 10 percent, but one can get quite a bit of leverage out of deductibility with a 50 percent rate.

I would note here that the group trying to encourage charitable contributions has developed a new gimmick. When it was found that contributions were of little importance among taxpayers whose marginal tax rates were only 15 percent, it was suggested that every dollar that was given to charity by low-income people be considered as $2.00 for tax purposes.

I am therefore not at all sure we could get away from these special pressures even if the tax rate were low and constant. And, while I applaud the efforts to broaden the income tax base, I think we will have a tremendous amount of difficulty in selling such a reform even though eliminating the special deductions and broadening the tax base would permit a reduction in average rates and reduce the distortion in resource allocation induced by the income tax.

Rather than relying on reform in the income tax, perhaps we should rely less on income taxation and more on expenditure taxation. An expenditure tax, whether progressive or proportional, seems to me inherently less complex and more egalitarian in the long run than an income tax because of its impact upon saving. Among its administrative advantages is the fact that there is no need to know where income comes from or how it was obtained. The taxpayer's earnings can fluctuate, can be obtained abroad as well as at home, can be interest from state and local securities or from capital gains, and yet none of these characteristics will have any relevance as far as the amount of the tax is concerned. It is what is done with the income, and not how it was obtained or its size, that is significant for expenditure tax purposes.

Among the other advantages of the expenditure tax is that it does not make the price of saving high, as does our current personal income tax. Although saving could be eliminated from the income tax base, as has been suggested, I think the administrative difficulties involved in this separation would be tremendous. Progressivity in an expenditure tax can be obtained with less distortion than in the income tax. I am confident that many difficulties with the expenditure tax that cannot be visualized now would appear if the tax were introduced. Certainly new forms of tax shelters would appear that are not easily visualized now. Nevertheless, it seems to me that expenditure taxation ought to be a part of the federal tax system. Perhaps the issue should be not whether we should have more or less progressivity in income taxes, but how much more taxation of consumption and less taxation of income we should have.

Norman B. Ture

Professor Tobin begins his interesting and thoughtful paper by asserting that "the case for a progressive income tax is still as uneasy as when Blum and Kalven examined it in 1953." I wholeheartedly concur with this assertion. I think Tobin is also on the right track in quoting Henry Simons that the case for progression in taxation rests on the ethical or aesthetic judgment that the prevailing distribution of wealth and income is evil or "unlovely." Tobin, early in his paper, disavows any effort to pursue consideration of tax progressivity on the basis of the economist's specialized expertise. He tells us instead that he is expressing his views as a citizen of a democratic society, appealing to shared tastes and values. I think, had he stuck to his guns as an economist, we would have been very well served, for in a free society, shared tastes and values need the continuous refreshment which is provided by the critical examination of our intellectual stars.

To be sure, Tobin has afforded us many valuable clues for such an examination, but regrettably, in my judgment, he has diluted its impact by attempting to resuscitate a utilitarian calculus, presenting us once more with issues which, one would have thought, we had long since resolved in the negative or agreed were moot. Tobin tells us explicitly that he rejects first principles as a means of establishing the rules of economic justice. Early in his paper, he asks, "If it were feasible to tax and redistribute these original endowments [the basic sources of inequality] without affecting their allocation among different uses [in an ideal competitive economy meeting all the conditions for Pareto optimality], would anyone be opposed to that?" If one eschews first principles, I do not know on what basis one is to reply. Suppose we could get past the analytical horrors of accomplishing the posited results, then, presumably, we could look ahead to the aesthetic or ethical questions. All I can say is that I hope that someone here will join me in answering Tobin's question affirmatively. You can bet I would be opposed to the redistribution.

I do not think we need the puny grounds for opposition which Tobin cites as a basis for answering his question negatively. I think the question, properly put, is why should we tax to redistribute original endowments? What is the ethic or aesthetic which urges any such transfer, which argues a society is better or more lovely if we are homogenized, rather than varied and disparate? What is the ethical or aesthetic principle that requires us to eliminate emulation, which obviously would become an irrelevancy in a society of permanently equalized endowments, wealth, and income? As a practical matter, to whom are we prepared to assign the authority for determining the transferers and the transferees and the amount of the transfers? How are we morally strengthened by the free lunch? Why would the community be made lovelier by the knowledge that efforts to increase our endowments would be to no purpose, other than to fund an endorsed donation to others?

Tobin also explicitly rejects "utility machine" arguments as a basis for opposition to (but not, apparently, as a basis for support of) progressive taxation. His argument is that the capacity to enjoy life is randomly distributed and independent of our endowments. I do not find this an appealing presumption, even from a heuristic viewpoint.

The argument seems to rest on the notion that there is a fixed stock and a fixed distribution of endowments without the intervention of the fisc. But initial endowments, of course, may be augmented, or they may be dissipated. Do we not generally observe a fairly substantial proportion of the population engaged in efforts to augment their endowments? What is the impetus for any such effort?

Without having investigated the matter, it strikes me as at least as good a presumption as Tobin's that the scale of such effort is functionally related to the capacity to enjoy. The assumption of random distribution of the capacities of utility machines, unassociated with endowments and efforts to change them, is not persuasive and neither, therefore, is the "probabilistic presumption for equality," which Tobin asserts follows therefrom. Even if it were feasible to base taxation on endowments rather than on the results of the use of endowments, the question is whether this feasibility supports the notion of a progressive (as opposed to any other) tax distribution. Presumably, a progressive tax will have incentive and disincentive effects that would alter an individual's efforts to change the amount of his endowments and would, in turn, change the distribution thereof, with results that are not laid out in any systematic way. I am certainly not arguing for the revival of the utility *esoterica* as a basis for determining the shape of tax schedules. I am asserting, rather, that such arguments are of as little use in defending progressivity as they are in attacking it.

Tobin does not hold to the assertion of uncorrelated endowments and utility capacity. His utilitarian calculus, at the close of his paper, restates some of the propositions about the relationship between endowments and utility functions on which the ancient arguments for progressive taxation were based. I think the case he makes is too tenuous to give us the basis for agreeing with his final challenge to Blum and Kalven—that is, that ethical "principles" and interpersonal evaluations are not sufficient to determine even the general shape of the optimal tax schedule. To repeat, this is not to say that these "principles" and evaluations are appropriate or useful means for determining the distribution of tax liabilities, but Tobin's argument has not advanced us a more useful guide.

The most alarming of his arguments for progressive taxes is the assertion that market prices and marginal productivities are not measures of the just deserts of the members of society; that some (presumably significant) part of one's earnings represents the return on the general societal overhead capital to be allocated equally among members of society as a social dividend. Even if one were to accept the notion, the analytical impediments to implementing it without the gravest abuse of justice, as perceived by those who would do the paying, are overwhelming. How do we identify such returns? How do we determine them? How do we measure them? How do we ascribe them, taxpayer by taxpayer? Is one to assume that the greater one's endowments, the more effectively they are used—and hence, the larger one's income—the greater the proportion of that income which is in truth attributable to this mystical "general societal overhead capital" which the state should feel free to claim for such redistributive purposes as it deems appropriate? At what bracket in the tax schedule should the taxpayers be told that they have not really earned all of the incremental income, that some market peculiarity has assigned to them the quasi rents of the organic collectivity—never mind the additional efforts they have undertaken to realize the additional income, and never mind the fact that the incremental income, or some substantial portion of it, properly belongs to those in lower brackets?

The assertion of this return to societal overhead capital may be appealing to a collectivist as a rationale for attempting to frustrate market outcomes which are, on some basis or other, deemed to be unlovely or undesirable; it must be appalling to those whose ethics and tastes call for promoting self-reliance and the freedom of the individual.

Conspicuously absent from Tobin's discussion is any examination of the success or failure of our increasingly redistributive fisc. To be sure, he does discuss briefly the disincentives of progressive taxation, but he gives very little weight to them as impediments to the use of such taxes to redistribute income. Here, it seems to me, lies the fertile field for economists to till. Why has a highly and

161

increasingly redistributive fiscal structure in the United States had so little effect on the shape of the income distribution? Surely, the answer must be found in delineation and measurement of the responses of the income transferers and transferees through the changes in relative costs and prices effected by redistributive tax and expenditure policies. The virtual invariance of Gini coefficients over extended periods of time seems to argue that these market responses substantially cancel the fiscal thrust toward redistribution.

It is a matter of secondary importance whether this presumptive finding—that redistributive tax policy has not redistributed income—is agreed to. The major value in pursuing this line of analysis is that it may disengage economists from efforts to justify someone's esthetic or ethical preferences and allow them to allocate their energies to the fields of their specialized competence. Whether the results of this use of their capacities will be fortunate for proponents of any given distribution of taxes is of consequence only insofar as it informs policy makers of the cost of indulging their (or their constituents') preferences.

At the beginning of my comments, I concurred with Tobin's assessment that the case for progressive taxation remains as uneasy as Blum and Kalven found it in 1953. Permit a slight amendment. For the economist qua economist, the case is not uneasy; it is virtually nonexistent. As a private citizen—and Tobin asserted he was addressing the problem thus—one can make the case for redistribution in much the same way as one might argue for holidays at the shore rather than in the mountains, for Beethoven rather than Bach. Perhaps a more persuasive case can be found in the fundamental ethics of a free society, but identification and convincing articulation of that ethos and of the unique set of fiscal arrangements it dictates are not yet on hand.

James S. Duesenberry

Let me first tell a story that illustrates some observations on diminishing marginal utility and also on tax codes. My brother-in-law, who is a trust officer for a large bank, encountered a corporate executive who was earning a couple of hundred thousand dollars and asked his board for a raise. The board said, "Well, you are doing a fine job. We'd be glad to give you another $10,000, but you're in a 70 percent bracket and there is no sense in that. We'll get the benefits people to fix you up with an option scheme or pension benefits and you'll be much better off that way." The executive replied, "No, no, I understand all about the taxes. I need the $3,000."

We should ask ourselves how we acquired our present tax structure. It did not come out of a social conflict between the rich and the poor as in some countries; it did not come out of a consensus for egalitarianism as in Sweden. It came as a result of some things that happened in the late 1930s and in World War II. When the war was over, the Congress found that it was more pleasant to vote expenditures than tax reductions. Most of the taxpayers did not seem to object very strenuously. Many of those taxpayers who did object managed to have portions of their income protected from taxation (through the so-called loopholes), so that, after that, they objected less. The result was that the tax stayed with relatively little change except for the accumulation of various kinds of loopholes.

Thus far we have been fortunate. In our society conflict over income distribution, and particularly between those with high income and those with low income, has been blunted, in part because we have had considerable social mobility. Our country has grown rapidly. We have had continuing immigration and it has been possible for one generation to rise in the social scale over its parents, while the immigrants themselves were better off than they had been where they came from. In recent years, there has been considerable upgrading in the quality of jobs, as viewed by the holders. At the same time, there have been relatively small increases in the population of adult men in the labor force and large increases in the number of working women and young people.

An unwritten paper of mine is called "The New Proletariats—Women and Children." Changes in the labor force have created new opportunities so that individuals have given their attention to their own mobility rather than to some political mechanism for redistributing income. Also, considerable political effort has been devoted to protecting the occupational positions of individuals or the positions of industries. But we have not had a war of "low incomes" against "high incomes."

Because the demographic pattern is going to reverse, we may find that there will be more conflict in the future. The opportunities for young men and for those young women who are career-oriented will probably be more limited in the future than they have been in the past thirty years. This may increase social conflict and give us more of the problems some other countries have had. This does not argue for a progressive income tax or for any particular tax; it does argue for some positive and visible political solutions to income-distribution problems. Whatever one's views about equality may be, I think we will have some important political conflict over equality. It may be more important for us to go at the whole question of redistribution from this point of view than to derive systems of taxation and so on from first principles.

Let me come to my second point, which is related to something that Norman Ture said and which I feel compelled to mention because there has been some discussion of utilitarian approaches. When I sat with Oswald Brownlee in a public finance course taught by Henry Simons almost forty years ago, it was taken as a proposition that there is no way to have a progressive income tax without some distortion of incentives that will result in a net loss to society. Pareto-optimality was thought to be always in conflict with redistributive measures. About thirty years ago, I concocted a relative income argument on the basis of which it can be shown that, on strictly utilitarian grounds, but without introducing cardinal utility, one can make a case for a progressive income tax as a means of eliminating some distortions arising from the interactions of preferences.

My third point is one which has already been raised and on which I have a couple of brief observations: When I read Tobin's paper, I was inclined to say that the major thing he left out was the pragmatic issue. It seems to me that right now there is some pressure on us to respond to the present disheveled state of the tax code that Wallis mentioned. Everyone recognizes that the redistributive power of the tax has been weakened by the existence of loopholes. Those loopholes benefit a variety of activities, some of which may be worthy of a subsidy and many of which may not be worthy on any grounds of general interest. There are those who say—I think, quite reasonably—that the tax is not doing much for redistribution. On the other hand, the tax is not only affecting individuals' work-leisure choices or work-saving choices but also is creating, by the operation of the code, some peculiar distortions in activity. This would be an argument for a flat-rate tax.

Allen Wallis said he thought that the problems of the code would become a lot less serious if we had a flat-rate tax instead of a progressive tax, and it is certainly true that some problems arise out of progressivity as such. But I think that Brownlee was also correct in saying that a flat marginal tax of any significant size will encourage a great deal of effort in the creation of loopholes. It seems to me that it is rather a dream to think that we could substitute a 30 to 40 percent flat rate tax with some exemptions and eliminate all the loopholes with the hope that the loopholes would not soon return.

We ought to approach tax reform in a somewhat more piecemeal fashion. We ought to be trying to narrow some of the loopholes now in the tax and broaden the tax base. We also ought to be changing the rates. But in changing the rates, we ought to have some concern for areas in which the elasticity of substitution between work and leisure is the highest. Some of the problems here are connected with income splitting and multiple-worker families where there is probably the highest elasticity between work and leisure. We ought not to believe too readily that some overall reform could wipe out all our problems and still leave us with the good aspects of a tax which, after all, generates the revenue used for redistribution.

This brings us to the question whether a consumption tax might be more suitable than an income tax. One can argue that there are a number of complications in the present code that would be eliminated if we went to a consumption tax. But in one of the coffee-breaks at this conference I listened to a spirited discussion on how to invent new loopholes for a consumption tax. I think it is by no means certain that we would be better off with a consumption tax.

I also believe we should be concerned about the inheritance tax. Part of the impetus for a progressive income tax comes from the belief, held by a large number of persons, that inequity arises, to a considerable extent, out of original endowments—which come from inherited capital, inherited education, inherited social class—or out of chicanery or luck.

I doubt there would be strong public acceptance of a consumption tax that did nothing about inherited physical or financial capital. It might be sensible to move in the direction of splitting the tax so as to have a consumption tax and an expenditure tax. This would not, in my view, be like the choice between collecting railroad tickets on the train or at arrival. I think it would make a real difference.

Finally I must align myself philosophically with those who take the position that Tobin suggested—that certainly if redistribution did not produce any distortions of economic activity (if people were like land), then one would find it hard to defend inequality derived exclusively from inheritance and not dependent on the individual's efforts to increase his own endowment. Tobin's question was based on the assumption that people are like land in the sense that nobody can do anything about his capacity to produce; in contrast, Ture focussed on the idea that land can always be improved. Naturally, there must be a difference in the outcome. But in the simple case where we do believe that inequality comes from original endowments, about which no one can do anything, there certainly is a case for removing a large part of this inequality—whenever we can do so without excessive disincentives that will adversely affect not only individuals but the whole society.

Richard A. Musgrave

I find myself in substantial agreement with most of what Professor Tobin said. There *is* no "law of gravity" from which the "true" schedule of progression can be derived; nor does the absence of such a law demonstrate that progressive taxation is wrong and that proportional rates are called for. Judgment on what constitutes the desirable distribution of the income tax burden or, for that matter, of the post-tax distribution of income is, in important part at least, a matter of social philosophy. If one believes that the existence of involuntary poverty in an affluent society is unjust and that too high a concentration of wealth at the top is undesirable, one may well end up with progressive taxation; if one believes that justice is in the rule of acquisition and does not relate to the end state, one may choose a head tax. The debate over what is just in the good society, I might add, is a serious matter, at least as serious as the debate over efficiency, and should not be belittled by being classified as "aesthetic." Clearly it is not a matter of aesthetics but rather, if one wants a Kantian classification, of practical reason.

As to my own views of the world, I find no difficulty in aligning myself with a philosophical position that shows concern for the end state and I therefore find myself at ease with the idea of progressive taxation. What I feel uneasy about, however, is the way in which we try (or should I say, do not try?) to implement it.

Let me then look at some of the major points raised by Allen Wallis and his reasons for thinking that the case for progressive taxation has become increasingly uneasy.

(1) Allen Wallis questions whether progressive income taxation does in fact reduce inequality. Perhaps the pains of progressive taxation are suffered in vain, leaving post-tax distribution as unequal as it would be under a proportional system. Can this really be the case? I agree that shifting may occur. Executives who receive high salaries may be more effective in raising their compensation to offset high-bracket rates than are employees who receive lower incomes, but this hardly disposes of the matter. If those who are subject to high marginal rates avoid tax by working less, efficiency costs are incurred but a reduction in inequality nevertheless results. In all, I find it difficult to see how post-tax income can fail to be distributed more equally, provided of course that society means business in applying a progressive tax. Sweden would seem to be a good illustration. If Wallis finds little evidence of reduced inequality in this country, the reason, I submit, is that our attempt at progressive taxation may be more apparent than real. Finally, I would note that changes in the Gini coefficient are not a very satisfactory gauge of changes in income distribution. The coefficient is notoriously insensitive and better results will be obtained by comparing the ratio of the income shares received by, say, the lowest and the highest quintiles in the income scale.

(2) Wallis notes the startling rise in transfer payments over the last decade and concludes that, those with low incomes having thus been taken care of, there is less need to apply progressive rates on high incomes. This seems to me a non sequitur. To be sure, one's concern with the distribution issue may place greater weight on raising the share of the lowest quartile than on reducing inequality as between the upper three. I would agree. Nevertheless, the issue of distribution among the upper three remains, even if the lowest quartile is provided for. Indeed, I would argue that if high transfers to the lowest quartile are to be made, there is an increased need for fairly arranging the pattern of withdrawal from the upper three. Undoubtedly, as the ratio of total revenue requirement to tax base rises, it becomes increasingly inevitable that taxable income be extended downward, and this has been the history of our income tax. But I do not agree that, therefore, rates applicable to higher income should be reduced. Indeed, as far as efficiency costs go, I am rather more concerned with the high marginal rates of tax implicit in giving to the lower end than with those applied in withdrawing income from the upper.

(3) Wallis argues that there has been a tremendous increase in the complexity of the income tax, deplores the Byzantine bureaucracy of the Internal Revenue Service, and points to the absurd length of some sentences in the revenue code. I share his displeasure with cumbersome language, but I would seek the appropriate remedy in changing the grammar rather than the substance. I do not wish to defend needless complexity, but it should be evident that a fair code in an exceedingly complex society cannot be simple. Consider expense accounts. The

166

law might be altogether lenient and permit the deduction of golf club fees as a business expense, or it might be altogether tough and disallow all expense accounts. Neither extreme makes sense. The law should (and in its imperfect way tries to) seek a reasonable in-between solution, a solution which inevitably is complex. To be sure, complexities can be avoided readily by a sales tax, a payroll tax or, better still, a head tax. But who pays it? The appealing case for simplicity readily becomes handmaiden to a less appealing case for a regressive burden distribution. The tax law, like other parts of our economy, should of course be efficient; but it should also be equitable. The fact that equity (like automobiles or vacations) is expensive is no reason for not buying it. I believe it is of crucial importance to the tax system and well worth paying for.

(4) Wallis points to Milton Friedman's conjecture that if top rates were cut back to 25 percent, declared taxable income in brackets above $500,000 would (by analogy to 1929) be six times what it is now. This may or may not be the case (who would doubt the veracity of so scholarly a publication as *Newsweek*), but again there are various ways of dealing with the problem. One is to reduce rates so that the benefits of tax avoidance are not worth the bother, and the other is to close tax preferences (as in the treatment of capital gains, tax exempt bonds, and real estate shelters), thereby increasing the required coverage of income. Combined with an integration of the individual and corporation tax and the resulting elimination of tax discrimination against distribution, such changes would serve to bring upper-bracket taxable incomes more nearly in line with what they should be, and what in fact they would be if income were channeled through less privileged sources.

Having made some critical comments, let me conclude with a point on which we all can agree. Surely our present income tax (superior though it is to that of most countries) is defective in that it combines high nominal rates with a quite incomplete base. This has two disadvantages: (1) people can complain about high nominal rates (which, in many instances, are in fact inapplicable); and (2) people with equal incomes (especially at high levels) who should pay the same tax are, in fact, taxed at widely varying rates. To remedy these defects, we should move to a fuller-base tax which in turn might permit a one-third reduction in rates. While I would not go along with the Wallis-Friedman maximum of 25 percent, I would *in such a context* (but only then) accept the reduction in the top rate for all income applicable to the 50 percent level which now applies to earned income only.

Finally, in appraising the general role of a progressive income tax, we must remember that it is part of an overall tax system that without income tax progression would be distinctly regressive. Once the tax structure is viewed as a whole, as of course it should be, the case for a global, personal, and progressive tax seems to me compelling. There may be some debate as to whether this role might not be played equally well or better by an expenditure tax, but I doubt that it would.

Since the case for such a tax was discussed earlier in this conference, and since Professor Feldstein and I have an ongoing discussion on this matter in our seminar, let me briefly put myself on record with three points thereon.

(1) I now agree that the income tax base is not as compelling a measure of taxable capacity as for a long time it was thought to be. The proper base, seen in a horizontal equity context, is an equal-option base, defined to include consumption plus bequests and gifts. It is not a consumption-only base.

(2) While the expenditure tax is administratively simpler than the income tax in some respects, I believe that it would be more complex in others. I do not think that it can claim a net advantage in this respect.

(3) If we are to make an experiment with an expenditure tax, let us do it outright, by substituting such a tax for part of the income tax while, at the same time, having as good an income tax as possible. But let us *not* permit the expenditure tax case to kill off such hope for income tax reform as we now have. In particular, let us not conclude that the income tax treatment of income components which are not consumed is unimportant. Such an approach would have the double disadvantage of blocking the improvement of the income tax while failing to establish a valid form of expenditure taxation.

DISCUSSION

DR. SMITH: With the permission of our speakers, I will first call on Walter Blum for some comments.

PROFESSOR BLUM: I think I am the only noneconomist on the platform. There is no need for me to add to the discussion of productivity or efficiency or incentives. I leave those issues to my colleagues. I would like to focus the discussion on a somewhat different matter suggested by ideas that Norman Ture expressed. I propose that we address this challenge: In what ways does progressive taxation bear on the nature of our society apart from economic implications? Perhaps the most instructive approach is to think of a progressive tax as a very heavy tax on the affluent in our society. In this context, I would like to make four points.

First, we are all aware that natural endowments of various kinds—beauty, leadership qualities, artistic abilities, psychological attributes, and so on—are not distributed equally in our society. Considering that a progressive tax operates to redistribute income and wealth in the society, we must ask whether our society would be better if the importance of the distribution of the other endowments were even more salient than it is now. If we were able to equalize income and wealth to a great extent, would this give us a better society or a happier society? Those with great qualities of beauty, leadership, and so on would come to occupy positions of high status more easily or automatically because there would be no rival route to status through dollars.

Second, we should examine attitudes about entitlement to income and wealth. I submit that, over the years, we have accepted the notion that someone who earns or possesses income or wealth is generally entitled to it, and much of what we prize in our society turns on that fact. When progressive taxes were introduced to pay for the burdens of government—burdens such as financing the military establishment, the post office, the justice system, and so on—it could still be argued that these taxes did not jeopardize anyone's entitlement to income and wealth, but simply arranged for each person to bear a "fair" share. But when a very large portion of the expenditures of government consists of direct and indirect payments to those at the bottom of the income and the wealth scale, we must ask what will be the resulting attitudes towards entitlement to income and wealth. Our whole notion of entitlement may change, along with many attitudes that accompany that notion.

The third point concerns the distribution of power between government and those outside government. For libertarians, who prize flexibility and individual initiative in our society, it is important that a considerable amount of power be kept outside of government to provide an independent source of initiative in our society. The question we should ask is what does very heavy taxation of the affluent do to this distribution of power between government and those outside the government?

My last point concerns the intrusiveness of government. In general, high taxes lead to increased government intrusion on the taxpayers. As taxes rise, taxpayers resort to various devices to reduce their taxes, and it becomes harder for government to collect them. I question whether a system of high taxation of the affluent can be maintained over a long period without increasing the instrusiveness of government.

DR. SMITH: I think it is appropriate now to turn to those who presented the two papers.

PROFESSOR TOBIN: I think, perhaps, that Mr. Ture misunderstood a couple of my arguments. I gave my individual opinion that if the state could fully tax the complete value of original endowments without introducing any distortions, there would be a strong presumption for equalization. However, since it is impossible to tax original endowment without distortions and without disincentive effects, inequality is justified, instrumentally. One must reach some compromise between the desirability of moving toward less inequality and the loss of social efficiency that results. Even a very self-oriented majority will not vote for confiscatory taxation since the members of that majority will consider the taxability and the social contributions of those to whom they might wish to shift the burden of taxation.

Thus a considerable amount of residual inequality would be justified on an instrumental basis. But I think Mr. Ture misstated the idea (or departed from the counterfactual assumption) of the initial question when he spoke about augmenting endowments, because at this point he again introduced incentives. Investment to augment endowments may indeed be affected by taxation, and this would be a distortion. I included in the *original* endowments their potential augmentation by investment, including human capital investments.

Incidentally, recent theory suggests that market signals may lead to over-investment in education. The possibility arises when individual productivity is not ascertainable, or can be determined only at considerable cost. Individuals are grouped into categories, and rewards are based on their classification. Although the reward in each category may equal the average productivity of its members, there is no close link between individual reward and productivity. In these circumstances, individuals have an exaggerated incentive to acquire the credentials that lead to high classification. Taxation might correct this distortion. But let me return from this digression to the main theme.

Perhaps Ture also misunderstood the role of the utility calculus in my presentation. On the one hand, some kind of ethical or aesthetic judgment, whether mine or his or that of voters in the country, is indispensable. On the other hand, the trade-off between equality and efficiency is a problem that can be treated both analytically and empirically, independently of value judgments. One would hope that some of the relevant marginal rates of substitution can eventually be estimated. Neither those theoretical models nor the empirical results with which they might be given content can ever solve the policy question, but they are as important as the ultimate ethical judgments.

It is certainly true that if one assigns individual utility functions and assumes that people behave according to them, the way in which one cardinalizes those utility functions to add them up across individuals will make a difference in the answer. Because the answer is thus subject to arbitrariness, one cannot expect to get anything conclusive out of such calculations. That is where value judgments on ultimate distribution come in.

I spoke in my paper about the interdependence of society and the dependence of the value of any individual's endowments on a highly complex social structure. This was not to suggest that we could thus reach a decision on distribution, but rather to counter the simplistic idea that the incomes earned before tax, in so complex a society, are clearly the just deserts of the earners.

But I have heard here a distinction between voluntary agreements and governmental coercion much sharper than does justice to the actual situation. Let us not forget that the complex economic life of a country like ours depends, among other things, on the enforcement of contracts, many of which are long-term contracts with exceedingly complex provisions. The coercion of the state is essential for the enforcement and judgment of those contracts.

MR. WALLIS: I have no systematic remarks to make here. Probably I should have made notes, particularly on Professor Musgrave's comments, some of which I believe need replies; some did not seem to me to come to grips with what I said. In any case, a good number of his comments sound rather unrealistic, particularly with regard to the complexities in the tax laws.

There is, however, one thing I have never really understood that Musgrave's remarks and Tobin's paper explained to me, Musgrave's remarks in particular. Much of the highly conservative—I mean socially conservative—literature attacking the progressive income tax focuses on what is called envy: The writers attribute the support of progressivity in the income tax entirely to envy. But I have never been able to understand this because I never knew anyone who supported progressivity on that basis.

171

I think this issue is what Henry Simons had in mind when he used the term "aesthetic"—a term which he coupled with morality. I do not think that to call this an aesthetic or a moral issue was to belittle the issue at all, but rather the contrary—to put it on a very high level. Much of what the supporters of progressive income taxes have had in mind is a basic revulsion against seeing people living in misery or living what seems like an animal existence. It is interesting to note that people feel more keenly about this the more the people are like them. If the people are foreign and far away and their whole culture is different, the feeling is somewhat less intense. Even so there is often a strong revulsion—calling it moral may produce fewer problems than calling it aesthetic. I have in the past thought that the case for progressive taxation has rested mostly on the desire to have funds to deal with poverty.

Now, from listening to Musgrave—and Tobin, to some extent—I see that he is as much interested in seeing that the people on the top are brought down as in seeing that the people on the bottom are brought up. I do not share that interest. Indeed, historically one can support the view that a tremendous amount of good has been done by persons with high incomes. Perhaps nobody in human history has done more good than John D. Rockefeller, Sr., not merely because Rockefeller accumulated so much, but rather because of his good ideas on how to use it effectively. He created the Sanitation Commission, the Rockefeller Institute, the University of Chicago, the General Education Board, and the Rockefeller Foundation, which have contributed far more to human welfare than anything else of a comparable order of magnitude. I have no antagonism for these creations, but I do feel revulsion at the sight of poverty.

I read the Blum and Kalven book when it came out, and indeed I was around the University of Chicago when it was being written. Certainly they were not keeping their work a secret and a number of people were getting into arguments with them and beginning to think about this issue. Nevertheless, I would have to say I did not feel strongly about it until about six or seven years later, when I had occasion to look into the way the progressive income tax actually works. I found that it does not treat people in the same economic circumstances even approximately the same, nor is it clear to me that it ever could. That was a big shock.

The more intrusive the tax becomes, the more this kind of inconsistency will occur, and this inconsistency tends to undermine the whole system. Our social system in the United States is dependent on the progressive income tax and on the people's respect for it and compliance with it. For all the little chiseling and corner-cutting that go on, most of our citizens treat the income tax with a fair amount of respect. But that respect will be torn down—is being torn down—through the obvious inequities of the tax, and once the tearing down is carried out, it is hard to imagine how our society will operate.

The other general kind of uneasiness, which is not touched on so much in the Blum and Kalven book—although Blum brought it out here very forcefully as did

Ture—lies in the broad long-run social implications of the progressive tax. This line of attack on progressive income taxation is in part a historical attack: the critics look to Roman times and the Renaissance city states and trace the kinds of things that have happened. Not being a historian, I cannot evaluate their case. Doubtless one can make a case for anything by going through history and picking out the right examples, and it takes a good historian to know whether the resulting generalization is valid. In any case, much of the historical argument is to the effect that the kind of thing embodied in the progressive income tax and in the modern welfare measures has invariably caused a deterioration in society—a destruction of the values we cherish.

DR. OKUN: This morning the show was the same as the show yesterday—a very interesting one—though put on by a different cast of characters. The issues remain exactly the same. We have come back to the question whether there is a case for equalization of income, whether there is a case for modifying the market's verdict, as opposed to treating it with ultimate respect. If we believe there is, then the case for progressive taxation is one we can be comfortable with. In either case, the principles are not coming from economics, but from outside economics. And I have been thinking how the discussion would have sounded if we had held a session on the case for economic growth, or the case for efficiency, or the case for price stability—easy or uneasy. On every one of these, we would have had to turn to some principles that come from outside the field. I repeat, the issues that were being discussed yesterday and are being discussed now are the issues that go to the heart of this debate, and they are philosophical issues.

DR. MOORE: I have a simple question I would like to ask Professors Tobin and Duesenberry. I would like to ask them to comment on the Friedman article in *Newsweek* mentioned by Wallis. If Friedman is right, that reducing the marginal rate to 25 percent would increase the tax taken by the federal government, would they support the reduction?

PROFESSOR DUESENBERRY: I must confess that I have not read the article and I am not sure about the answer. But I have some concerns that go beyond merely collecting enough revenue to do something. There is, in my view, a social function here. Let me put it this way—though this may not be an answer to the question—I would like to emphasize what Professor Musgrave said. There are some strong equity considerations supporting the idea of redistribution to low-income people. The middle-income groups who are neither winners nor losers ought to feel—and I say "ought" from the standpoint of the political health of the system, not from a standpoint of morality—that a good share of that redistribution is coming from the winners and going from the winners to the losers, though these middle-income groups may pay some of it because they are at least not losers. The redistributive effect of the tax has some real merit. May I also say that the

173

income distribution figures being cited have almost no relevance if the composition by age and sex of the lowest part of the income distribution is totally different now from what it was twenty-five years ago. If that is the case, merely comparing the lowest 20 percent now and the bottom 20 percent thirty years ago, in terms of shares, would make no sense at all.

PROFESSOR TOBIN: If Friedman's choice—of either reduced rates or less revenues—were the only choice you offered me, I would support his proposal. I do not, however, believe that it is the only choice available. There are other improvements in the tax code that would broaden the tax base and yield a closer approximation of both equity and efficiency.

Professor Feldstein is right. Okun and I have talked a great deal about tradeoffs between equality and efficiency. But some things in the tax and transfer system are wrong on both counts and suboptimal from all points of view.

I must say, it is not attractive to me to reward the people who have, by seeking and using all kinds of loopholes, put us into a position where the Friedman proposal might be right.

PROFESSOR BUCHANAN: As Okun says, we have had two shows, yesterday and today, that were basically the same. And I have been surprised that a fundamental point has not been raised—though Wallis almost raised it a minute ago. There has been no discussion whatsoever about how to define an appropriate size of the group within which equality is to be imposed. This is a vital point.

Implicit in all this discussion is that we draw the line around the nation state. Now do we say that its members are the appropriate members of the tribe to be subject to equality, or do we not? Or is the group smaller than the nation state? The external constraints and the opting-out problem are vital and I do not see how we can have gone through two sessions and not raised this issue, though that is the case.

DR. SMITH: I will take the liberty, as chairman, to note in one minute what seems to me the main points that have been made.

One, there have been comments from virtually all speakers, regardless of ideology, that value judgments are of determinative importance in decisions about a system of taxation. Okun summarized it very well: principles of taxation do not come from economics alone. Some of us regret the fact that this point is not more frequently recognized in economics books, where it is seemingly presumed that the only proper attitude favors a certain degree of egalitarianism. But that is a value judgment and should be recognized as such.

Second, many of the speakers have referred to the fact that there is now a great deal of redistribution of income in the pattern of expenditures with people at lower income levels getting a disproportionately large share of the benefits of government expenditures. To the extent that that is so, one might, of course, argue that a proportional tax or a degressive tax, viewed in the entire context of government activities, involves a redistribution of income.

Third, I note that there have been a series of references to egalitarianism. The philosophers thus have been brought in—more power to those who are broadening the discussion by making it interdisciplinary. If psychologists had participated, I suspect they might have drawn distinctions on the basis of the effects of various aspects of taxation on motivations.

PART FOUR

WHERE DO WE GO FROM HERE?

WHERE DO WE GO FROM HERE?

Robert Nisbet

At the end of the second volume of *Democracy in America*, Tocqueville wrote: "The nations of our time cannot prevent the conditions of men from becoming equal, but it depends upon themselves whether the principle of equality is to lead them to servitude or freedom, to knowledge or barbarism, to prosperity or wretchedness." [1]

It is interesting to set that passage against the lines with which Tocqueville had concluded the first volume of the work, published in 1835, five years earlier. There, in one of his more notable predictions, Tocqueville declares the United States and Russia the two major world powers of the future. All others, he writes, would appear to have reached their natural limits, but these two "are proceeding with ease and celerity along a path to which no limit can be perceived." [2] Tocqueville's contrast between the two nations is instructive:

> The American struggles against the obstacles that nature opposes to him; the adversaries of the Russian are men. . . . The conquests of the American are therefore gained by the plowshare; those of the Russian by the sword. The Anglo-American relies upon personal interest to accomplish his ends and gives free scope to the unguided strength and common sense of the people; the Russian centers all the authority of society in a single arm. The principal interest of the former is freedom, of the latter servitude. Their starting-point is different, and their courses are not the same; yet each seems marked out by the will of Heaven to sway the destinies of half the globe. [3]

Two Kinds of Equality

Whether Tocqueville, when he concluded the second volume of *Democracy in America* with the passage that opens this paper, had Russia and the United States specifically in mind as paired opposites, I do not know, but he might well have. With even greater force, he might have them in mind were he writing today. I do not suggest that the United States and the Soviet Union are the only alternatives to

---

[1] Alexis de Tocqueville, *Democracy in America* (New York: Vintage Books, 1945), vol. 2, p. 352.

[2] Ibid., vol. 1, p. 452.

[3] Ibid.

be considered when it comes to the uses of equality; clearly, a variety of inter-mediate possibilities exists, in fact as well as theory. But it would be hard to find, at this moment, two countries which serve better as examples of the two contrasting philosophies of equality in the contemporary world: on the one hand, equality before the law, with equality of opportunity as its corollary, and on the other, equality of condition or result, at least so far as the masses are concerned.

The distinction between the two kinds of equality is vital, and no one has ever made it more luminous in his thinking than Tocqueville. Most of Tocqueville's often-noted ambivalence, even inconsistency, on the subject of equality clears up in our minds when we make our way to the sense in which he is using the word. When he writes, "Personally, far from finding fault with equality because it inspires a feeling of independence, I praise it primarily for that reason," [4] he is referring strictly to political and legal equality, to equal access by citizens to the Constitution and the liberties and protections it provides. It is equality in precisely the same sense that he has in mind when he notes the development of compassion in modern democratic morality and law.

Very different, though, is equality of social and economic condition. Such equality cannot be achieved, or even undertaken seriously, without measures that tend to destroy political freedom. It is equality of this sort that Tocqueville has in mind when he writes: "Every central power that follows its own natural tendencies courts and encourages the principle of equality, for equality singularly facilitates, extends, and secures the influence of the central power." [5] His growing pessimism on the future of liberty sprang from conviction that in the democracies when an ultimate choice had to be made between equality and freedom, it would be the former that was chosen.

In Europe Tocqueville could see the beginnings of redistribution. "The wealth of the country is perpetually flowing around the government and passing through its hands; the accumulation increases in the same proportion as the equality of condition; for in a democratic country the state alone inspires individuals with confidence, because the state alone appears to be endowed with strength and durability." [6]

It is unlikely that Tocqueville, were he living in any Western country, including the United States, would write that last passage in quite the same way. Confidence in government is a good deal less at the present time than it was even a couple of decades ago. The same acids—so largely political in source—that have eaten away at economic and social institutions in modern society have begun to eat into the political fabric itself. For years now, every major poll and survey has confirmed what ordinary observation tells us: that respect for President, Congress, and now, most recently, the whole judiciary—the imperial judiciary as it is increasingly being

---

[4] Ibid., vol. 2, p. 288.

[5] Ibid., vol. 2, p. 295.

[6] Ibid., vol. 2, p. 307.

called—has diminished year by year, as has respect for and confidence in leaders in other spheres of society.

I find it a striking (if melancholy) fact that the decline of liberty in the economic and educational spheres of life has been accompanied by a decline in the actual authority of government—its authority in the preservation of domestic order and in its conduct of foreign affairs. The evident decline of patriotism is a register of the government's diminished capacity to arouse respect and trust in the minds of its citizens. We may regard with some sense of relief the passing of certain once-clamant forms of patriotism in the Western countries—patriotism in which the spirit of religious revivalism was dominant, often at the expense of personal freedom. But patriotism in some degree is the necessary cement of any kind of organization, and without it no government can long conduct its business without passing into outright military rule. The liberties guaranteed by the Constitution are real only in proportion to the authority placed by the Constitution in government.

Why are liberty and authority both declining at the present time, and why does an assessment of the present suggest further decline in the future? The answer lies, I suggest, chiefly in the extraordinary power that equality has come to have on the intellectual and increasingly on the political person. Equality before the law, I repeat, is fundamental to both liberty and authority: that is, equality among citizens of access to those rights and protections set forth in the Constitution and the laws. I do not of course pretend that we have achieved such equality or even that we are likely to—that is, in full. The values, variables, and mechanisms of this or any other kind of equality are numerous and complex. But as an ideal, equality of access to law is important in itself and indispensable to any free society. It is the kind of equality most obviously lacking in the totalitarian countries of the world, countries where a different measure of equality has succeeded in obliterating freedom and legal equality alike.

I take the time-honored phrase "equality of opportunity" to mean, basically, equality of access to the law, to the rights and privileges and freedoms guaranteed by law. Certainly, this is what equality of opportunity meant to the Founding Fathers, including Jefferson, and has meant until very recently.

Today, however, equality of opportunity has increasingly become subtly fused with equality of result or condition. And this kind of equality—equality of result—lies at the heart of the egalitarianism that confronts us in government, the media, the universities, and other habitats of the political intelligentsia—or, to use a term I prefer, the clerisy. Redistribution of income, property, and other goods through taxation has become an honored aim. Once the purpose of taxation was simply to raise enough money to meet government expenditures. Today it is aimed at reconstruction of economic and social conditions.

The point is, equality has become more than a time-honored value—one among a plurality of values. It is by now tantamount to religion, carrying with it (at least in the minds of many intellectuals, leaders of special-interest groups, and

181

a rising number of politicians and bureaucrats) much the same kind of moral fervor and zeal, much the same sense of crusade against evil, and much the same measure of promise of redemption that have historically gone with religious movements. The difference is this, however: whereas the religious movements I speak of have traditionally had man's spiritual condition principally in mind, the new religion of equality and the clerisy of power that serves as the church for this new religion have nothing spiritual in mind—only the economic, social, and political. It is one thing to declare Everyman a priest as Luther did, or to declare men created equal in the highly limited sense Jefferson intended when he drafted the Declaration of Independence. Expectations are not aroused, or do not become consuming. It is an entirely different matter when equality of economic and social condition becomes a god for the intellectual or politician. Expectations cannot do other than increase exponentially. Envy—of all passions the basest and most destructive of personality and society alike—quickly takes command, and the lust for power with which to allay every fresh discontent, to assuage every social pain, and to gratify every fresh expectation soon becomes boundless.

Mr. Justice Holmes, writing to Harold Laski, put the matter into focus: "I have no respect for equality, which seems to me merely idealizing envy." No doubt it is this very fact that explains the rather mean status equality as a value has had in Western thought: from Plato's rendering of it in *The Republic* all the way down to Faulkner's memorable treatment of the Snopes family. I do not say equality and envy are the same thing, but envy is the secret canker in equality—that is, equality of result or condition.

My guess is that the great majority of the American people share this view of the dangers inhering in any policy of large-scale redistribution, of legislated equality. To say this is in no way to accuse them of inhumanity. On the record Americans in large numbers, in majorities, dislike racism, are in favor of the abolition of extreme poverty, of improvement in conditions of work, child-rearing, old age, health, and so on.

But here the humanitarian spirit is limited to a finite goal. It is a very different matter, though, when equality is invoked with redistribution of wealth as its mechanism. I doubt that many Americans favor this; they sense the nature of the measures—political, economic, or social—required to institute it in significant degree. They sense also the fact that equality, once entered into as a systematic policy by and for a population, could never seem adequate. Most people are wise enough, I believe, to understand, if only subliminally, the inevitable and unceasing acceleration of expectations that must go with egalitarianism as social policy. And I believe, finally, that most Americans also understand that "equality" and "redistribution," as now used by the political clerisy, are really code words for a degree of revolutionary reconstruction they do not wish to see.

I do not say Americans are satisfied with the present economy or social order. Opposition to "malefactors of great wealth" or "economic royalists" can certainly be heard from time to time. Big business clearly arouses ire on occasion, as does big labor or big anything when pollsters are around. But if the simple existence of great disparities of income and property were really important to Americans, I assume their resentment would extend to those such as Muhammad Ali, Robert Redford, Barbara Walters, Woodward and Bernstein, Frank Sinatra, and the occasional millionaire textbook author. But it does not. In fact, on the evidence, even the poorest of people seem to take pleasure, vicarious pride, in the millions gained annually by an Ali or Barbara Walters. (That is why Rousseau, master egalitarian, chose to bar from his good society all artists and performers.)

The Growth of Egalitarianism

But it seems unlikely that the present wishes of a majority of the American people will be decisive with respect to egalitarianism, or substantial redistribution, in public policy during the years ahead. For intellectuals, their self-serving modesty notwithstanding, have a great deal of influence upon the makers of public policy—through what they teach and write, through the fascination businessmen and politicians seem to have for them (even if only as court jesters), through the media, and through the innumerable relationships intellectuals have with those forming the infrastructure of government, the bureaucracy. It is the intellectual—the social or physical scientist—not the ordinary member of the middle class, who is likely to be called on by the federal judge for crucial advice in an affirmative action case, or by the candidate for high office. How revealing it was to read recently of the supposedly idiosyncratic and austere young Jesuit become governor of California—after he decided to put his name in after all for the presidency, Walter Heller and Christopher Jencks were bidden immediately to come to the governor's modest pad for consultation. One assumes that John Rawls will not be far behind. Admittedly Professor Rawls's prose style is anything but seductive, and meaning is often a morass in the pages of *A Theory of Justice*. But there are enticing phrases, all the same, and how can one regard a theory as other than benign, if not actually divine, that insists, as Rawls's theory insists, upon equal distribution of all social primary goods (among which he specifically includes "self-respect") *except* when unequal distribution works to "the advantage of the least favored." [7]

How nice to have that escape clause. But can we assume that it will work, be allowed to work in the good society, in the interest of the businessman, the investor, the oil explorer and developer, and the successful retailer, as well as the interest of the best-selling author, the film or football star, or the tenured holder of the illustrious academic chair? It is impossible to be sure, but one somehow doubts that that is precisely what Professor Rawls has in mind.

Professor Rawls is insistent that public policy must lead toward nullification of all "accidents of natural endowment" and "results of social circumstances." For the

---

[7] John Rawls, *A Theory of Justice* (Cambridge, Mass.: Harvard University Press, 1971).

life of me, I do not know why public policy should work in this fashion, but the statement that it should comes *ex cathedra* from Professor Rawls and from many another priest of the New Equality. Again I ask: Will the doctrine of nullification be applied to the fruits (economic and other) of the Nobel scientist, the United States senator, the heavyweight champion of the world, and the stars of *All the President's Men*, as well as to the businessman?

How do we account for the burning sense of mission among intellectuals today? Be assured, intellectuals will have a great deal of shaping influence on any national policy of redistribution, though their habitual posture as one of society's discriminated-against minority groups will no doubt disguise this influence. I offer the following as reasons for the dedication to egalitarianism by the large majority of academics and other intellectuals in the West.

First, there is the by-now deeply embedded humanitarianism that William Graham Sumner so admirably described in *The Forgotten Man*—A and B getting together to decide what C should do for X.[8] Needless to say, C is Sumner's forgotten man—the individual who works hard, pays his bills, seeks to save, not bother anyone, and look out for self and family. Understandably, as Sumner had come to realize, reformers love X and detest C. Egalitarianism makes for a bully pulpit from which to excoriate C and sentimentalize over X.

Second, egalitarianism, or large-scale redistribution, is capable, as history plainly shows, of generating a high degree of millennialist response. The Levelers during the Puritan Revolution, the Jacobins in 1792-1794, the Bolsheviks in 1917-1918, not to mention the leaders of a few score subsequent revolutions in this century, all demonstrate this affinity between equality and evangelism. Marx himself thought redistribution a *petit bourgeois* fancy, but look at what the dream did to an Anthony Crosland!

Third, equality can be made the pivot of a philosophy of history. Even Tocqueville, tortured though he was by the implications of egalitarianism, built his whole philosophy of history around it, pointing out how every major event from the Crusades to his time seemingly worked toward the spread of equality in Western society. In all truth, no one really knows what the "movement" of history is, whether indeed there is any such thing as concerted long-range "movement" by civilization. But among the idols of the Western intellectual-philosophical mind, none ranks higher than belief in such movement, and equality lends itself superbly to predictions grounded in assumed knowledge of historical inevitability.

Fourth, equality has a natural affinity with the whole idea of centralized rationalist government. Edmund Burke said, correctly: "Believe me, sir, those who attempt to level never equalize." But it is hard nevertheless to prove a difference between leveling and equality when large masses of people are involved, and when central bureaucracy, working in the name of humanitarianism or social justice, is

---

[8] William Graham Sumner, *The Forgotten Man and Other Essays* (New Haven: Yale University Press, 1919), pp. 465-95.

at the helm. Even if one were indifferent to equality as such, adoration of central planning, central management, of economy and society would, I think, necessarily bring one around to adoration of equality.

Fifth, equality is the only possible value that can really serve revolutionary aspiration. All revolutions in history, the American Revolution possibly in part excepted, have been mounted on an assault against inequality. Freedom can serve as the point of departure for liberation movements—liberation from whatever kind of imagined or perceived tyranny. But freedom, in any genuine sense of the word, cannot be successful as the *continuing* theme of a revolution, for, once a revolution has been successful in military or political terms, the people are, by definition, made free. But not equal. Not immediately. Hence the need for a process of permanent revolution in society that can be best generated by the value of equality and that can be justified by incessant references to the surviving consciousness of aristocrats, businessmen, Trotskyites, Confucians, and so on. Moreover, equality has a built-in fascination for those, religious and lay alike, who seek, like the Grand Inquisitor and like Rousseau, a total remaking of human consciousness. In *Inequality* the gentle and scholarly Christopher Jencks can write:

> We need to establish the idea that the federal government is responsible not only for the total amount of national income, but for its distribution. . . . If we want substantial redistribution we will not only have to politicize the question of income equality but alter people's basic assumptions about the extent to which they are responsible for their neighbors or their neighbors for them. . . . As long as egalitarians assume that public policy cannot contribute to economic equality directly, but must proceed by ingenious manipulations of marginal institutions like the schools, progress will be glacial.[9]

Rousseau, it might be noted, stated the same point much more grandly and encompassingly in his famous chapter, "The Legislator," in *The Social Contract*.

Finally, and here I skirt the edge of moral prophecy, egalitarianism is likely to grow and spread simply because we are living in one of history's twilight ages. The authority of traditional values and institutions seems to recede almost constantly, and it is in precisely such circumstances, as much comparative history demonstrates, that a preoccupation with substantive equality intensifies. The same forces which make for an increase in subjectivism, for a retreat to ego or consciousness, for a decline in the work ethic, for a materialistic hedonism, and for a diminished sense of personal responsibility in one's own life also make for a spreading concern with equality or at any rate with the leveled conditions which pass for equality.

Solzhenitsyn (an authentic prophet, I believe) thinks the West generally and the United States particularly are about seventy-five years behind Soviet Russia in

---

[9] Christopher Jencks and others, *Inequality, A Reassessment of the Effect of Family and Schooling in America* (New York: Basic Books, 1972), p. 264.

historical time. The conditions spreading so rapidly in the West today are very similar, he argues, to those present in Russia at the beginning of the century. Prophets, even the best of them, err on occasion. We can all hope that Solzenhitsyn has erred here, but I should not wish to bet much on it.

Indicators of the Future

Where do we go from here? Can we realistically hope and plan for relief from the bureaucratic Leviathan that now, in the sweet name of humanity, occupies more and more social and economic space? Is there a possibility that the public sector will begin to recede and the private regain the ascendancy it once had, in culture, education, mutual aid, and voluntary association, as well as in business enterprise? Will the clerisy of power—sanctified in this country since Woodrow Wilson's New Freedom and his war totalitarianism—suffer a retreat for its generally sorry performance in the making and execution of social policy during times of peace and war? I am afraid the answer to each of these questions is No, and I shall explain why presently.

But first it must be admitted that some strange sights and sounds are perceptible right now, few of them predictable even a decade or two ago. Words like *decentralization, localism, neighborhood,* and *voluntary* have today an acceptability if not prestige they did not have a few years ago. It is possible today, as presidential candidates have discovered, to utter imprecations on Washington, D.C., and its bureaucracy, and be applauded for them. The governor of Colorado can write a piece for national circulation begging his fellow Democrats to heed the people on such subjects as localism, neighborhood, and hatred of centralization, and to try to forget the New Deal as "The Only Chosen Way" to salvation. There is, in sum, much unfamiliar rhetoric. True, a Benjamin Cohen, now eighty, still fighting economic royalists as valiantly as in 1934, argues for still more centralization of government. Hubert Humphrey not only declares that Washington-based bureaucracy is a good thing in itself but that racism underlies much of the assault on this bureaucracy. And, as I shall indicate shortly, the clerisy of power has neither forgotten nor learned anything since 1934. From academy to foundation to national capital, its conventional wisdom continues to perceive, define, and seek to solve problems very much in the fashion of the New Deal.

Still, I cannot deny the existence of patterns of thought and behavior that fly in the teeth of this conventional wisdom of the clerisy, that must outrage it beyond power of expression. A Harris poll in April 1976 tells us that the American people overwhelmingly regard high federal spending with deep concern, as they do the diminished confidence or trust of people in their government. The same poll indicates that 94 percent of the people consider inflation the greatest single problem facing the United States. And there is reason to believe that more and more people are coming to understand the vital role of big government and its regulatory agencies in the generating of inflation. Some 79 percent of the people believe that welfare reform must be given high priority, and 85 percent express serious misgivings about the once-sacred social security system. Once the prospect of such sentiment could have been dismissed. It could have been relegated to passing fancy. But the evidence is very strong that we are dealing with reasonably solid public—rather than mere popular—opinion.

There are other indicators of change in this country which cannot help, I should think, but gnaw at the clerisy's conscience. Consider the 10,000 to 15,000 communes, urban and rural. One may dislike them, or many of them, on moral or hygienic grounds, but that has nothing to do with the matter here. They tend very strongly to be nonpolitical, even "retreatist," so far as the political mentality is concerned. Much energy that would once have gone into radical politics or doorbell-ringing for latter-day New Dealers goes instead into hoeing corn or child care. How wasteful this must seem to the heirs of Harry Hopkins!

There are the pentecostals and evangelicals. The number is estimated at 50 million, and growing. I do not mean that there is anything in the way of retreat from politics to be found here (in fact, it works the other way, I would guess), but it is safe to conclude the politics of these people differs significantly from the politics of the National Council of Churches of Christ.

Observe the renascence of localism, of neighborhood. Marx said class conflict was the only way class consciousness could grow. I suggest it is local conflict with the federal government in such matters as busing that helps stimulate a renewal of consciousness of neighborhood and local community. We shall see much growth of this consciousness, I believe, in the years ahead. In some degree it will be reaction to diminished confidence in the national state in a variety of respects.

Nor can the rebirth of ethnic loyalty be dismissed from mind. This too may present problems, may augur future fragmentation most of us will not like. But as an indicator, the renewal of ethnic consciousness is useful. Whatever else it suggests, abandonment of the melting-pot ethic, a manifestation of monolithic democracy, is certainly present. I do not assume that ethnic groups are politically chaste, but it is interesting nevertheless to see a Jesse Jackson urging blacks to fend for themselves, to drop efforts to remake the political government.

There are still other indicators, of diverse kind and importance. Revenue sharing has only barely gotten off the ground and is certain to be the object of egalitarian witch hunts, with diversity among states made to seem rank inequality of constitutional right. But the fact is that revenue sharing exists. So in smaller degree do hopes for direct family assistance—so well on the way, despite the political clerisy's opposition, prior to the Watergate disaster. And there are signs of interest in the negative income tax, educational vouchers, and other devices for reducing the administrative Leviathan. There is the fact that for even the saintliest of the clerisy, a size of national budget exists that begins to suggest caution where for so many years there was only a kind of Rover Boys' spirit of derring-do, of tax and spend, spend and tax, and the devil take the hindmost.

After all, we have by now a national budget that not even John Kenneth Galbraith would have dared dream of—in size, that is—when his influential *The Affluent Society* was published a couple of decades ago. Size of military budget notwithstanding, a very high proportion of this annual budget goes to programs with humanitarian purpose. Who, in the 1950s, could have imagined an HEW of present size, complexity, and impact upon economy and social order? It is unlikely, to be sure, that Professor Galbraith is happy. In the first place, large as the budget is, it doubtless does not seem large enough to him. Or perhaps its divisions and categories do not seem quite right. And in any case a certain spirit of disenchantment has set in, even among members of the clerisy of politics. Memories are too ripe of Model Cities, the War against Poverty, and certain other programs of the New Frontier and the Great Society which first gladdened, then dampened, the hearts of the clerisy.

Can we, then, from what I have just written, take some comfort? Will the public sector be reduced, the private expanded? Will the Leviathan begin to diminish in size? Will the allure of political solution to social and economic problems lessen? I wish I could think so, but I cannot. There are altogether too many persisting currents visible to encourage optimism along this line, any hope that the clerisy of power, after a near half-century of dominance in government, the academy, bureaucracy, the foundations, and elsewhere, is finally in retreat.

First is the still-formidable size of the clerisy, a few defectors or heretics notwithstanding. I venture the guess that it is if anything larger than two decades ago, if only because of the attraction of its promises and the time-worn appeal of its conventional wisdom. As great as ever, I fear, is the clerisy's preference for the public over the private, the big over the small, the national-centralized over the local, the bureaucratic over the voluntary, the metropolis (especially the Boston-Washington metropolitan axis) over the small city or town—the more so if the latter is actually solvent, able to handle its own problems. Observe the continuing appeal of wage and price controls in the clerisy despite the dismal record of such controls.

Second, and very important, is the seemingly ineradicable affinity between the clerisy and some variant or other of what can be pronounced, or secretly thought of, as left, or Socialist, or revolutionary in however bland degree. There is an almost tropistic character in the formula: left is good; right is bad. There are many ways of illustrating this "adversary mentality," to use Lionel Trilling's memorable phrase. Think of the general response of intellectuals to anything smacking of business, large or small, or profits of free private enterprise. Recall the headlong rush in the early and middle 1960s to support of the destructive turmoil on the campuses—a turmoil that—though in large degree generated by faculty members and other intellectuals—was safely designated from the start as "the student revolts." And as I noted above, *equality* and *redistribution* are code words for economic and social reconstruction that are revolutionary in implication. No one needs be told how much fascination the clerisy of power finds in these magic counters. Then there is the double standard applied to despotisms abroad—what reams of copy on the "unspeakable atrocities" of, say, Chile's current government or the Greece of the colonels, and how little on the executions by the millions, the forced migrations, the exiles, and the tortures which have gone and continue to go with governments of the left, the Soviet Union, China, Cuba, North Vietnam, and so on. How else does one account for an acceptance of Maoist China ranging from the ecstasies of a Shirley MacLaine to the contemplative pipe-smoking indulgences of Harvard professors?

What is fundamental, I suppose, is the clerisy's abiding dislike of anything strictly economic except insofar as it may be brought within the iron hand of the bureaucrat, call him what we will. Heroes abound in the clerisy's halls, but they tend to be political, even military, eleemosynary, literary-artistic, and intellectual. Never are they drawn from the ranks of business, at least not until a generation or two has allowed a business name to become cleansed (through politics or philanthropy) of its association with profit, money getting, capital expansion, and economic growth.

Nor has the clerisy of power had much affection for the middle class, from the time Hobbes blamed it for the English Civil War. Rousseau, Bentham, Marx, the Webbs: the list is a long one. Its proud motto is: *épater le bourgeois*—shock the middle class! The *philosophes* in eighteenth century France delighted in sketches of the bourgeoisie in which the heads and faces were made to resemble donkeys. That a majority of our clerisy of power is itself middle class has nothing to do with the matter. One deplores middle-class values while enjoying them in a Berkeley hillside house or a very comfortable upper Westside apartment in New York. One must.

It is said of the Puritans that their opposition to bearbaiting sprang less from the pain inflicted upon the animals than from the pleasure excited in the spectators. Of our clerisy of power it is fair to say: its delight in affirmative action springs less from any good done the ethnic poor than from the manifest discomfort of the middle class, black or white.

These, then, are my reasons, or some of them, for taking small hope from the indicators of change I noted above and for believing the Church of Politics, the clerisy of power, is still too large, still too powerful in influence on school, media, university, foundation, Congress, and the bureaucracy, to offer likelihood of substantial change. I could be wrong. I hope I am wrong, but, so far as our Leviathan is concerned, until the spirit of eliminating it—of *écrasez l'infâme*—replaces the spirit of simply joining it (and this latter spirit has come to infect business and labor as well as the intellectual class), there is manifestly little to look forward to.

Equality and the War Society

Additional grounds for concern lie in the prospect of war and all of its egalitarian, power-centralizing, and bureaucratizing potentials. There is no intrinsic reason why the United States could not have a powerful military without at the same time creating something akin to a war socialism around it, but American experience throughout the twentieth century suggests that such a military is not likely. Far more likely is a continuing system of matching funds for HEW every time an increase in the military budget takes place. Merely observe the steps toward socialism taken in this country in both world wars.

I find this an unhappy situation. I believe we could have a much stronger military than we now have, one quite capable of meeting the increasingly dangerous threats posed by the Soviet Union and its minions. The reason we do not have such a military is the development of the philosophy of nineteenth-century writers as diverse as Clausewitz and Marx—that a strong military demands something approximating a war society, defined commonly from an egalitarian, humanitarian viewpoint. We might have a military duly insulated from civil society—much better undoubtedly than the one we now have—if some of the currently huge budgets and bureaucracies, inspired by goals of equality and entitlement, were substantially reduced. As I have said, nothing so weakens the legitimate authority of government (and adequate military force in its proper place is a part of government) as the government's assumption of burdens so vast, so heavy, so costly that they tend to suffocate the performance of its normal activities. If survival in the military-socialist world (a world increasingly aggressive toward the United States and certain to remain so) is a matter of genuine importance to us, then the time has surely come to develop a very different theory of government and also of the military. There is in theory no sound reason whatever for basing our war potential upon war socialism.

But to see possibility in strictly theoretical terms is in no way to see likelihood, or even probability. The fact is, the wars the United States has fought in the twentieth century, starting with World War I, have carried with them enormous increases in social entitlements, in programs generated by war-sprung egalitarianism. The Jacobins, during the French Revolution after foreign wars had begun, set the example for this. Side by side with Western Europe's first universal military conscription lay the promise, if not the actuality, of Western Europe's first venture into a collectivism that reached almost every detail of French life, with glittering entitlements inevitably involved. From the Revolutionary and Napoleonic wars down to those of the twentieth century, national warfare has tended to mean national socialism in some degree in every Western country.

It is a commonplace that today the Soviet Union feels no obligation whatever to supply social, cultural, and intellectual entitlements to its people, even to offer the rhetoric of egalitarianism as a cushion on which to rest its massive awesome military establishment. In the Soviet Union the military govern, with even the Politburo, as Solzhenitsyn has recently told, a committee of impotence, a mere facade.

But seemingly in the West, certainly in the United States, the union has been fixed between the military establishment and the vast amalgam of social entitlements, given cement by egalitarianism. What I am saying is that, in addition to other forces working toward (or potentially working toward) an increasingly bureaucratic and centralized egalitarian society, war (or its prospect) must certainly be counted. Memory is too fresh of the intoxicating experience we knew in two world wars (if not in Korea and Vietnam)—the experience of an extended moral crusade linked to economic prosperity, of a sense of national community serving as anodyne to ordinary irritations, torments, and alienations.

Think too of the number of academic intellectuals reminiscing nostalgically about their experiences off and on over the past thirty-five or forty years running large federal agencies, especially in wartime, when one could know the heady experience of meeting payrolls and not having to maintain a profit-and-loss register. I can think of at least one economist who to his dying day will surely think his finest hour was in service as deputy administrator of the OPA during World War II. If we increase the 39,000 employees he had then for the subsequent inflation in all areas, we see the visions of power-cum-humanitarianism that must surely dance in any academic intellectual's head.

War also attracts because it contains a revolutionary potential. I think of the historical linkage between the progressive-populist-socialist state of mind which took shape some seventy-five years ago and the state of mind produced first by World War I, then by World War II. After all, war and revolution have always been close in history. All men of military genius like centralized power, wrote Tocqueville, and all men of centralizing genius love war. And centralization of power is, of course, the very cornerstone of successful revolution—all cant about liberty and rights notwithstanding. When power is sufficiently centralized, the result, in effect, is a revolution. When a revolution is conducted successfully, the result is extreme centralization of power. Despite the flow of myth on the subject, this is for the most part all there is to the matter. It is no wonder that a Napoleon could become the idol of the intellectual left in France. Hitler would almost certainly have become the idol of the intellectual left in Western Europe had it not been for his consuming and pathological hatred of the Jews. The image of Gaullism is lustrous at this moment in the United States, as well as the rest of the West. Fortunately, no Charles de Gaulle seems to be in sight. But that may well change, and quickly.

The reason centralization of power so easily results from revolution and war, so evidently links them, is its ineradicable relation to equality—or, at very least, to leveling. It is not possible to centralize power in a society without, in some degree, equalizing. Correspondingly, it is not possible to effect equality, in sudden and calculated fashion—or at least to effect a claimed equality of economic and social condition—without in large degree centralizing and bureaucratizing political authority.

If there were no other reason for my less than sanguine view of the American future, it would be this last: the bureaucratizing of power. Despite Max Weber's great studies of bureaucracy, there is still much we do not understand or appreciate about it. Bureaucracy on the large scale is, or can be until one simply acquiesces in it, formidable and at times frightening. There is a small, interesting literature by those who, fleeing some highly personal despotism of the non-Western world and coming to take residence in a Western country, have found a form of tyranny they never dreamed of when power, however intense, was confined to one man.

In some recent remarks reflecting on the machine, Robert Penn Warren noted the fate of the albatross in Coleridge's *Rime of the Ancient Mariner*. The albatross was killed, as will be remembered, not from hatred or malice, but because the machine, the crossbow, was there to be used. Bureaucracy is a machine, and once present in mass and power it has to be used.

When I think of despotism in the world today, I do not think of a Hitler or Stalin or Mao. I have come to think, rather, of the bureaucrat—that is, the head of the powerful agency or commission, or any of scores of subheads of such bodies, or, for that matter, of the solid ranks of underlings in bureaucracy—immovable in his job security, implacable in his enforcement, his bloodless execution of ordinances and rules he never made. The brutal despotism of a Hitler or Stalin does not, on the evidence, last long; too many sadists are required to give such despotism effect. There are cheaper, blander, and more powerful ways of imposing power, among them psychiatric, narcotic, and, not least, bureaucratic.

To paraphrase an ancient principle, I would say there is far more in common between two bureaucrats, one of whom is Communist and the other democratic, than between two Communists, one of whom is a bureaucrat and the other an ordinary citizen, or than there is between two democrats, one of whom is a bureaucrat and the other an ordinary citizen. Such a truth has behind it the wisdom of a Max Weber and a Robert Michels.

Bureaucracy tends, in short, to acquire a sameness everywhere except insofar as it is checked, limited, and (as it were) humanized by counterpowers in a social order: business enterprises, professions, churches, families, labor unions, and voluntary associations, all largely autonomous, free in some degree from bureaucratic inquisition.

Unchecked by strong forces in the economy and society, then, bureaucracy becomes its own immovable—or perhaps irresistible—force. It is precisely the kind of despotism Tocqueville had in mind when he wrote the extraordinary and now celebrated chapter near the end of *Democracy in America* entitled "What Sort of Despotism Democrat Nations Have to Fear." Such despotism, Tocqueville wrote, will be different from the harsh tyrannies of the past. It will not kill or torture human beings for their opinions; it will, rather, seek to prevent or suffocate these opinions. It will not so much restrict as extinguish free thought as it will cover society with a network of tiny rules and regulations, one so tightly constructed that even the most energetic and original of minds will not be able to break through. Such despotism, Tocqueville tells us, will not so much terrify as enervate and stupefy.[10]

We may be permitted slight dissent from that last. Bureaucracy can and does terrify. The greatest artists and prophets of the last century—Dostoevsky, Dickens, Balzac, Burckhardt, and Nietzsche among them—saw and foresaw this in one more instance of how art precedes science in understanding of the new. In our own century, then, are the stories and novels of Kafka. On April 3, 1976, the *New York Times* reported the Swedish actress Bibi Andersson's story about the Swedish tax bureaucracy. "I was shocked. I was scared. . . . If there are taxes that I have not paid, I will pay all of them with enthusiasm. It is the bureaucracy I speak about. They did not behave to me as if they wanted money. They seemed to want to prove that I had committed a conscious act of cheating, that I was a criminal."

Of course. Dostoevsky's parable of The Grand Inquisitor in *Brothers Karamazov* should have prepared us for this, not to mention Huxley's *Brave New World* and Orwell's *Animal Farm* or *1984*. But desire to prove someone mischievous or evil is, *pace* Miss Andersson, less motivating, I believe, than simple desire to use the machine that has been constructed—Coleridge's crossbow. If there is an antitrust, an antifraud, an antipollution, or an "antianything" division numbering thousands of individual persons, among whom desires for advancement and fame are surely as great as among newspaper reporters, it follows that the division must on occasion go into action. If there is no real (or at any rate important) case at hand, one can quickly be contrived. What is vital is that the machine be used. If it is not, it becomes rusty from disuse, and its servants morose.

The *New York Times* also reprinted (on April 10, 1976) that the eminent civil libertarian Charles Morgan, Jr., obliged by his American Civil Liberties Union superiors to resign from the Washington office, wrote: "Bureaucracy tends to blandness. It tries to turn everyone into carbon-copies, and in Orwellian ways executive directors recast themselves as executive editors and, finally, as censors." He was referring to the hierarchy—the bureaucracy—of the ACLU, of course, but his words have equal relevance to all other bureaucracies: business, professional, academic, religious, and others. But they have extraordinary relevance to government bureaucracy simply by virtue of its size and its union with political sovereignty. There is some possibility (if only theoretical) of escape from other bureaucracies. There is no escape, though, from the government's bureaucracy, save possibly by

---

[10] Tocqueville, *Democracy in America,* vol. 2, pp. 334-39.

corruption. No wonder Orwell saw susceptibility to corruption in government as the last great hope of freedom.

As I say, I am not charging bureaucrats with inhumanity, malice, vindictiveness, or sadism. The vast majority are honest, efficient, and hard-working, and a great many of them are dedicated. That is precisely the problem of bureaucracy: the better it is, the worse its impact upon culture and social order. It is not the occasional evidence of venality or cruelty in the bureaucrat that makes one apprehensive. It is, rather, the much more common evidence of dispassionate, bland, emotionless fulfillment of job responsibilities.

The great German philosopher Lotze compared the crushed worm, writhing in pain, with the angel endowed with consummate intelligence but without feeling, watching from the heavenly ramparts. The modern world is filled with bureaucratic "angels." Ideology does not seriously matter. I can do no more than speculate, of course, but behind the seeming paranoia of Chairman Mao there may have been a tormenting fear of the kind of bureaucracy his sense of history tells him is the inevitable spawn of revolution, of large-scale remaking of social order and human consciousness.

A large journalistic literature attests to the torments, and then the illegal steps, of the Kennedy, Johnson, and Nixon administrations, the results of White House struggles with the Pentagon, the State Department, and other bureaucracies in Washington. Max Weber correctly saw bureaucracy as first the spawn of the democratic revolution in modern history, and then the nemesis of democracy—taking that word in the sense of popular participation through elections in the actual governing process. One can measure the progress of democracy, according to Tocqueville, by the progress of the civil service in scope and influence. The old "great unpaid" becomes supplanted by the "great paid." No matter what the purpose, there is much in history that suggests the fettering of purpose by the instruments devised to fulfill or achieve the purpose. The administrative machine tends to triumph.

If I were to prophesy, I would prophesy the triumph of the Swedish model of bureaucracy. We generally have read about Swedish "social justice," but now we are beginning, at long last, to gain sight of the machine. I venture the guess that the Soviet Union—internally at least—will more likely come to resemble Sweden than Sweden will resemble the command-economy structure once so dominant in the Soviet Union. Sweden's approach is easier, cheaper, and in the long run more effective.

The Servile State

This, then, is where I am obliged to believe we go from here. It is not, god wot, where I want us to go, but where I am convinced we are (almost irreversibly) headed at the present time: to the peculiar form of despotism—grounded in humanitarianism and popular currents but largely formed by bureaucracy—that a score of prophetic artists and philosophers and historians foresaw a century and more ago. As I say, I hope I am wrong, and no one has higher respect than I for the operation in history of the random event, the maniac, the prophet, and the genius. None of these is ever predictable. One or all may be around history's corner.

But we are forced to deal with present evidence and probabilities, however tenuous these may be. The dead hand of the recent past is a heavy one, far more so because of the current political clerisy's worship of it. "Things are what they are," wrote the great Bishop Butler in the eighteenth century in one of his sermons, "and the consequences of them will be what they will be; why, then, should we desire to be deceived?"

The political habit of mind, the political clerisy consecrated to state as the medieval clerisy was consecrated to church, the whole machinery of political power brought into being by Renaissance and Reformation kings, all of these, obviously, have grown stronger and spread more widely under modern nationalism, democracy, and socialism. The political has clearly triumphed over the religious, the social, and the economic. Tribute is of course paid: the glossing over of what is political and bureaucratic through the use of the rhetoric of the "social." Our clerisy's cant notwithstanding, today's "democratic" state is in fact a vastly more powerful structure, reaching further into the lives and minds of its citizens, than any divine-right monarchy of the seventeenth century ever was. But to try to sell this truth, this platitude, in the halls of the universities, in the ranks of most of our intellectuals, is foredoomed to failure.

I suspect we are headed for what Hilaire Belloc so eloquently and accurately termed *The Servile State*. In that remarkable but little-read book, Belloc wrote: "The definition of the Servile State is as follows: 'That arrangement of society in which so considerable a number of the families and individuals are constrained by positive law to labor for the advantage of other families and individuals as to stamp the whole community with the mark of such labor we call The Servile State.' " [11]

The secret of accomplishing the Servile State is really simple. By concentrating upon the inequalities that exist in any more or less free society, especially the inequalities observable in the economic sphere, it is possible through astute use of redistributionist legislation, and through the invisible government of bureau, agency, and commission, to achieve forms of inequality that are actually greater than those eradicated. These inequalities are rendered more or less painless by the rhetoric of egalitarianism and social justice. The economic and social inequalities native to any free society are transformed into the far more destructive, but less immediately galling, inequalities that go with centralized political power and its numerous strata of privilege, status, affluence, and authority. Freedom will die. As Goethe once

---

[11] Hilaire Belloc, *The Servile State* (London: T. N. Foulis, 1913), p. 16.

wrote: "Lawgivers or revolutionaries who promise equality and liberty at the same time are either utopian dreamers or charlatans." But if the process is gradual enough, as it is likely to be in this country, I am not sure many people will even notice when the final line between freedom and collectivist servitude has been crossed. If we have a few more years of egalitarian and redistributionist rhetoric, a few hundred more "entitlements," another million or so members of the federal bureaucracy pledged to achievement of equal rations, equal housing, equal social esteem, equal strength and beauty, how would we possibly know of the transition?

This is how the situation seems to me, and I would be lacking in candor if I did not say as much. Still, on the right day of the right week in the right month, it is possible for me even yet to take hope. There are strange specters hanging over the landscape, none exactly welcome to the clerisy of power. We cannot, I repeat, ever forget the random event, the maniac, the genius, and the prophet in history. What appear to be iron trends and irreversible laws of movement so often turn out not to be such. Lenin's "locomotive of history" becomes derailed. Event or personage or calamity confounds.

Think of the Church of Rome at the beginning of the sixteenth century. To its enemies as well as its own clerisy, it must have seemed permanent, if not actually eternal. In its way, the church was as omnicompetent, penetrating of life and mind, and as monolithic as our contemporary national state. Its clerisy was mighty, and it is easy to imagine the sense of history-endowed superiority this clerisy had as it looked out on the land.

But as every schoolchild knows, there came a Reformation, the church's and the religious clerisy's power notwithstanding. Perhaps we are at the beginning of a Reformation ourselves, one that will dislocate and fragment the national state and its clerisy just as the earlier one dislocated and fragmented the Church, with something in the nature of a new feudalism resulting. No one can know, of course. The future is subject for speculation only. But just as the behavior of chickens, goats, and tigers is said to portend earthquakes, so may the current, bizarre behavior of many politicians and political intellectuals portend a different kind of earthquake. No doubt we shall soon see.

WHERE DO WE GO FROM HERE: OPTIONS FOR THE FUTURE

Wilbur J. Cohen

It is an interesting and even significant observation that tax policy and major aspects of income maintenance policy are handled by the same committees in Congress— the House Committee on Ways and Means and the Senate Committee on Finance. Yet the legislative considerations of the two policies have traditionally been kept quite separate. On the other hand, economic and fiscal policies have played a role in determining income maintenance policy at a given time, though within limits decided in past years primarily by the chairmen of the two committees.

As the size and importance of income maintenance programs have grown, there has been, I think, an increased congressional recognition of the interrelationships between tax, expenditure, economic, and fiscal policy on the one hand and income maintenance policy on the other. But I am not at all sure where we will come out on this matter over the next eight years. There is more to the resolution of this issue than economic policy alone: Psychology and politics play important roles. There are, therefore, many different options available to the American people and to the Congress.

While redistribution of income in terms of income classes is of vital concern to economists and some of the American people, redistribution of income over one's lifetime is probably of interest to fewer economists but to more working people. The average head of family is concerned about the distribution of his or her income over time for such purposes as to purchase a home, to provide for accidents, disability or premature death or for retirement and medical costs, and, in many cases, to meet the cost of educating his or her children.

Because of the nature of the relationship between private and public sector in this country, the resolution of the crucial issues in income maintenance has been related more to the philosophy underlying this relationship than to income redistribution. It is therefore essential, in my opinion, for us to comprehend the larger context within which our social welfare programs and expenditures operate rather than judging them solely in relation to the way they affect the Lorenz curve.

I first should like to summarize briefly what has happened in the past twenty-five years in our expenditures for health, education, and welfare in both the public and the private sector. I believe the size and nature of existing obligations and expenditures will determine the choice of options for future policy in health, social security, and welfare reform.

Table 1
PUBLIC AND PRIVATE EXPENDITURES FOR SOCIAL WELFARE PURPOSES, 1950 AND 1975, AS PERCENTAGE OF GROSS NATIONAL PRODUCT

Net Total	1950 (13.4%)	1975 (27.3%)	Increase, 1975 over 1950 (2.04 times)
Income maintenance	4.1	10.7	2.61 times
Health	4.6	8.3	1.80 "
Education	4.1	6.9	1.68 "
Welfare and other services	.8	1.7	2.13 "

Source: Alfred M. Skolnik and Sophie R. Dales, "Social Welfare Expenditures, 1950-75," *Social Security Bulletin,* vol. 39, no. 1 (January 1976), p. 19.

The Growth in Expenditures, Public and Private [1]

In 1975 all expenditures, public and private, for health, education, and welfare were equivalent to 27.6 percent of the gross national product. Eliminating duplication resulting from the use of cash payments to purchase medical care and educational services produces a net figure of 27.3 percent.

In 1950, the comparable figures were 13.6 and 13.4 percent. In absolute figures the total grew from $35.3 billion in 1950 to $388.7 billion in 1975.

The change in the components is shown in Table 1.

Private expenditures in 1975 represented about 27 percent of the total. During the twenty-five-year period public expenditures as a share of the total moved from 65.9 percent to 72.7 percent. The share of public expenditures moved up in health primarily as a result of Medicare and Medicaid while the share of private expenditures in income maintenance moved up a bit as a result of the increase in private pension and related plans. The share in education remained relatively unchanged at about 85 percent.

Some Options in Social Policy in 1976–81

I have selected for my discussion here some of the principal options still open for debate and decision in three major areas of social policy. These areas are national health insurance, social security financing, and welfare reform. I have not prepared definitive answers on the options discussed, which would have required a paper about five times the length of this one.

[1] Alfred M. Skolnik and Sophie R. Dales, "Social Welfare Expenditures, 1950-75," *Social Security Bulletin,* vol. 39, no. 1 (January 1976), pp. 3-20.

Options in National Health Insurance. I believe it is fair to say that there is now widespread agreement on the general principle that everyone in the nation should be covered against all or a large part of medical costs. This decision has been reached after years of experimentation with both private and public insurance arrangements. The American public is very insurance-minded and appears to support the extension of insurance covering medical costs.[2]

It is significant that at this time there is no substantial organized movement in the United States advocating the establishment of a public medical service program such as in Great Britain, the Soviet Union, or several other countries.

There are, however, two major policy areas where there are differences of opinion about national health insurance: (1) whether the insurance coverage should involve deductibles and coinsurance in order to place upon the individual some financial responsibility or whether the coverage should be for first-dollar costs; and (2) the respective roles of the public and private sectors in implementing universal and comprehensive coverage.

Before analyzing these two controversial areas, I should like to point out two areas in which I sense there is general agreement: (1) that any overall plan should include persons of low income, and the costs for these persons should be the responsibility primarily of the federal government; and (2) that the scope of medical care coverage should be comprehensive and include home, office, and institutional services with incentives for noninstitutional and outpatient care. A review of the various proposals introduced in Congress indicates that these are the only two major areas of agreement. In addition, there is an implied recognition that to achieve these objectives some federal legislation is necessary and that there are additional costs to the federal budget.

The controversy over deductibles and coinsurance is a longstanding one. Those who favor them argue that they reinforce personal responsibility for meeting part of the costs, cut down on unnecessary use of scarce services, and reduce insurance costs. Those who oppose them argue that they retard early access to medical care, retard preventive services, increase administrative costs, and cause an increase in overall health costs.

There is both a deductible and a coinsurance feature in the present Medicare program, and these features are widespread in private health insurance policies. Nevertheless, it is also possible to purchase insurance coverage which will cover some or all of the deductibles and coinsurance. In fact, it is now possible to over-insure—that is, by purchasing more than one private policy an individual can receive more than out-of-pocket costs.

It would be possible for Congress to enact major medical insurance coverage such as the Long-Ribicoff proposal which provides for substantial deductibles and

---

[2] For an examination of the tax burden at representative income levels under four different national health insurance proposals, see Bridger M. Mitchell and William B. Schwartz, "The Financing of National Health Insurance," *Science,* vol. 192 (May 14, 1976), pp. 621-29.

a coinsurance provision but allows first-dollar coverage to be handled by private insurance. In this case individuals would have complete or almost complete coverage for all medical care costs. Another option would be the provision of medical care coverage for mothers and children without any deductible or coinsurance with a family limit on out-of-pocket costs.

The public sector/private sector issue is much more fundamental and complex than the deductible/coinsurance issue, and the resolution of the public/private problem may set a pattern for many years, as with the federal/state pattern set for unemployment insurance in 1935. The major options as I see them in connection with the public/private sector issue are these:

(1) A system of requiring employers to provide a defined level of benefits for employees and their dependents through private insurance. This is similar to the plan proposed by the Nixon administration, the insurance profession, and the medical profession.

(2) A system of providing for collection of the contributions and payment of the bills through the public sector. This is similar to the Kennedy-Corman bill and is supported by labor organizations.

(3) A system of providing for the collection of the contributions through the public sector with payment of the bills through the private sector. This is the model used by Medicare and could be used under (2).

(4) A system requiring employers to provide *basic* benefits with a public system for major medical benefits ("catastrophic" coverage) as in (2) or (3).

(5) A system requiring employers to provide *basic* benefits with a public system for all aged persons, all children under age eighteen, for the birth of children, and for major medical benefits as in (2) or (3).

(6) Under each of these five, an additional option could be given for each state to decide whether it wished to choose a different option for the people within the state. For example, a state could decide that it wished all bills to be paid for by: (1) a private insurance company, (2) a nonprofit health agency, (3) a state agency, or (4) the Medicare agency.

In the consideration of these options, a major policy issue is, Should one comprehensive plan be adopted at a given time or should an incremental phased plan be adopted? One option, for instance, would be to put into operation a comprehensive program in the following steps:

(1) Extension of Medicare to persons between sixty and sixty-five and to all disabled persons receiving social security benefits—about six months after enactment, with a family limitation on out-of-pocket costs. These changes along with some broadening of the scope of benefits could be implemented promptly and efficiently since they would be an extension of the present system.

(2) A single federal system for low-income persons replacing a large part of the existing Medicaid program—about eighteen months after enactment. There would probably still have to be a residual federal-state program for those services

(such as dental care or intermediate nursing home care) which might not be included under the federal program.

(3) A comprehensive program for those under age eighteen and for prenatal, childbirth, and postnatal care—about two years after enactment, with no deductibles or coinsurance.

(4) A major medical coverage (sometimes called "catastrophic" coverage)— about two years after enactment.

(5) Coverage of all other aspects—about three or four years after enactment.

Options in Social Security Financing. In this discussion of the financing of social security I am attempting to isolate, as far as possible, the financing questions from those relating to revisions in the benefit structure. There are a substantial number of important questions relating to the benefit provisions, but these would take us into other complex issues. I shall, however, deal later with the question of changes in the retirement age. But here I propose to discuss the general question of the way to finance the costs of the existing social security program.

When the social security system was being considered in 1935, the original plan submitted by the President's Committee on Economic Security envisioned a financing structure which involved a direct government subsidy from general revenues beginning in 1965. The estimated federal contribution was about 28 percent of benefit payments in 1975 and about 35 percent in 1980.[3]

This plan was opposed by Secretary of the Treasury Henry Morgenthau, who did not favor a general revenue contribution to the system. A substitute plan was adopted, based on the principle that the system would be wholly self-supporting from contributions and interest from the reserve fund. In 1980 the interest from the reserve fund was intended to yield about 40 percent of the cost of the benefits.

Both the proposed plan and the 1935 law contemplated a schedule of contributions which increased over a period of years in order to enable the economic system to adjust to the cost. During World War II it was decided by Congress to postpone the scheduled rise in the contributions and an amendment was included in the law to authorize a government subsidy if needed at some future time. This amendment (the Vandenberg-Murray amendment), enacted in 1944, was repealed in 1950. Since that time the system has been on a pay-as-you-go basis with a modest contingency reserve fund which at the beginning of the recent downswing of business was equal to less than one year's benefit payments.

During the past several years there have been a number of issues raised on the financing of social security:

(1) There has been an attack on the regressivity of the payroll tax, led largely by economists who favor financing of the program from general revenues or who favor exemptions from the tax in relation to family circumstances as in the federal

---

[3] U.S. Committee on Economic Security, *Social Security in America* (Washington, D.C., 1937), p. 212.

income tax. The rebuttal to this argument is that, taken as a whole, the system of taxes and benefits is not regressive and that any general revenue financing must be considered in a broader context of policy affecting the entire social welfare system.

(2) There has been a concern that the tax on low-income and blue-collar workers is very heavy and in most cases greater than what these individuals pay in income tax. The pressure here is for a reduction in the cost on these individuals and pressure for increasing the cost on higher-income persons. One development has been the increase in the maximum earnings base for contributions and benefits from the $3,000 limit in 1939 to $15,300 in 1976, with pressure for further increases in the next few years to $24,000 or $30,000.

It should be noted in passing that the federal tax law was amended for the year 1975 to enable individuals with earned income of $4,000 or less to receive a tax credit of 10 percent, which is approximately the amount of the employee and employer contribution under the social security system. In addition, individuals with earned income between $4,000 and about $7,000 could receive a credit which phases out at about $8,000 of earned income. In this way, to some extent, the Congress responded to the argument on the burden on low-income persons. This tax credit would have to be extended by Congress for 1976 and succeeding years. It now only applies to taxpayers with dependents.

(3) This pressure for a higher maximum earnings base has been countered by opposition that it would cut into the private sector area where private pension plans operate, result in an increase in social security benefits, provide a "windfall" to higher-income individuals, and discourage private savings by higher-income individuals.

(4) At the present time, the expenditures under the social security system exceed the contributions, and the difference is made up from withdrawals from the reserve fund. The newspapers characterize the present situation as the "bankruptcy" of the program, thus creating anxiety among the 32 million beneficiaries, the 100 million contributors, and the business community. Economists respond by saying this is just the kind of economic situation in which withdrawals from the reserve fund are appropriate, that no increase in contributions of any kind to the system should be levied during the economic recession, and that any kind of resolution of the system's financial problems can be deferred for a while.

On the other hand, President Ford has proposed that the short-range financial problems of the system should be met by an increase in the contribution *rate* upon employers and employees. This proposal has been opposed in Congress because it would impose a heavier burden on low-income earners than on those with higher incomes. On the other hand, the opposition to both an increase in the maximum earnings base and any general revenue subsidy has resulted in a stalemate which serves to assure the continuation of the "bankruptcy" anxiety.

(5) An important complicating factor in the solution of the short-range problems is the periodic publication of long-range cost estimates of the system that are appreciably above present costs. In part this is due to the future reduction in the birth rate estimated from extrapolations of the present trend and in part to conservative estimates of future economic growth based upon present pessimistic attitudes. The long-range cost estimates are subject to a substantial margin of error and need not be resolved in our dealing with the shorter-range problems.

(6) The social security amendments of 1972 made a significant change in the program by providing for an automatic increase in benefits tied to an increase in the cost of living and an automatic increase in the maximum earnings base and retirement test based on increases in wages. In addition, the legislation included an unintended error by "coupling" together price and wage increases, thereby producing benefits higher than are justifiable and costs higher than intended. Hence, there is general acceptance of the need for an amendment to "decouple" the benefits—a course of action which will probably reduce the long-range costs by about 1 percent of payrolls. On the other hand, the increase in benefits under present wage-price conditions does not make the financing of the system in the short run any less difficult.

(7) There is a concern about the impact of social security financing on savings, investment, and economic growth and about the relationship between the social security system and private pension plans. Pervasive and long-run questions of this sort must be explored, along with many other factors in the larger total saving-investment-economic growth and tax alternatives.[4]

In summary, the situation at the present time seems to me to be as follows:

(1) Legislation should be enacted as soon as possible to deal with the short-range financial situation but the date of any new contributions should be postponed until 1978 so as to avoid any adverse impact on economic recovery. In addition the changes should be phased in over several years.

(2) The existing law provides for the establishment of an advisory council to be set up after February 1977. The existence of this council would enable the Congress to consider the longer-range problems and possible changes in the benefit provisions.

(3) Consideration of changes to provide general revenue financing for social security should also involve calculating the cost of general revenue financing for national health insurance and welfare reform and comparing it with future overall tax yields, economic growth, and other priorities.

Options in Welfare Reform. There is one similarity between welfare reform and national health insurance: there is widespread support for the general principle

---

[4] For a review of some of the recent financial and benefit alternatives in social security, see *Reports of the Quadrennial Advisory Council on Social Security,* House Document No. 94-75, 94th Congress, 1st session, March 10, 1975. This council was appointed in 1974.

and wide disagreement on all the essential elements necessary to implement the principle. In both welfare reform and national health insurance, there are a wide variety of plans and provisions, and there probably will be still more plans suggested.

Several factors seem to indicate that welfare reform will not be a "one-shot" matter. Some of the proposed solutions involve a substantial additional cost to the federal government. With the problems involved in financing social security, unemployment insurance, and other programs, it is doubtful whether a thorough and comprehensive reform is feasible in one step.

Moreover, it appears that a really satisfactory solution of the problem of income levels for a federal welfare reform program cannot be achieved without solving the problems of food stamps and Medicaid eligibility. In fact, welfare reform would be facilitated if Medicaid were absorbed into some kind of national health program either previously or simultaneously.

The basic element in any welfare reform is the establishment of a nationwide standard payment. It is clear that what is acceptable and needed for New York is too high for Mississippi and what is acceptable for Mississippi is too low for New York. Any plan which is likely to be adopted would involve a compromise between these two levels with the likelihood that the standard will be toward the lower level and necessitate supplementation by the states for a number of years. One option would be to establish a given level of payment but provide for automatic increases over a five- or ten-year period to reach the desired level.

A much more difficult problem to solve is the relationship of the basic benefit to the incentive to work. Most economists urge that any person who works have only one-half of his or her earnings subtracted from the basic benefit. Thus, if the basic benefit for a family of four persons were $5,000 a year, an individual earning $9,000 a year would receive $500 in benefits for a total of $9,500 in annual income plus any income exempted as "work expenses." Such a plan would not only be costly but would also involve millions who do not now receive a federal payment. In order to provide a reasonable basic benefit for a mother with three children who cannot or should not be required to work, there must be a costly plan to accommodate a reasonable incentive to work. Otherwise, the basic benefit for the nonworking head of family would be inadequate to provide a reasonable incentive to work at a more reasonable cost.

This dilemma could be resolved by establishing two different plans: one for families with a working member, the other for families where the head cannot or should not be required to work. This double-headed plan may involve some difficult marginal problems.

Most students who have studied plans to provide a basic income in lieu of the existing welfare system have recommended that it be administered by the Internal Revenue Service as part of the income tax collection system. I am sure the IRS is not overjoyed at this vote of confidence since they are understaffed for carrying out their present responsibilities. The assignment to administer a basic income supplement would require not only millions of additional income tax forms to handle but also millions of clients, who are unfamiliar with concepts such as adjusted gross income, deductions, credits, and similar matters, to service.

The states might well be encouraged to experiment with a real plan. This could be done by amending the present welfare law to authorize four states to adopt one of the suggested plans and to receive federal matching for the additional cost. We could then see what the bugs were and how to eliminate them before involving the whole nation in a new and untried system.

Concluding Remarks

My observations in this paper may be highly frustrating to economists. I have not discussed the options which would make our income maintenance programs less regressive or more progressive. Over the past forty years such a direct approach to the problem has been unsuccessful. Most congressional leaders and most presidents have not approached the problem in that fashion. There are some indications that a change is under way. Nevertheless, I believe that the major decisions in the three areas I have discussed are not likely to be based solely upon income distribution factors. Broader influences are likely to come into play, even though underneath all these influences such elements as incentives, savings, and economic growth will be involved.

COMMENTARIES

Edgar K. Browning

Dean Cohen indicates that he is going to limit his attention to reform proposals in three areas and make no attempt to provide definitive answers. To provide definitive answers, he pointed out, would have required a paper perhaps five times as long as the one he wrote. Frankly I would have preferred to read a paper five times as long if it provided definitive answers to anything in the area of income redistribution. But I doubt that the approach Dean Cohen is using in discussing the various options for reform would have provided definitive answers regardless of the length of the work.

Basically, the approach is to examine each area where we already have a welfare policy or where there is one proposed to see if minor alterations in the policies would improve them. I call this a piecemeal approach to reform of the welfare system. It seems to me that it invariably leads one to take a narrow view and to ignore many of the common factors involved in different welfare programs.

There is a common denominator in all three policy areas that Dean Cohen discussed in his paper. That common denominator is that the motivation for the reforms is to redistribute income downward. In other words, the proposals he discusses are, it seems clear, largely motivated by a desire for greater equality. Once this is recognized, it is clear that these various programs must be considered as alternatives to one another. Is it better to cut social security taxes on the poor, *or* to raise welfare payments, *or* to enact national health insurance? Dean Cohen looks at each of these policies separately and does not seem to realize that these proposals are alternative ways to redistribute income. Which is the best way? Dean Cohen does not attempt to answer this most fundamental question.

What he does is adopt a piecemeal approach that often leads to his ignoring the ways many existing programs interact and overlap. This, I think, can often give a somewhat distorted view of the problem. For example, in his discussion of welfare reform when he mentions negative income taxation, he does not seem aware of the fact that many low-income families already face marginal tax rates greater than the 50 percent figure he mentions. He does not seem aware of the fact that adding a negative income tax to the present system—at least a negative income tax of any size—would invariably raise tax rates to prohibitively high levels for many low-income families.

He also seems unaware that the reforms of the social security tax he discusses are really quantitatively trivial questions. He discusses the possibility of lowering or eliminating the tax burden on poor families by reforming the social security tax through the use of exemptions, or some such device. As a matter of fact, the burden of the social security tax on officially poor families is probably no more than 2 percent of their income when cash and in-kind transfers are counted. The reason is that the social security tax only affects earnings, while cash and in-kind transfers, which are not taxed, are approximately four to five times as large as the earnings of the poor. So any reform of the social security tax in the name of helping the poor is really a trivial question.

The point I would like to emphasize is that it is extremely difficult to take a broad view of the welfare system in this country. This difficulty is due to the fact that the system is so complex no one can understand it fully. The present system is composed of perhaps a dozen quantitatively important programs, and another 200 or so minor programs that interact and overlap in ways so bewildering that no one has ever been able to put together a coherent overview of the whole system. At least it is clear that nowhere in the literature is there a coherent picture of how all of these programs fit together and what their overall consequences are.

For example, no one, to my knowledge, knows with any degree of accuracy how much income is redistributed annually to low-income families. One can find a number of very crude estimates—in fact, I have developed some of my own—but these estimates are recognized as extraordinarily rough, and it is obvious that we really do not know exactly how much redistribution is going on in the present system.

I find it interesting that this topic was hardly discussed at all at this conference. We are discussing how far in the direction of equality we want to move, and yet there is no agreement as to exactly how far we have already gone. How can we talk sensibly about redistributing more if we do not know how much is already being redistributed? To repeat, it is the complexity of the current welfare system that leads to our inability to understand what exactly is the present state of affairs.

I think the piecemeal approach to policy analysis that Dean Cohen and many others have used is not likely to improve matters much because it leads to neglect of the most important questions. It leads one to ignore many substantive questions such as whether a well-designed negative income tax would be a suitable alternative to virtually all existing programs. I think that most people, on examining (or trying to examine) the way the present system works, recognize that this would be an attractive alternative. It has the advantages of smaller administrative costs, probably smaller distortions, and, I suspect, somewhat greater equity in the distribution of transfers among low-income families.

These advantages have, of course, been widely discussed in the literature on negative income taxation, and I do not have space to go into great detail on any of these matters here. I would, however, like to emphasize two points. First, as long as we follow a piecemeal approach to policy analysis, trying to patch up each one of innumerable and uncountable programs, we are unlikely to move towards any obviously more sensible type of transfer system.

Second, there is one frequently overlooked advantage to a simple welfare system like a negative income tax, and it is, to my mind, one of the most important advantages: a simple system could be understood. Under the present system, it is clear that members of Congress and the American public do not realize how much redistribution is actually occurring, or what the consequences of further redistribution would be. From a political viewpoint, it makes a lot of sense to try to use policies having easily understood consequences. Democratic political institutions do not work well when the public cannot understand what is going on.

I realize that simplicity in the welfare system comes at some cost: we would lose the advantage of being able to balance benefits and costs precisely in each of dozens of policies. Professor Feldstein emphasized the importance of having numerous policies in the welfare area. But when our imperfect political process appears unable to achieve an optimal balancing of benefits and costs anyway, we might be sacrificing little by moving toward a simpler system.

Let me turn briefly to Professor Nisbet's paper. In reading it, I was reminded of Joseph Schumpeter's book, *Capitalism, Socialism and Democracy*. As may probably be recalled, Schumpeter raised the question: "Can capitalism survive?" And his answer was: "No. I do not think it can." [1] As I understand Professor Nisbet's paper, he is raising a similar question: Can freedom survive? And his answer is much the same as Schumpeter's.

Professor Nisbet clearly interprets the topic of this session somewhat differently from the way I do: his paper is concerned with the political and social trends and where they are leading us. He believes they are leading us along the road to serfdom, to use Hayek's trenchant phrase. As I understand him, the major reason is the existence of a large intelligentsia whose members are predominantly egalitarian. Indeed, this may be a factor in determining political trends, but I think there are forces at work that he neglects. In short, he isolates one force in the political process and claims that this force overwhelms all other influences. This is not very satisfactory as a theory of how the political process functions.

I think the real interest in his paper is in the questions it raises, rather than in the answers it gives. For example, he clearly believes that existing political institutions are not working very well in the area of redistribution. Why is this so? Do political institutions work better in other areas, so that there must be some peculiarity about redistribution that causes the process to go haywire here? Are there reforms of the political process which would improve matters? Unfortunately,

---

[1] Joseph A. Schumpeter, *Capitalism, Socialism and Democracy*, 2nd ed. (New York: Harper & Brothers, 1947), p. 61.

Professor Nisbet does not consider these questions, but instead simply concludes that things will continue to get worse.

I think the questions Professor Nisbet raises are important, and I wish we had the time to pursue them further. But, even if I did have five times as much time as I have to spend in considering the questions Professor Nisbet's paper suggests, I would be unable to arrive at any definitive answers either.

Henry J. Aaron

This concluding session of the conference has been given two papers that could hardly be less alike. In response to the question, "Where do we go from here?" one seems to answer, "toward philosophical speculation," and the other by answering, "toward legislation." Actually, we need both, but not, I think, of exactly the kind suggested in the two papers. I shall devote most of my time to Professor Nisbet's paper, because it is longer and because in my opinion, it is more seriously and obviously flawed than Dean Cohen's.

I divide my comments on the paper into three unequal parts. First, Nisbet poses the issue of equality in a highly dramatic, and I think unproductive, fashion. We are asked to choose between a completely egalitarian world, a leveled society of revolutionary equality, and a world of equality only before the law in which any outcome is acceptable, so long as it occurs under law. On the one hand, we may observe property rights and cherish liberty; on the other hand, we may choose equality and sink gurgling into a bureaucratic morass, our freedoms choked.

While such an approach lends itself to colorful contrasts and urbane rhetoric, it is ahistorical and (I think) essentially irresponsible. It is embarrassing to have to point out that we already redistribute income, and that the choice for both ethics and policy is not between complete equality or cessation of redistribution, but rather between doing a bit more or a bit less than we do now to deal with specific kinds of problems—health care, housing, income support during old age, unemployment, or periods of grossly inadequate income. Unfortunately, Nisbet's suggestions that we do not redistribute substantial amounts of income make the statement of this obvious point necessary. It may be philosophical fun to joust with Rawls, as is done in the paper, or to suggest that one can no more support a little equality than be a little bit pregnant, but to do so is frivolous. The evidence is palpable that we can redistribute without losing all freedom; that we can carry out some redistribution without excessively sacrificing efficiency. When Nisbet asserts that there are two contrasting philosophies of equality in the Western world —neither more nor less than two—he badly strains my capacity to take him seriously. For there are, in fact, many approaches to equality, most of them quite far removed from either of the pure types to which he directs our attention.

210

The American people have repeatedly ratified the modified welfare state that redistributes some income, and they continue to do so, in public opinion surveys and at the polls. The same public that mistrusts political and legislative leaders (who—not incidentally—committed criminal acts, lied repeatedly, and led the country into a bloody and futile war) also indicates support for social security, for transfer payments, for better health protection, for full employment, in short, for the very essence of the moderate redistributionist ethic which Nisbet would have us think has fallen on hard times. The issue, in fact, is not whether to redistribute, but how much, and the consensus seems to be that we should do about what we are doing, or perhaps a bit more.

In fact, it is simply impossible not to redistribute income in the modern nation state. So long as the government provides any services at all and collects taxes to pay for them, some citizens will gain more than others and some may lose. This will be true no matter what the services provided, or what the taxes collected. It is true, in particular, even if, as Nisbet suggests, taxes are imposed only to collect revenue. The nonredistributive state, like the unicorn, is a myth. Nisbet may be suggesting that we should blind ourselves to the redistributive effects, but I cannot really believe that he supports such an attitude of contrived ignorance. He may be arguing that all acts of the state should be kept to a minimum in order to hold down the redistributive effects of government. But even then, redistribution is inevitable, whether we like it or not. He may think equality, per se, is a bad thing but he never quite says so, reserving his attacks for the consequences of trying to redistribute and his scorn for those who advocate it.

Which brings me to a second point—the tone and manner of the paper. In Nisbet's hands, the desire to reduce inequality becomes a religious movement and motivated by envy, almost indistinguishable from leveling. Its advocates suffer from an adversary mentality.

I can only conclude that Nisbet sees different egalitarians from those I know. Most of the ones I know are motivated not by envy but by a sense that equality of opportunity has not yet been achieved. They even think it is worth fighting for such equality and feel genuine satisfaction from waging that fight. At their best, they live the statement by Camus, "I belong to the world through all my gestures, to men through all my pity and gratitude." Some egalitarians are hypocrites and some are motivated by envy. But for each one of those, I know a hypocritical advocate of the status quo guilty of callousness. All such motives are ugly, but fortunately they are not typical, and, in any case, we must still evaluate actions.

Finally, Nisbet's paper is marred by elementary logical and factual errors and by passages that substitute rhetoric for argument. The allegation that revolutions stress equality is used to support the absurd proposition that the desire to reduce inequality is necessarily revolutionary. He seems unaware that the federal sector, measured as a fraction of full employment GNP, is almost the same size as it was in 1960, before the Great Society was ever invented. Those passionate for less inequality of income are dismissed as followers of a new religion, but equality before the law seems to come to us from time's anvil a hard and perfect truth. In Nisbet's telling, the negative income tax was opposed by the clerisy of equality. In fact, support of the NIT is perhaps the best single indication of support for additional income redistribution.

Having read Nisbet's paper before I read Dean Cohen's, I was reminded of the old story about the beauty contest with two entrants. The judges took one look at the first entrant, and gave the prize to the second.

Unfortunately, the second contestant is wearing an overcoat that hides his philosophy, and all we can see are his policies. Being on the same platform with Wilbur Cohen reminds me of Gottfried Haberler's famous introduction of the prolific author and editor Professor Seymour Harris at his retirement dinner: "I'd like to present Seymour Harris," Professor Haberler said, "whose books you have all either read or written."

I would like to comment on Dean Cohen's remarks about social welfare problems, most of which he has either solved or created, for no single person deserves more credit or blame for existing social welfare legislation to the reform of which he addresses himself. My judgment is that the credit vastly outweighs the blame.

The great strength and weakness of Cohen's paper has been that he has largely ignored philosophical issues of the kind Nisbet addresses. He has also ignored the issues of economic efficiency—he calls them incentives, saving, and economic growth—that obsess economists. He has focused, instead, on redistribution between the old and the young, the employed and the unemployed, the well and the sick and disabled, widowed, divorced and deserted mothers and the rest of us. Income inequality—a palpable issue to healthy, well-fed, non-aged intellectuals—may be an abstraction to many others, while poor kids, untended illness and impoverished old age are real to everyone. These matters are related to income inequality, to be sure, and redistribution among these groups constitutes the major part of such redistribution as we have today.

But Cohen's paper, like his entire career, is more or less silent on the issue of income redistribution. He does not tell us whether he wants more or less; he does not use his considerable political standing to promote distributional issues in the public consciousness, and I do not know why. I am sure he is not indifferent to inequality, but I do not know whether he believes that income inequality just is not as important as are income needs of the aged sick and one-parent families or whether he would like to reduce inequality but feels that direct efforts will not succeed.

This vagueness is a strength because legislation based on it can unite people who would be divided on income redistributional issues. Indeed, the inefficiency he alluded to this afternoon was a source of strength when programs were few and expenditures low, because it broadened support.

But inefficiency is now a weakness, and I think vagueness on the issue of distribution is becoming a weakness because it has led to increasingly serious anomalies in the social welfare system. It was an approach that sufficed when the coverage of social welfare legislation was incomplete and overlaps were few. But coverage is now extensive and overlaps are numerous and bewildering. Expenditures are high and getting higher. The cost of inefficiency has gone up accordingly.

Once one recognizes that problems in food stamps, Medicaid and welfare reform are tied to one another, as are those of veteran's pensions, black lung benefits, unemployment insurance, and the tax code, and that all are related to income distribution, the need for directly facing the problems of income distribution is evident.

I had hoped Dean Cohen would give us his thoughts on distribution, but he did not. He continues to believe that an issue quite properly ignored in the past should be ignored now. But I agree with the premise of this conference that we should directly consider the issue of income distribution.

Alan A. Walters

As I heard Professor Nisbet's survey of the prospects of Western man's freedoms and as he generated the gloomy forecasts of their demise, I could only nod assent again and again. The fascination of "equality" with its ethical preemptions, its opportunities for a splendid display of moral superiority (indeed of self-righteousness), its possibilities for expiating guilt feelings, and above all its idealistic, romantic and sentimental appeal to "all that is best in man" has created a force which liberals (and I use that term in its literal, old-fashioned sense) seem ill-equipped to counter. So irresistible is the tide that the very term *inequality* carries with it a stigma of disgrace—an undesirable state brought about by man's cupidity and society's indifference.[1] Furthermore I suspect that Professor Nisbet is entirely correct in interpreting the modest reactions against centralized power as too feeble and too thin to make any substantial and lasting effect on the hegemony of clerisy and bureaucracy. There *is* a hope—but that is all.

It is tempting for one who has lived in Britain these many years to illustrate the path of a society, similar in culture and institutions to the United States, that has pursued egalitarianism (sometimes resolutely, sometimes casually) for many years. Perhaps we lead the United States by some ten or twelve years—but the evidence is that the United States is catching up. In Britain all the ingredients described by

---

[1] The phrase *inequality of income and wealth,* embalmed in all economic textbooks, naturally suggests that anything other than equality is second best. Attempts by noted liberals to substitute the less emotionally charged term *income differences* in place of *income inequalities* have not met with any observable success.

Professor Nisbet are to be found in larger measure and more virulent form. The amalgam of academic and bureaucrat (still quaintly called a civil or public servant) and politician and their contempt for the businessman—or more particularly the enterprising profit-seeking businessman—has been made clear in the edicts of governments.[2] He has been taxed to near bankruptcy, nationalized and banished, or controlled into that twilight sector where private business subsists only by leave of bureaucratic indulgence. If he behaves—that is to say if he conforms to price controls, wage controls, planning restrictions, investment "suggestions," and the long list of other unknown restrictions—then he may be allowed to continue his unsavory and demeaning pursuit.

Of course even in the United Kingdom there are strange signs to be seen and odd noises to be heard in the land. There are revolts against the leveling of schools and the allocation of pupils by a centralized bureaucracy. There are vigorous complaints against the escalating bureaucracy and its inflation-proof pensions. But nevertheless the egalitarian circus still rolls down the road. In the finance bill that is at present proceeding through the Houses of Parliament there is yet another wonderful attempt to prevent people making themselves rich—by imposing taxes, at horrendously high marginal rates, on what an American would call fringe benefits, such as occupation of a company apartment, even on business. However, it has been calculated that if such taxable income were assessed for cabinet ministers, both the prime minister and the chancellor of the exchequer would receive *negative* money salaries after tax; the tax payments on their occupation, of 10 and 11 Downing Street, and their respective country houses would exceed their ministerial stipends. Imposts at more than 100 percent rates— certainly in real terms—have not been uncommon in the United Kingdom, and have been "justified" on egalitarian grounds. Now indeed the squeeze may cause the pips to squeak.

There is, however, one point where I would like to push Professor Nisbet's argument further. I do not think that Tocqueville was correct in contending that democracy leads to egalitarianism. Certainly it is true that there will be a redistribution of wealth associated with considerable expropriation, but not necessarily a redistribution towards greater equality. Consider, for example, the archetypical democracy where government power is unlimited by constitution or convention or custom and where the government is in the control of a simple majority. Then in order to obtain authority in this land, a contender for power will be induced to offer 51 percent of the electorate virtually 100 percent of the national income in order to win votes. Almost half the electorate will be expropriated to provide the bribe for the government's supporters. Of course such unconstrained democracies do not last very long; power is soon disposed from the barrel of a gun—as we have seen in many countries. The basic lesson is that democratic societies must,

---

[2] It was immortalized by Mr. Heath when, as prime minister, he condemned the "unacceptable face of capitalism."

by custom or constitution, severely limit the power of government to tax and expropriate and to control and regulate. To ensure a free society, government must be in chains.

These reflections lead me to doubt the wisdom of attempting to rationalize a Rawlsian justice. For in the very nature of the contract which individuals are supposed to form as the cement of society, Rawls has argued that no one knows when or if he will be the least favored. It is the turn of fortune's wheel. But it is too easy to arrange coalitions based on class, religion, race, or simply mutual interests to form an expropriating majority. Fortune's wheel can be fixed. (We note that in the process the production of useful goods and services will decline rapidly; why should one labor if the fruits are to be taxed or taken away? Political activity becomes the most rewarding pursuit and engages virtually all men.) Of course we shall never reach such a parlous state of affairs—but the approximation of many new democracies to some similar forms of tyranny should give us pause before dismissing such reflections as irrelevant.

The process envisioned by Professor Nisbet, however, is not my nightmare of a people's democracy. Characteristically it is the slow inexorable suffocation of our liberties by the bureaucracy under the heel of humanitarianism. That invisible government, which in Britain takes the form of political appointee boards of nationalized corporations, administrative courts such as rent tribunals to fix "fair" (well below market) rents, planning bodies, and the immense and pervading power of the great departments of state to penalize, punish, and promote, has not merely captured the "commanding heights" (government spending now accounts for 62 percent of total GNP) but is suffocating the productive plains. But one would be naive to suppose that an egalitarian society is the real aim of this colossus. Indeed the bureaucracy is designed to generate greater inequalities and additional "problems"—housing problems, pollution problems, welfare problems, and so on.[3] Although such inequalities and newly spawned "problems" are the result of the political-bureaucratic process and, one might expect, are consistent with expectations, the plain facts of life tell us that the egalitarian hopes are always frustrated. New fortunes are made by those with inside knowledge or political pull; the poverty fighters do well, but somehow the poor seem to be left poor. The answer of the bureaucrats is inevitably a bigger and more highly paid bureaucracy, better to administer these egalitarian measures.

Often they get away with it, as one can see in Britain over the past decade or so. But sometimes they do not, especially when the scandal becomes more obvious and demonstrable, and when the normal attempt to cover up fails. While the free press continues there is at least a good chance that the pseudo-egalitarian

---

[3] Britain has an immense public housing sector, a system of rigidly controlled rents and tenures, and massive subsidies to housing in general and rental housing in particular. Britain has about an 850,000 "excess supply" of houses—and also approximately 1 million "homeless" persons; in order to deal with this problem there is a vast army of civil servants administering subsidies, contracting new house building, inspecting, and regulating rents and tenants.

measures will be exposed for what they are. The next step, however, is clearly the silencing of dissent; again this may be done in subtle ways by using the machine's immense patronage and promises of rewards and threats of punishments.[4]

But exposure of quack cures and the most effective accumulation of evidence on their malignant impact are unlikely to affect the fundamental drift towards the egalitarianizing bureaucracy. Modern egalitarianism is the product of emotional needs closely associated with personal interests. To do well and good at the same time *is* an achievement.

And, I believe, that there is another overriding reason. The levelers have put their faith in a simple idea with a messianic tone. The opponents have no such simple faith. On the whole they are pragmatic men who scorn simple ideologies. They are not much interested in ideas. Thus on the ideological front—and who can teach in any university and not appreciate how important ideas are shaping peoples' values and ambitions—the levelers have enjoyed a virtual monopoly.[5] And for this reason above all, I must join Professor Nisbet in his assessment of the sad prospects for our Western society.

Irving J. Goffman

It is somewhat uncomfortable being the only bureaucrat on this panel. However, Professor Nisbet's comments are gratifying in a way—during my six-month tenure in Washington thus far I have felt rather powerless and was delighted to read in the professor's paper that that was not really the case. In fact when I read his paper, I felt like a New York streetwalker suddenly told by Mayor Beame that not only is her profession legal but that it is the highest form of public service.

It is difficult—if not impossible—for the social scientist qua social scientist to criticize the artist, since the latter invokes the aid of the muses in his search for beauty while the former seeks truth based upon facts and logical formulations. Nisbet must be, I suspect, a frustrated poet, for his presentation this afternoon has absolutely nothing to do with the world as it is observed by the intellect. Poetic license permits all forms of unsupported and insupportable assertions and allegories—an admirable goal but nothing whatever to do with social policy in general or this conference's topic in particular. It is not so much his conclusions that offend me but rather his methodology of presenting a plethora of revealed doctrines which must have been targeted directly from the heavens to Morningside Heights. I do

---

[4] Again Britain has recently set an example in measures designed to create a closed shop in the profession of newspaper journalism—not to mention influential left-wing proposals that that news media should all be nationalized.

[5] Moreover, the young will find it in their personal interests to join the egalitarian clerisy; they are more likely to get well-paid inflation-proof jobs in the rapidly expanding bureaucracy. The bandwagon has developed its own impetus; on it rolls.

not know whether God revealed himself to Nisbet in a dream, but whatever his source, he has kept it a closely guarded secret. Either one blindly accepts the gospel according to St. Robert or else one simply dismisses it out of hand as the scriptures of a false prophet. I choose the latter, recognizing full well that I may regret it on the judgment day. But who are those intellectuals, politicians, and bureaucrats, who are not only members of the power elite but are vocal and clear in their insistence upon absolute economic equality?

Nisbet knows better than to foist his theology upon us. We have come together this week to find solutions to our social ills based upon learning and wisdom and not to be fed yet another dose of snake oil. In a pre-Adam Smith world, perhaps the clerisy of power did rest with the church and was perfectly egalitarian in its ultimate objectives, but that notion is at least 200 years out of date and 99 percent wrong.

It might be fun to debate Nisbet on his theories of history and the bureaucracy whereby otherwise decent men and women have been turned into fanatics chasing after power and equality. It might even be instructive if we were provided with even more good thoughts for the day, but it would not get us to the subject at hand—what lies ahead in income redistribution policy? Here, Dean Cohen's paper is more relevant and revealing.

On the whole, Cohen's presentation of the issues is sound, and while I suspect that I would disagree with him on how far we should go in certain areas, his detailing of the options is reasonable. What is particularly helpful about his paper is that it reminds us of the principal reasons why we engage in income transfers. First, we collectively insure ourselves over our life cycle to smooth out our income upon the occurrence of certain events such as retirement, death, unemployment. For a variety of reasons the caprice of the capital markets in the case of retirement income, the random nature of the event in the case of unemployment, we have decided to socialize the insurance function. Second, there is a humanitarian desire to sustain those whose own efforts—for one reason or another—are inadequate to bring them up to the level that we as a society deem to be necessary for basic consumption.

There are those—John Kenneth Galbraith and Christopher Jencks among them—who would argue for income transfers on the grounds that it is somehow unseemly that the rich are rich. But I agree with Professor Kristol, that equality for equality's sake is not a very strong force in this country, even among the option makers.

I noted the two reasons for income transfers partly to indicate to Cohen—I hope to his relief—that there are those in the economics profession and the analytic community of Washington and elsewhere who do recognize the social insurance function of income transfers. How can we not recognize that function when we compare the some $140 billion going through the cash social insurance programs

217

to the $25 to $30 billion going into the cash and near-cash welfare programs? It is quite clear where the society is placing its priorities.

While we should be careful to make the distinction between social insurance and income assistance, it is also important not to make the distinction too sharp. Most welfare reform proposals that call for a general income maintenance program are variants of Professor Friedman's negative income tax. We should remember that his concept, though it has earlier parallels, grew out of his work on lifetime income and income averaging in the positive tax system. Inherent in the negative income tax concept is the notion that we should smooth out the income flow of a rather large portion of the working population whose income floats above and then below the so-called breakeven point—that point in the income distribution where we divide entitlement for an income supplement from tax liability. Viewed in this manner, a negative income tax for at least some in the population is not much different from a social insurance program justified by the "earned right" concept.

On the other hand, we should remember that we have had a significant income redistribution or "welfare" component in our social insurance programs for many years. The replacement formula tilt in social security is the best example of this welfare in the guise of social insurance. Not that the commingling of welfare and wage replacement in social insurance is necessarily wrong, but, right or wrong, we should recognize that it is going on.

What is going to happen over the next several years is likely to be the result of the need to separate and rationalize these two functions. Now that the social security system has fully matured, we no longer have the situation in which every retiree is a relative winner. If we use as the alternative world a fair rate of return on investment, then roughly half the retired drawing social security will be losers and half winners. Given the fact that social insurance is, as we know, by and for the middle class, how long can the redistributional component in social security stay unnoticed and unquestioned, especially now that we have passed a supplemental security income program? I doubt that it will be for very long. One of the very important decisions will be the relative roles to be played by social security, supplemental security income, and private pensions and savings accounts, which have been encouraged and protected by increased federal regulation and tax preferences.

The so-called welfare mess continues without much improvement since the family assistance plan was shelved. It is true that the welfare system is now much less inadequate than it was then, given the growth in the in-kind benefits, especially food stamps. Though my staff and I have severe reservations about aspects of his methodology and his assumptions, Professor Browning is quite right in pointing out that we do not measure fully how far we have come in income redistribution to the bottom quintile. But we still have problems of horizontal inequity and federal-state relations that can only be solved by substantially overhauling the present patchwork system.

There exist obvious difficulties with the unemployment insurance system. Benefits were extended to sixty-five weeks during the recession partly because we lack a comprehensive cash income assistance program open to all low-income families. But, judged on the basis of household income and assets, this is an extremely expensive and unfocused way to help low-income people. It is equally true, of course, that the executive and the Congress—responding to messages being given out by a risk-averse middle class—were trying to protect total household income, lest significant portions of the middle class were to suffer a severe decline in life style and were forced to liquidate their assets.

Dissatisfaction with the tax system continues to be a running (often acrimonious) dispute, even though it appears that we are as unable to reform the income tax as we are unable to reform the welfare system, social security, or unemployment insurance.

And, finally, there is the debate over health insurance. Here again I think Cohen's comments are useful and I would like to restate them a bit differently.

On the one hand, there is the fear of "catastrophic" medical expense. I agree with Cohen that there is a strong middle-class constituency that wants (and in many cases needs) protection against this event just as much as the middle class has desired protection upon the events of retirement, death, disability, and unemployment. This is what I think we can fairly label the social insurance aspect of health insurance reform.

On the other hand, there is the equity issue of guaranteeing better access to health care for the low-income population. Here the parallels to welfare reform are obvious—some in the poverty and near-poverty populations are covered by Medicaid, even to an extent that I would argue is too generous, while others have virtually no coverage at all. In any event, the access to health care for low-income people is an income redistribution or welfare issue and should to some extent be distinguished from the social insurance issue of catastrophic expense coverage.

As is probably obvious from my comments until now, I believe that the issue of horizontal equity runs through all these areas—welfare, social security, unemployment insurance, health insurance, and tax reform. To a very large extent, it is our constant attempts to manipulate behavior and fine-tune equity that has resulted in the high marginal tax rates and work disincentives that Browning and other critics have focused upon. Ironically, it has been our attempts to negotiate equity on the basis of specialized characteristics that have led to the very severe inequities throughout the tax-transfer system. Here, Nisbet has a glimmer of a point—who wins from all these preferences and fine-tunings in the tax-transfer system? Let me quickly point out, it is not the bureaucrats. It may come as a surprise to Professor Nisbet, but one of the strongest constituencies for simplification of the tax-transfer apparatus and the elimination of all these horizontal inequities will be found in the Washington and state bureaucracies that administer the current farrago. If he so desires, my staff and I will be happy to introduce him to fellow bureaucrats at Health, Education, and Welfare, Labor, Treasury, and the Internal Revenue Service who will bear witness to my assertion. The winners are, of course, people more directly in the political process—senators, congressmen, and representatives of special interest groups. But the entire structure has become so complicated and inequitable overall that even among those people there is a growing movement to simplify the tax-transfer system and to make it more equitable.

Thus, let me suggest that what we are likely to witness over the next several years is a drive to change the following programs in the following ways:

First, there will be some sort of welfare reform along the lines of a negative income tax. Whether that reform comes about exactly as Friedman originally proposed remains to be seen. In my opinion, there are three likely outcomes: (1) a classic negative income tax with state supplements (Cohen is quite right to point out the necessity for state supplements in this model); (2) a two-tier federal negative income tax (such as the Canadians are considering) under which the aged, disabled, and single-parent families with children below a certain age receive a high guarantee with a high reduction rate, and other households receive relatively low benefits with a low reduction rate (presumably the breakevens for similarly sized households would be the same); or (3) a negative income tax that leaves so-called employables entirely out of the basic benefit but gives zero tax range equivalents to the household instead. It will not be easy to get the political process to decide which of these proposals it should adopt, but it is my prediction that one of these three approaches will be adopted. Let me add here a point on net costs. I do not think that the net federal cost will much exceed the amount of fiscal relief being given the states. Here I clearly depart from both Cohen's analysis of what is needed and Browning's fears about what will happen. I do not think that the federal price tag will much exceed $5 billion as an outside estimate.

Second, I see two things happening in social security. Primarily there will be a movement to adjust benefits so that *households* with similar lifetime earnings will be treated equally. This will not be easy to accomplish inasmuch as it demands taking on such controversial issues as the dependent's benefits, the treatment of two-earner families, coverage of government workers, and social security's relationship to the supplemental security income program. In addition, I sense the beginning of debate on the issue of vertical equity in social security. This is, of course, even more controversial, but I think that it is an inevitable debate given the passage of the supplemental security income program and the increased payroll tax rates necessary to finance the social security system. As the wage base and the rate go up, one is going to hear more questions asked by the top half of the population about that which they are buying in this so-called earned right program.

Third, while I am not optimistic that we will ever achieve a comprehensive tax reform that eliminates all the present horizontal inequities in the tax system, I suspect we will begin to see some movement in that direction. As should be clear from my comments, I do not expect to see much change in the progressivity of the average tax rate since I believe that the amount of additional redistribution in welfare reform or its health insurance analogue will be extensive.

In closing, let me return again to a comparison of our social insurance outlays of some $140 billion compared with some $40 billion in welfare. However regrettable those figures may seem to those who genuinely desire more equality in income distribution—the Lorenz curve devotees—they reveal a fundamental fact. We are a middle-class society with a great deal of income equality already achieved. Thus, it is predictable that most of our income security effort is in the social insurance programs. A rational and calculating middle class which is reasonably risk-averse is protecting its income over its life cycle. As Tocqueville pointed out, the principal drive for equality comes from the middle class. It is not a plot of a political-intellectual and bureaucratic clerisy of power. The so-called welfare state is here because the middle class wanted it. The task before us is to restructure its components and operations so that it is less grievously inequitable, so that people understand and agree to the correlation between their payments (made through whatever tax) and what they should expect to receive, so that its bureaucracies are reduced and made more objective in the criteria they apply, and so that the entire system operates to enhance liberty and economic productivity. These ends are not compatible with the welfare state, but to make them compatible will take cooler and more rational analysis than Professor Nisbet has given us and will take more of a willingness to upset conventional political wisdom than Dean Cohen seems to possess.

Permit me to conclude with a plea for unity among professionals interested in welfare reform. Let us strive for consensus, so that we prevent the debate which occurred at the time of the family assistance plan. In many ways Pogo was right when he said, "I have met the enemy and it is us." Conferences such as this one can assist greatly the ultimate outcome, if and when welfare becomes a serious political issue. Otherwise, I fear that none of us will have much impact on eventual policy. The late Bishop Pike summarized this most succinctly:

> One day, God called together the leaders of all of the major faiths:
> Ladies and Gentlemen, God said, I have a brilliant idea—
> Catholic: Is it ecumenical?
> Methodist: Is it moral?
> Baptist: Is it non-alcoholic?
> Jew: Is it Kosher?
> Quaker: Is it quiet?
> God: Oh! Forget it.

DISCUSSION

PROFESSOR NISBET: First, I should like to consider Mr. Aaron's comments on the amount of "redistribution" and my seeming unawareness of the fact that we have already redistributed. Of course, all history is in very large degree a process of redistribution. Call it mobility, call it dislocation, call it circulation of money, affluence, wealth, status, power—regardless what you call it, it is what history is about. But it is neither accurate nor fair to point to specific ad hoc welfare programs of the late 1920s and the 1930s and the New Deal—programs such as social security —and call them redistribution.

There has been redistribution ever since the Garden and the Fall, but we have been perhaps for a decade or two in an era in which the word *equality* or the word *redistribution* has taken on a dynamic sense. I do not recall that social security and unemployment insurance were originally justified in terms of the ethics of redistribution or the ethics of equality. I do not think they were.

I have no objection to a properly conducted assault on poverty. Poverty is its own degradation, its own disgrace. It is a horrifying thing. But why seek to bring it within the rhetoric of the new equality?

As for my implication of revolution in egalitarianism, Aaron is correct— I not only implied but also stated that when redistribution reaches a certain point, it becomes revolutionary. That seems to me elementary history. The essence of the French Revolution, for example, had very little to do with the few thousand individuals who were guillotined. It had little to do with *sans-culottes* running around the streets. It had everything to do with the legislation that was passed starting in 1790 in the national convention—the legislation on class, on family, on money, on property. This was largely egalitarian legislation, and when it had reached a certain point, a revolution was accomplished.

To label something a revolution does not necessarily make it one. The ideologues on the campuses in the 1960s said they were having a revolution, but, of course, they were not. They did not make one iota of difference in the basic structure of the university. Despite the rhetoric and window-breaking, no revolution was accomplished. But, by simply passing enough laws and setting up enough agencies in the name of redistribution or equality, a revolution may be accomplished before you know it.

I have carefully avoided, in my paper and my comments, the slightest suggestion that my word clerisy implies a conspiracy or plot or anything of that sort. It is simply a word that describes a significant number of highly educated people in a society linked by a central or preponderating dogma or ethic or allegiance. Their mentality is in no way conspiratorial or insurrectionary or revolutionary by intent. On the evidence, they overwhelmingly prefer a public to a private approach. They overwhelmingly prefer to do things at the national level rather than at the level of the local community. On the record of the last thirty-five years, they have shown a preference for centralized administration over decentralized administration, and for the executive over the Congress, and for the Congress over state legislatures or city councils.

In the colleges and universities in this country, in the high schools and junior high schools, in the media and the foundations, in our huge bureaucracy (whether state, federal, or other), the overwhelming thrust of mind of the clerisy is toward the dogma of redistribution—of equality—and it is highly important for economists to understand this.

I recognize the theory of the economic determination of history, but it is a seriously flawed theory. Admittedly, there is a human survival level that may be called economic, above which people have to live. But when this is reached, questions of dogmas, status, and right and wrong begin to take precedence. It is a great mistake to underemphasize the importance of great dogmas brooding—hovering—over civilizations at given points in history.

In my opinion, right now, in Western society, the dogma of equality is brooding, hovering. Sensibly and insensibly it shapes strategies, techniques, and approaches that were once pragmatic, piecemeal, ad hoc, and problem-directed.

DEAN COHEN: Let me make two general statements in order to explain my response to the comments on my paper. First, I think that, by and large, in the American situation, there is no substantial stress on equality of income, though there is a consensus on equality of opportunity—and that is a very important distinction. Except in a very small minority of economists and some other minority groups, there is little demand for absolute equality of income or near equality of income. There is, however, vast agreement that certain elements in our society prevent equality of opportunity—that is, access to jobs, education, or the opportunity to earn an income. Over the years, those persons who have been advocating improvements in the income maintenance and education and health programs have not attempted to obtain absolute equality or even to approach equality, but rather to provide a greater degree of equality of opportunity, which is what the middle class and the blue-collar workers (as well as others) stress as an important objective.

My second point—and here I am dealing with what Aaron has said—is that, in carrying out these programs, it is neither wise nor necessary to debate the philosophical issue of whether we are for or against redistribution of income from one income class to another. That would be a fine discussion for the American Economic Association, or for the Brookings Institution, or for economists generally, but I do not think it is the kind of discussion that throws much light on policy or program development in the United States.

A good case can be made that more redistribution would be a good thing, but that does not necessarily mean I would argue publicly for redistribution as the major reason for welfare reform. I do not think that redistribution of income by income class is important to 75 or 80 percent of the American public in its evaluation of changes to be made in the welfare system. They may think the distribution of income is inequitable, or wrong, or immoral, or wasteful, but they do not approach the problem of welfare reform in terms of the redistribution of income by income class.

These two points must be kept in mind when we deal with other questions that concern these programs—questions of the work ethic, savings, the sense of dignity and self-respect, and discrimination. These questions relate not to income redistribution per se but to other values that many of the American people think are much more important institutionally than income redistribution.

When Professor Browning says I attack the problem on a piecemeal basis, he is correct; a piecemeal approach is in my opinion the only way of making progress. His view that some simplified system will resolve all these inequities and disparities—through some simple negative income tax—in my opinion is not realistic. The very fact that we have not been able to agree on the key elements in a negative income tax is an indication of the difficulties that must be faced in trying to develop a plan which will be acceptable.

Milton Friedman's proposal was raised as the basis for the solution of the problem. Friedman advocates a negative income tax that supersedes all existing programs. Only a man from Mars would think of the negative income tax as a practical political solution for all existing programs. I would agree that in five years or fifteen years we may have something like the negative income tax—but to assume that it is possible in one fell swoop to devise a politically acceptable program that will solve all of our problems is not realistic.

All the different plans to simplify the system have been immediately attacked for their cost, or for their level of benefits, or for their marginal tax impact, or for their effect on work incentives, or for the number of people that would be included or excluded. A negative income tax with a $5 billion price tag on it would probably require supplementary programs, including the food stamp plan.

I might be willing to accept a $5 billion program, but that program would not supersede the other systems. The only way we can have a program that would supersede all the other systems and have some kind of a work incentive would probably be to establish a system that would cost around $30 or $50 billion a year. We are therefore faced with the problem that we cannot have such a program adopted immediately. While I would agree that such a program may ultimately come, it will come only after certain other conditions are met. The notch problem with Medicaid must be resolved in some kind of way, we must have reasonably full employment, the number of people within the poverty group must decline substantially below the present 24 million. It might well be that all this will happen five, ten, fifteen years from now, so that it would then be possible to put a negative income tax as an underpinning for a number of the other programs, but not necessarily to supersede them.

Taking both economic and political factors into account, welfare reform is probably not the highest priority in dealing with present income maintenance programs. As I said earlier, I would first deal with the problems of health. I would then deal with redistribution of costs of social security. I would use some money for new education programs. Welfare reform would be fourth on my list of priorities.

DAVID LINDEMAN, Department of Health, Education, and Welfare: Those in the audience and on the panel interested in the history of ideas and the sociology of knowledge, reflecting on Dean Cohen's remarks, are asking themselves why he has come to his conclusions. We are faced with a classic case of saying it is so making it so. His analysis is self-fulfilling. He believes that the political process will come out in a certain way and the evidence is no more than his statement that it will.

I would ask the panelists the following question: Would they find it desirable to construct a negative income tax system that would be essentially redistributive within the bottom 20 to 30 percent of the population?

DR. AARON: I can do little more than repeat Dean Cohen's comments on the difficulties of a negative income tax. A variety of minority groups seek certain objectives in welfare reform, but I have yet to see a single plan that could put together majority support. I have felt for some time that a simplification of welfare through a negative income tax will not occur until Medicaid is reformed. Without reform of Medicaid, any plan can be made to look as bad as Senator Williams of Delaware made the family assistance plan look. I would guess that "reform" can occur only through some form of national health protection, and, like Dean Cohen, I doubt that it will be effected. But I think that it would be a prerequisite.

I have not always agreed with Wilbur Cohen, as he knows, but over the years I have learned to respect his forecasting abilities. He turns out to be right more often than wrong. If he says it is so, that does not make it so, but it does lead me to wonder why he said it and to think hard about it.

MR. PHILIP LYONS, House Budget Committee: I was taken by Professor Nisbet's concluding remark about the dogmatic cloud that had come on the American horizon, the cloud of equality. How did this particular cloud happen to settle on the American horizon, and why does it seem to be moving toward aggressive redistribution of income?

PROFESSOR NISBET: The dogma of equality has been an active and vital influence for two or three centuries but limited largely in the first place to the religious field, and then eventually becoming a legal and constitutional concept. The great justification of the public school system, for example, was to equalize opportunity. But it is the movement of the Western nations into a high degree of welfare activity that has recently tended to convert the older ideas of equality to the one that is now the dominating idea.

We cannot measure such things. They do not calibrate easily—they do not lend themselves to econometrics or any mathematics. But we cannot read history without a sense that there are powerful values that can hang over civilization and that these values change.

Solzhenitsyn, perhaps too pessimistically, says that we are seventy-five years behind the Soviet Union in our historical trajectory—that what is happening in Western society today is remarkably similar to what was happening in Russia from about 1890 to about 1900 and 1910. Even great prophets err, but I do think something different has come over Western society in the last two or three decades. Part of it is this spreading dogma of egalitarianism—the paying of moral reparations, if necessary, in the effort to redistribute.

I wish I could be more specific, more concrete about this dogma. I admit that, in part, my ideas about it result from an awareness, a reading, a feeling of things, but I do not think this cloud is going to be just wished away by logic or argument either.

MR. LYONS: It is almost as if we just became entangled in it.

PROFESSOR NISBET: Yes. In the period of my coming of age—in the late 1920s and early 1930s—there were bold, imaginative programs. These programs sometimes proved to be all wrong—the AAA or NRA for example—but they were not justified in terms of redistribution. And I have never read the history of the income tax, but I would be very surprised if many justified the progressive income tax on the grounds that it would help bring about equality or a redistribution of income. I think it was entirely a revenue-collecting measure. But now we talk about the progressive income tax in terms of its effort to "redistribute" and whether it succeeds or fails by that standard. Today, using the retrospective view of history, we are beginning to reassess aspects of the New Deal—and even actions under President Hoover. No doubt we will go back to the times of Teddy Roosevelt and say that such and such a move was the first step toward "redistribution" or toward "egalitarianism." This is a bad way to read history.

THE SOCIAL ALLOCATION
OF CAPITAL

George H. Dixon

Some forty years ago, I believe, that noted commentator on the American scene, Will Rogers, quipped that Americans don't get all the government they pay for . . . and that's probably a very good thing. I would like to share with you a few brief thoughts about one aspect of the government that Americans *are* getting, and for which the price tag remains as yet unknown. It is an issue which has interested me ever since some of my Treasury associates spoke of it, and it has to do with the social allocation of capital in this country. By that, I mean any action by the government that attempts to direct the flow of savings toward some specific investment objective. Let me amplify.

There are four ways by which a government can affect the flow of savings in financial markets. It can borrow directly in those markets and then relend to a savings and loan association, a corporation, a housing authority, or a municipality. The rate charged here is lower than the ultimate borrower would pay in the market. Perhaps the most famous current example of this is the federal government's loan to New York City.

Another means of socially allocating capital occurs when the government guarantees the debt of the borrower to private lenders. A case in point is the Lockheed loan, which is guaranteed by the federal government and administered by the Emergency Loan Guarantee Board of the Treasury.

Capital flows are also affected by regulations. Take, for example, the interest rates on savings accounts—savings and loan associations are allowed to pay a somewhat higher rate of interest than commercial banks. The purpose is to direct savings to a mortgage lending institution in order to stimulate housing. For the same purpose, the minimum denomination for purchase of a Treasury bill is normally $10,000. This is meant to limit disintermediation out of savings institutions in times of rising interest rates.

Yet another means for socially allocating capital is the straight subsidy. An example of this is a mortgage subsidy either to the borrower or to the lender. In a recent bill known as the Financial Institutions Act, it was proposed that the holder

Note: This is the edited transcript of the speech given by Mr. Dixon at the luncheon on May 20, 1976.

229

of a mortgage receive a tax credit for a percentage of the interest income received.[1] This, of course, would be to encourage mortgage lending and housing.

Thus, there are four basic methods by which the flow of savings in the United States can be directed or nudged to some socially desirable objective: (1) financial intermediation in which a government or agency borrows directly in the market and relends for the purpose intended; (2) the federal guarantee of loans; (3) regulations establishing rate ceilings, rate differentials, or the amounts that can be borrowed or loaned; and (4) direct subsidies.

Although some may say that these arrangements are largely a thing of the past—that they no longer are important, if they ever were—most plans for the social allocation of capital in this country were developed within the past five years and new plans are being developed all the time. Consider the following litany of events—not an inclusive listing by any means, but enough to give you a flavor of what has happened in recent times:

- The guarantee of the Lockheed loan occurred in 1971.
- The Government National Mortgage Association (GNMA or Ginnie Mae) was formed in the late 1960s and activity in guaranteed pass-through instruments has mushroomed in the 1970s.
- The activity of government-sponsored agencies—the Federal National Mortgage Association (FNMA or Fannie Mae), the Federal Home Loan Bank, and the federal credit banks—also have grown. While these agencies are not guaranteed by the federal government and there is no statement of moral obligation printed on any of the instruments they issue, there is— in the final analysis—an implied backing. The federal government simply is not likely to let them fail. Moreover, Fannie Mae and the Home Loan Bank have the ability to borrow from the Treasury.
- In late 1975, after extensive debate, New York City obtained a $2.3 billion revolving credit arrangement with the federal government under which it borrows from the Treasury at a rate only slightly higher than the rate paid by the Treasury.
- The Federal Financing Bank Act of 1973 authorizes most federal agencies to borrow directly from the Treasury at one-eighth of 1 percent above the Treasury borrowing costs for like maturities. Major participants in this program include the Export-Import Bank, Farmers Home Administration, Amtrak, Rural Electrification Corporation, TVA, and the U.S. Postal Service.
- Many of the agencies now borrowing from the Federal Financing Bank previously borrowed in the open markets under federal government guarantee, but not so easily nor at as favorable a rate. The purpose of the Federal Financing Bank is to assure greater coordination of agency borrowings with

---

[1] S. 1267, 94th Congress, 1st session, March 20, 1975. Passed by the Senate, but not the House.

overall Treasury borrowings to minimize disruption in the financial markets. In this regard, the concept has been successful, but it also has enhanced the social allocation of capital to specific causes.

These examples give some indication of what has already occurred. There are also a number of other schemes afoot:

- The FINE study (Financial Institutions in the Nation's Economy) proposes that the Federal Home Loan Bank borrow directly from the Treasury in order to finance the mortgage market.
- The $100 billion Energy Independence Authority proposed in the 94th Congress would provide loans and loan guarantees to encourage domestic energy resource development. In essence, the EIA would borrow in the capital markets at favorable interest rates (because it is a federal government agency) and then relend to private sector energy projects.
- Senator Javits recently proposed a bill whereby the federal government would lend to municipalities in financial difficulty.[2]
- A bill was recently introduced to establish a $1 billion government bank to make loans to consumer cooperatives.[3]

This listing is not all-inclusive, but it does give one an idea of what is happening. The social allocation of capital in this country is coming of age. Special interest groups and politicians see "government banks," "government guarantees," and other devices as a panacea to solve many ills. The logic is simple. By borrowing from the federal government or with its guarantee, one avails oneself of capital which otherwise might not be available in the marketplace or which would be available only at significantly higher interest rates.

Proponents of these schemes will even claim that the federal government gains because it receives a higher rate on its loan than it pays for the money or, in the case of a guarantee, a fee. Have we at last found a way to provide manna from heaven without cost? We know that the housing sector, the city, the energy project, and the consumer cooperative gain as direct recipients of this allocation of capital. Seemingly everyone gains and no one loses.

But is there really no cost? Can we socially allocate capital to one cause and then another without making someone else worse off? The contention of this paper is that we cannot—that there is a cost—that parties not favored in the social allocation formula suffer relatively—that the cost of channeling savings to housing falls heavily on low- and moderate-income families—and that under most schemes for social allocation of capital, our nation's financial markets become less efficient—which, in turn, hurts us all. In short, there is a real cost to the social allocation of capital, and unless we recognize this fact, we will soon reach the point where

[2] S. 1833, 94th Congress, 1st session, May 22, 1975.
[3] S. 2631, 94th Congress, 1st session, November 6, 1975.

what is at stake is no longer the division of the proverbial eggs, but the salvation of the goose.

Let us take a look at the situation in greater detail, starting with the guarantee arrangement. In the New York City case, the original plea was that the federal government guarantee the financial obligations of the city. Now what would have happened if this had happened? For one thing it would have made the obligations more valuable than Treasury securities. Not only would they carry the obligation of the U.S. government, but their interest would be tax-exempt as well. Imagine the windfall gain to investors. Contrast this gain with the return to a person who invests in the securities of a well-run municipality. This investor accepts a lower initial yield because the risk is lower than that of New York City. All of this, of course, is in keeping with equilibration in financial markets according to risk and return. But the relationship between risk and return is altered when the federal government steps in to guarantee the obligations of one borrower and not those of others.

This alteration would explicitly favor a city or corporation which is not well managed financially. If, through political pressure, it is able to get the federal government to enter the scene and guarantee its securities, it will be able to borrow at a lower rate than it could otherwise. This explains what happens to the return; but does the underlying risk go away? Of course not. It is merely shifted from the investor to the federal government and to taxpayers at large. If default should occur, the federal government will need to make good on the obligations. Where will it get the funds? Either by forgoing programs, increasing taxes, or increasing the federal debt. In addition to the future burden on taxpayers, increasing the debt may bring immediate pressure on interest rates paid by all borrowers.

Therefore, there are costs to the guarantee, though they are somewhat hidden. One is the contingent or potential cost to present and future taxpayers. Another is the possibility of increased cost to other borrowers in the financial markets. A third is the increased element of government risk which accompanies each successive guarantee. And finally, there is the unfair economic advantage that a government guarantee provides to the guaranteed party.

Guarantees also alter the normal function of financial markets. We know that this function is the efficient channeling of savings to the most productive investment opportunities, whether these opportunities be private sector investments or public sector investments with a social return. The mechanism by which funds are channeled is the trade-off between risk and return. When the federal government explicitly directs funds to certain investments which, because of the risk involved, either would not be able to attract funds or would be able to attract them only at a rate higher than the government rate, it tampers with the workings of the marketplace. This tampering can lead to less efficient financial markets with the result that savings are allocated in our society at higher costs and/or with greater inconvenience than they would be otherwise. In turn, this has adverse implications for capital formation and for economic growth.

From this discussion, it is easy to go to a case in which the federal government, or some agency thereof, borrows in the financial markets and relends to another party. The purpose is to provide funds at a lower rate than the individual, city, or corporation could obtain in the marketplace. In short, the credit-worthiness of the federal government is substituted for that of someone else.

The effects of this form of socially allocating capital are more or less the same as the previous case. In whole or in part, the federal government absorbs the risk of default, and the costs of this absorption are ultimately borne by taxpayers. In addition, other borrowers in the marketplace may be at a disadvantage. Clearly they are at a disadvantage relative to those to whom capital is allocated socially. However, they also may be at a disadvantage in an absolute sense—they will have to pay a higher interest rate to secure the sums they need.

Again the equilibration mechanism in financial markets is distorted. Funds no longer flow on the basis of risk and return. One set of potential borrowers moves to the head of the line and capital is allocated to them on the basis of government decree, not by the rules of the marketplace. No longer must these borrowers justify a project's social or private rate of return in relation to any market-determined standard of efficiency.

The result is that some projects are undertaken which might be otherwise rejected if the borrower had to compete in the financial markets. In society as a whole, then, investments are undertaken which are not optimal in terms of economic efficiency. As a result, at the margin there is an adverse impact on the real economic growth of the nation.

Moreover, if distortions in risk-return relationships lead to less efficient financial markets, this also has an adverse effect on economic growth. These markets simply become less effective in channeling savings to investment projects on a risk-adjusted return basis. For all of these reasons, economic growth and want satisfaction in our society may be less than otherwise would be the case.

Turning now to government regulations which divert the flow of savings in our society away from that which would occur in the marketplace, we find that the effect is similar. In this case artificial restraints are established which bias the flow of savings toward socially desirable causes. The best known and most important case is mortgage financing. By establishing ceilings on savings rates of mortgage lending institutions and by making investments in alternative money market instruments more difficult or less attractive, the government hopes to enhance mortgage financing at rates of interest lower than what otherwise would be market-clearing rates. This, too, allows projects to be undertaken that cannot be justified in terms of a market-determined cost of capital. It may also lessen the efficiency of financial markets with results similar to those described before.

233

However, there is another direct cost effect. Rather than falling on taxpayers in general, it falls on savers who must accept lower interest rates on their savings than would otherwise prevail. In other words, by placing limits on the maximum rate paid and by establishing barriers to investing elsewhere, savers must accept rates of interest lower than what would be the market-clearing rates in the absence of these restrictions. This is particularly true in times of rising interest rates.

Fortunately, the forces of competition are not long shackled. During the last several years, money market funds, which enable individuals to invest in money market instruments in smaller denominations than is possible with a direct investment in a Treasury bill, commercial paper, or other form of investment, have become quite prevalent. This financial innovation has met a previously unmet need by providing alternatives to traditional depository institution savings programs.

There still exists a barrier to investment elsewhere by low- and medium-income individuals. We said before that the direct cost of socially allocating capital to mortgages falls on savers at savings institutions. More specifically, this cost falls on low- and middle-income persons who do not have alternative investments for their savings. They must accept lower savings rates than would prevail in free and competitive financial markets. Who benefits from this social allocation of capital? Homeowners, residential building owners, and, to a lesser extent, commercial building owners. These owners typically are middle- to high-income individuals. Comparatively few low-income people own homes.

Is this subsidization of housing by low- to moderate-income families likely to continue? Perhaps not on the same scale as it has. If the Financial Institutions Act had been passed, greater competition would have developed for savings as interest rate ceilings were gradually lifted over a period of five and one-half years. Market-clearing rates of interest could then be paid, and the burden for subsidizing housing (if it is to continue to be subsidized) will not fall so heavily on savers as it does now.

So far we have covered three of the four means of socially allocating capital. The last one I wish to discuss is the interest rate subsidy, which can be a subsidy either to the borrower or to the lender. If social allocation of capital toward some objective is deemed appropriate, I would contend that the interest rate subsidy to the borrower results in the least disruption to financial markets and is the most equitable. For one thing, the subsidy goes directly to the party one wishes to benefit. For example, the government may not wish to subsidize all borrowers in the mortgage market, but only low- to moderate-income persons.

If the market-clearing rate on a mortgage were, say, 10 percent and the subsidy were 2 percent, the effective interest cost would be 8 percent. The risk-return equilibration mechanism in financial markets is not distorted. The borrower must compete for funds, but he knows that part of his interest cost will be picked up by the government in the form of a subsidy. In other words, the financial markets are allowed to perform their function in the same manner as before. The borrower must attract a loan and pay an interest rate to the lending institution commensurate with the risk involved.

Moreover, the subsidy comes from the federal government or, more specifically, from taxpayers as a whole. It does not fall directly on low- and medium-income savers who are forced to accept lower interest rates on their savings than otherwise would prevail. Therefore, it seems to me that it is both more efficient and more equitable to use the interest rate subsidy approach than it is to use any of the other means for socially allocating capital.

The interest rate subsidy could also go to the lender. Here the government would subsidize certain categories of loans—such as mortgages or loans to cities. A subsidy of this sort would result in a rate of interest on these loans lower than would otherwise prevail. However, this type of subsidy is more generally a shotgun approach in that it benefits all borrowers in a particular category. While this may be appropriate in trying to stimulate housing and construction in general, it is not so effective in trying to enable low-to-middle-income individuals to purchase housing. Here a subsidy to the borrower would be better.

While the subsidy is the most effective way for the social allocation of capital, one should not conclude that there are no inefficiencies involved. Projects are accepted which would not be accepted if a market-determined cost of capital were employed. Thus, the subsidy shares with other methods the shortcoming of altering the risk-return acceptance criterion for projects. However, we must bear in mind that by definition the purpose is the social allocation of capital as opposed to its allocation strictly on economic grounds.

In summary, it is important to recognize that the cries for the social allocation of capital are increasing. The political appeal is irresistible—there seemingly is no cost, or at least the cost is so hidden as to be illusive. Now we all want to do what is socially right with respect to our cities, pollution, the less fortunate, or what have you. If there were little or no cost to socially allocating capital, I think we all would agree that it would be the right thing to do.

But, as we have established, there is a cost—though it is not readily apparent. As a result, hard decisions are necessary in judging the benefits of a plan for the social allocation of capital in relation to the "opportunity cost" to taxpayers, to other borrowers, and to savers. It is paramount that these costs be recognized and evaluated before a decision is made. In that old vernacular, "there is no such thing as a free lunch."

PART
FIVE

WELFARE REFORM: WHY?

In the final session of the conference, a distinguished panel and a well-informed audience discussed whether major modifications are needed in the American public welfare system. The discussion was videotaped for educational and commercial TV and the edited transcript that is presented here has been published separately as an AEI Round Table.

ROUND TABLE DISCUSSION

ROBERT H. BORK, solicitor general of the United States and moderator of the Round Table: This Round Table, which is jointly presented by the American Enterprise Institute and the Hoover Institution, will consider the issue of welfare reform.

The welfare issue appears to have become a permanent feature of the American political landscape. The problem has always been with us and, as we become increasingly egalitarian, is likely to remain with us. Our dilemma is that we want the poor to have better lives, but we seem also to be unhappy about the results of our attempts to achieve that goal. Federal spending on income security has risen more than $100 billion since 1964 when President Lyndon Johnson called on his countrymen to wage a war on poverty. Yet, more than 20 million Americans still live below the officially defined poverty level. The public perception, whether accurate or not, is that something is very wrong.

To begin our discussion, let me turn first to Senator Abraham Ribicoff, a former secretary of health, education, and welfare. Why, senator, do you think there is so much criticism of the nation's welfare program?

ABRAHAM A. RIBICOFF, United States Senate (Democrat, Connecticut): I think, first, because politicians, from the President of the United States down, have found it politically profitable to play the demagogue with respect to the poor and the black. Second, the criticism reflects a guilty conscience of the American middle class because American society has failed to solve its problems.

Our annual welfare bill, some $40 billion, is high. But, when you compare that with our gross national product of $1.4 trillion, you find that less than 3 percent of GNP represents the overhead of American society for its failure.

Beyond these reasons, I believe the dissatisfaction arises because political leaders really don't have the guts to face up to the problem.

MR. BORK: Congressman Conable, as a senior Republican member of the House Ways and Means Committee, can you tell us why welfare costs have skyrocketed in recent years?

BARBER B. CONABLE, United States House of Representatives (Republican, New York): Well, it is a very expensive program. The $40 billion the senator mentioned is the cost of only the three largest programs—cash payments, food stamps, and Medicaid. There are lots of other programs, as well as severe costs, because of an administrative hodgepodge.

Also, costs have gone up sharply in recent years primarily because more people now, a total of about 29 million, are participating in these major welfare programs. Welfare is a needs program, and the poor are hit hardest in an inflation as the value of the dollar goes down. Obviously, needs will go up and welfare costs will increase in these circumstances. Third, administration is expensive. It costs over $3 billion a year to administer our welfare program at this point—8 percent of the total cost.

All these things have combined to make welfare not just a highly visible part of our governmental system, as the senator mentioned, but a controversial and increasingly expensive part.

MR. BORK: Dean Cohen, as a former secretary of HEW, do you think our present welfare system is the most efficient way of helping the poor?

WILBUR J. COHEN, dean, School of Education, University of Michigan: No. The present system is not only inadequate, but it has been built up over the years in such a way that it fails to benefit all the poor equitably. There are better ways of helping the poor, but all of them involve more cost and more problems, economic, political, administrative, and otherwise. Part of the reason why we don't have a better welfare system, or a substitute system, is because it is difficult, in a country as large as ours, to agree on what an adequate standard is for, say, both New York and Mississippi, and because of various other complex decisions which are necessary to administer a system in a country as big and diverse as the United States.

If one were to attempt to develop a better system to meet the needs of the poor, one wouldn't start with the current system.

MR. BORK: Dr. MacAvoy, you now serve as a member of the President's Council of Economic Advisers. How well do you think our present welfare programs are meeting their objective of helping the poor?

PAUL W. MacAVOY, member, Council of Economic Advisers: Robert, I'm intimidated by the prestige and seniority of the other members of this panel. As the youngest member of the panel, it's not my position to judge these distinguished gentlemen, who all played some role in the development of the existing institution. [Laughter.] I might add that they have done that job very well themselves. Their remarks were severely critical of where we now are—in other words, they're tearing down their own edifice. So perhaps I should be in the position of building it up a bit. As I understand the original intent of these programs, it was to help persons who are in no position to help themselves to obtain the necessities of life—food, clothing, shelter, the minimum of transportation, and other goods and services. These persons may have been ill; they may, for one reason or the other, be incapacitated for various periods. The programs have attempted to help them as part of the American dedication to equality. In good part, the programs have done that.

The criticism that I could make, as an economist, of present operations is that they have gone beyond their original intent by helping many individuals who may not qualify under these standards. If we were to take the expenditures that Representative Conable mentioned and distribute them only to those who meet the original qualifications, we would provide 130 percent of the poverty level of income; that is, we are spending more than enough to bring above the poverty line every member of the population who is considered poor. That poverty still exists indicates that others who do not meet the original qualifications must be receiving substantial amounts of income through the programs for one reason or the other.

We also have an extensive federal and state bureaucracy administering the programs—so intricate that it is extremely difficult to find out how much we spend on them. Members of my staff, back in the Executive Office Building, are tracing these expenditures now, trying to find out how much goes to which part of which program. They will be late for the session this evening. [Laughter.] But when I left to come to this meeting, they had found well over $2 billion of annual outlay for salaries and other operating expenditures for overlapping federal, state, and local programs. It might be a very good idea to redesign programs, not to achieve perfect government, but to reduce costs by reducing the specificity of the programs, the extreme detail, the opportunities for legalisms to determine who qualifies and who does not that add up to a lawyer's and bureaucrat's dream.

MR. BORK: I am going to object: we don't use *legalism* as a pejorative term here this evening. [Laughter.]

DR. MacAVOY: You were brought on to this panel to prevent violence from breaking out, not to create it. [Laughter.]

MR. BORK: I thought I heard a murmuring on my left. Senator Ribicoff?

SENATOR RIBICOFF: Well, I think Barber and Professor MacAvoy make a good point—that the administrative costs are high. The reason is that there are some 1,150 separate agencies throughout the United States, administering every conceivable type of welfare program. It makes no rhyme or reason.

I think the professor makes another good point. I too am convinced that we could take this pot that we spend on welfare, simply divide it up—without any administration—and put checks through the computer, and we'd end up saving the American taxpayers billions of dollars. I think President Nixon tried to do that, to a certain extent, with his proposed family assistance plan, which was very well conceived, but, while the House did act—twice, in fact—the Senate couldn't agree; and then Mr. Haldeman and Mr. Ehrlichman finally did in the plan.

DEAN COHEN: But doesn't that illustrate the problem? It's very easy to criticize the system—which I have done—but it's very difficult to find a solution that everybody will accept.

When welfare reform is discussed in any kind of a general situation, one person will go away and say, "Well, I'm for that because it will cut the welfare rolls in half." But the fact is that most of the working poor of the United States are not in the present welfare system, except for food stamps.

If we were to generalize the program in the way you just did, senator, we'd end up spending $15 billion to $25 billion a year more. That's the reason why the Nixon plan and the other proposals for a negative income tax have not passed both houses of Congress. The solution to the problem is to find a plan that includes an equitable level for the whole United States and an income disregard that will be a work incentive.* I haven't yet seen a proposal that meets those criteria that costs less than $15 billion a year more than the present program. Now, is that what the American people mean when they talk about welfare reform?

SENATOR RIBICOFF: I think the problem is that no one in this country has the answer. I lived with it as secretary of HEW, before that I lived with it as governor, and now I live with it as a United States senator. I am convinced that there is no one solution, no one answer. And I think that we ought to realize that, before we put into action any particular program involving millions of people and billions of dollars, we should undertake a pilot effort.

I would like us to take some of the best ideas, and spend some money for four or five pilot programs to see if they work. As a matter of fact, one of the tragedies of President Nixon's family assistance plan is that when it was stalled in the Senate Finance Committee—and I had been able to obtain unanimous agreement for the expenditure of $500 million for a four-year experiment on pilot programs—the secretary of HEW and the President wanted all or nothing. So they ended up with nothing. I would hope that, when we approach welfare reform again, when some President has the courage to come up with a proposal, men like Barber in the Ways and Means Committee, myself, and others would try to test it out before we commit the country to a $40 billion program.

CONGRESSMAN CONABLE: Senator, I have a different version of what happened to the family assistance plan. It was my understanding that the Senate Finance Committee was unwilling to accept the standards that were laid down in that plan because it felt they were too low. And because it couldn't get agreement on a higher level of benefits, the whole thing died.

---

* Editor's note: See Dean Cohen's remarks on p. 256 for a definition of "income disregard."

SENATOR RIBICOFF: No, Barber. Before it got to that—

CONGRESSMAN CONABLE: We sent you a bill in early 1970 that provided for an income floor of $2,400 a year, for a family of four.

SENATOR RIBICOFF: And then the so-called liberals wanted more, the conservatives wanted less. To break the impasse I suggested pilot programs. Then Senator Long, Senator Williams, everybody around the Finance Committee table— liberals, conservatives, the middle-of-the-roaders—agreed unanimously to go up to $500 million to try it out, to see if it worked. I thought that was a great idea.

But the Nixon administration wanted to go for broke, so nothing happened. Later on, in 1972, when Secretary of HEW Elliot Richardson and I had worked out a compromise for an income floor of $2,600, it collapsed because the secretary could not even get by Ehrlichman and Haldeman to talk to the President of the United States.

MR. BORK: Well, let's try the future before we replay that loss.

DEAN COHEN: I think that the problem that Senator Ribicoff just discussed is still here today. What amount could be agreed on as a proper minimum for the entire United States? At the present time the poverty yardstick for a family of four is around $5,500. Now, could you get Congress to approve, as a political compromise, a federal minimum that is close to $5,500? Obviously, I would say—and you gentlemen may correct me—the amount would have to be substantially lower than that. But the lower amount wouldn't satisfy many states, particularly the industrial ones; and you wouldn't be able to get a compromise, since there are two senators from every one of those states.

DR. MacAVOY: You're not asking the right question. The question for us is not to determine a specific minimum level of income for everyone, but how we can best help those who are, in some way, unable to work within the economic system to raise their level of income.

There are many people who have temporarily low incomes, and they would be caught up, and rewarded, in any program that simply sent out checks to everyone whose income was below a certain level. But we're not really aiming at guaranteed incomes. As a first priority we seek to provide the opportunity to consume to those unable to generate their own assets and income.

DEAN COHEN: Well, what income level would you propose?

DR. MacAVOY: This is just the problem. We shouldn't propose a single level of income that would apply universally. We should propose a new program, one which can be so specific as to separate persons without income, wealth, or any

243

opportunity to earn from those who have low levels of income or the capacity to earn a steady income, albeit a low one.

DEAN COHEN: All right. I ask you again: for people who have no income, what level would you set?

DR. MacAVOY: My next door neighboor is a medical student who has no income and who would qualify under a check-receiving program during this period when he's in school—before he begins to earn $20,000 or $75,000 or $150,000 a year.

DEAN COHEN: Well, I'm perfectly willing to exclude all physicians and medical students, because they are going to have a lot of income.

DR. MacAVOY: Ah, but then you have a special program, and there are lots of other exclusions that you must make, Mr. Cohen, as well.

DEAN COHEN: Make all the exclusions you want, and tell me what is the income level that you would propose for a minimum?

DR. MacAVOY: Now we're back to the present program.

MR. BORK: No. We're not back to the present program.

DR. MacAVOY: Yes, we are. We're back to 1,100 programs.

SENATOR RIBICOFF: What bothers me with Professor MacAvoy's points— and this is the problem every time you look for welfare reform—is that everybody talks in generalities. You're one of the President's economic advisers, professor. Give me a specific program that you would advise President Ford to submit to the Congress of the United States.

DR. MacAVOY: Mr. Ribicoff, I have that program in hand.

SENATOR RIBICOFF: Good. Let's hear it. [Laughter.]

DR. MacAVOY: You keep tearing down your building, and I keep trying to patch it back together again.

MR. BORK: This is a historic moment, I think. [Laughter.]

DR. MacAVOY: Our existing welfare programs can be improved. They can be made more efficient by introducing more advanced government-operation techniques and by removing from these 1,100 programs those that we all agree are clearly redundant—

244

DEAN COHEN: The computers broke down on the SSI program [Supplementary Security Income].

DR. MacAVOY: —and that suggestion differs from Mr. Cohen's, which is to tear the current system down and start issuing checks.

CONGRESSMAN CONABLE: Can we agree on this, gentlemen—that we're not likely to achieve the millennium overnight, and shouldn't expect to? Can we agree that we should be taking concrete steps toward a more rational welfare system, through a process of consolidating some programs, cashing out others, building a federal floor under benefit levels in order to reduce the disparity between the high- and low-welfare states, and so forth?

SENATOR RIBICOFF: Barber, would you go for national standards and for the federal government's assuming the entire welfare load? Those two changes would begin to eliminate the disparities, and would also eliminate the tragedy of New York City, the only city in the United States that has an annual tax bill of $1 billion for welfare. If New York City were like practically every other city of the United States and did not have to pay for welfare, its budget would show a surplus instead of a deficit.

CONGRESSMAN CONABLE: Senator, that's the point. We can't have a single national standard because it's politically unachievable. But we can move in that direction. We could start building a floor under the existing structure.

SENATOR RIBICOFF: I believe we could have regional standards reflecting the different standards of living throughout the United States. Certainly, it doesn't cost as much to live in, say, Mississippi as in New York City. There could be one standard for New York City, Chicago, the other industrial parts of the United States; another for rural areas; another for farm states; and another for the Deep South. I think we could have national standards built on a regional basis.

In other words, what I am arguing for is not a uniform program for this country—that just couldn't be done—but for a common sense approach, for pilot programs that are developed cooperatively by the legislative and the executive branch. Before we spend $40 billion we should first spend $500 million over three or four years to find out what works. Then we can adopt those that do and junk those that don't.

MR. BORK: We've heard remarks that the welfare system is terribly complicated— it's balkanized, it has 1,150 different agencies, and so forth—and that must be part of the problem. Yet Dr. MacAvoy says he doesn't want a check-writing program because it would necessarily include all kinds of people we don't wish to include. What would be wrong with combining all of these programs—in fact, doing away with individual programs like social security, aid to the disabled, aid to the blind—and simply using a check program? Wouldn't that eliminate a large portion of bureaucracy, a lot of overlap?

CONGRESSMAN CONABLE: We supposedly took that step with SSI. We combined three programs—

DR. MacAVOY: But you took another step in that case, congressman. Once you cashed the programs out, you started adding benefits on top. And that may be the real problem—the Congress just can't keep from adding a few more goodies.

CONGRESSMAN CONABLE: Part of the difficulty there is that everybody wants a piece of the action. There are eleven House committees, ten Senate committees, and nine executive agencies all participating in welfare,and they operate on a competitive basis. The minute you cash out, say, the food stamp program as part of any cash welfare program, you'll find the agriculture committees fighting to create some new type of food stamp program in order to get a piece of that action for the jurisdictional benefits it will give them in getting through their agricultural bills.

MR. BORK: Are you telling the American public, tonight, that the welfare problem is entirely a jurisdictional problem?

CONGRESSMAN CONABLE: Oh, I didn't say entirely. All I'm saying is that that's a serious complicating factor; and the competition among participating agencies and committees is unseemly.

DEAN COHEN: Could I join my colleagues in agreeing on two points that have been made here? One, I think it is possible to improve the present welfare system without having a millennial program. Two things could be done. First, we could remedy—as we have tried to do for many years—the exclusion of the working poor, who are not covered, for the most part at least, by Aid to Families for Dependent Children [AFDC]. Of course, broadening the program to include the working poor would require an increase in cost, and that presents a difficulty. But I think that the discriminatory treatment that now exists, where a man or woman who tries to keep the family intact cannot, except in some states and localities, get on welfare, embodies a wrong philosophy. It gives the head of the family an incentive to desert the family, and it ought to be corrected.

Second, I think that Barber's suggestion for minimizing interstate disparities is a good one. It would not preclude having a different system later on if we moved now to set some kind of minimum and then raised that over a period of five years, so that when we did get an opportunity for more comprehensive welfare reform, the disparities wouldn't be as large as they now are. It's my understanding that one of the major reasons why the family assistance plan couldn't be enacted was the size of the disparities.

CONGRESSMAN CONABLE: Wilbur, it's always entertaining to see people advocating the federalization of welfare when, I think, almost half the welfare passed out in the country is passed out through three states—California, New York, and Massachusetts. Thus, the federal representatives of the other forty-seven states would have to pay a substantial fiscal dividend to those three states, a politically unlikely vote under the circumstances.

SENATOR RIBICOFF: That's unfair, Barber. The Supreme Court has eliminated the residency requirement. Keep in mind that New York City, for example, has been the magnet for the blacks from the South and for the Puerto Ricans, who have a right, as citizens, to move there; and New York has been defenseless. Welfare is a national problem, the obligation of the whole country. And if New York is defenseless against poor immigrant U.S. citizens, why should the people of New York—or Connecticut, or Massachusetts, or Washington—suffer the burdens alone?

CONGRESSMAN CONABLE: Senator, I wish I could agree with you. I agree that that's an unfair condition, but nothing is a national issue that is not recognized as such by the national legislators. And I think it's still unlikely that the federal representatives of forty-seven states will give a major fiscal dividend to the representatives of three, no matter how equitable the latter's claims.

SENATOR RIBICOFF: Well, once we lifted the welfare burden from their states and counties, they might do it. Because, don't forget, in that event they too would not have the bills to pay.

This is why I don't believe, gentlemen, that we are ever going to have welfare reform until we have a courageous, farsighted President who is willing to go to the American people to explain it, and go to the Congress to fight for it. The problem is so complex that none of us, as individuals, can galvanize public opinion and public understanding to do this job. The opportunity can only come with a President who is concerned and is willing to take his lumps. But, having been a cabinet secretary and a senator, I have seen that most Presidents are unwilling to do that. As I mentioned today, the reason we have had so many secretaries of HEW is that no President is willing to go as far as a secretary of HEW must go in order to try to solve the problems facing the country. Politically, a President finds that unacceptable.

CONGRESSMAN CONABLE: I think we've had a good many more lumpy Presidents lately than we've had congressmen. [Laughter.]

MR. BORK: I have a feeling that some member of the executive branch should have a right to answer that, but I'll pass it by.

I really want to know whether you think that, at the national level, there is anything to be gained by moving towards a check system, a negative income tax,

247

or a family assistance plan, and by doing so eliminating the large bureaucracies that give specific programs.

DEAN COHEN: I agree that it's entirely desirable to have what you call a check-writing system, whether you call it a negative income tax or a family assistance plan—which is really a basic payment plus an income disregard as a work-incentive provision. But I think that it shouldn't be established until the computers are able to handle that problem. Judging from experience with existing programs, I don't think we've done so much better with the computers than we did with individualized treatment. Therefore, I am very skeptical about computerization without adequate attention to the human side of the equation—to making it possible for these people to get their checks and their eligibility in their local community.

MR. BORK: I understand that. But are there savings to be gained—and in this company I hesitate to say it—by the abolition of bureaucracies like HEW and HUD—savings large enough to make a check system viable?

SENATOR RIBICOFF: I never thought I'd disagree with my friend Wilbur on anything when it comes to welfare. But I think eventually that's where we must go. It makes the most sense. It's the simplest way, and we must face up to it. Why are people poor? It's very simple: they don't have money. When we face up to the simple fact, we'll start to understand how to solve the problem. But all the social workers and all the welfare bureaucracies certainly compound the problem. I think, too, that HEW should have been split up into its three basic components —health, education, and welfare—a long time ago. I thought so back when I was secretary of the department, and I still do.

I also think that eventually we'll have to take the Milton Friedman approach, the negative income tax approach.

DR. MacAVOY: Robert, let me provide a somewhat different view. It appears to me that some people are poor because they have low incomes at present, but that those same people might have much higher incomes in the future. My daughter is in that class; she's thirteen. Then there are other people who are poor because they have low incomes even though they have considerable wealth. That's my grandfather; he's eighty-six. Finally, there are of course the people who are truly poor because they have little or no income, wealth, or earning power.

This third class is the one, I think, that we seek to aid in welfare programs. At this time it is not possible with our information systems to differentiate among those three classes with a check-writing program that provides negative income taxes.

MR. BORK: You mean, suppose you had to fill out a questionnaire like an income tax return?

DR. MacAVOY: Yes. Put it to the IRS officer to compare the IBM salesman, who fills out a tax return in which he pays taxes on an income of $85,000 a year, with a welfare mother, who pays taxes on the basis of negative income. Now, the first has assets, a pattern of expenditure, previous income levels, and the names, addresses, and birth certificates of his children. But the second may have none of these. In the second case all of the indicators that an IRS officer would use to determine the level of income and wealth, and to determine how wealth has been generated in the last year or two, are not there. So the problem of ascertaining whether one qualifies is compounded enormously. That's what Mr. Cohen is saying.

MR. BORK: You mean an audit system wouldn't do it?

DR. MacAVOY: Mr. Cohen is saying that the computer systems would not do that well. And, even though I criticize the level of expenditure on bureaucracies now, it's my judgment that the savings on staff and the like in HEW would be more than cancelled out by increased expenditures in the IRS, plus the additional cost of payments to persons who would receive checks even though they would not qualify under the original intent of the program. Mr. Cohen is saying that it would cost $15 billion more under a check-writing, negative income tax program because that approach is so general that it cannot get at only the people one wants to help. And, therefore, we would have to spray the landscape with that much more expenditure.

MR. BORK: And you would say that even if we could eliminate programs like subsidies to housing, subsidies to agriculture, and all of those bureaucracies?

DR. MacAVOY: I would eliminate subsidies to housing, which I consider among the redundant programs. There are serious problems of excess coverage in the food stamp program; those are now being dealt with administratively. I believe there are other programs where there is a specific record of waste.

MR. BORK: But you're telling us that the elimination would not free enough funds to finance a negative income tax program?

DR. MacAVOY: I don't think we need that program when we can reform the present system, program by program, and have a structure of half-a-dozen specific programs that get at what we're trying to do—which is to provide necessities to those who have no income and no wealth.

MR. BORK: It sounds like the welfare mess is a mess without a cure.

SENATOR RIBICOFF: I think that the professor's comparisons are so invidious that we're never going to solve the problem if we take his explanation. How can he put his thirteen-year-old daughter in the same category of not having any money with someone without education, without a skill, without a job, without a house, without clothes, without a piece of bread for his belly, for heaven sakes? I think Wilbur is wrong too. The two professors are wrong.

MR. BORK: Not unlikely, not unlikely. [Laughter.]

SENATOR RIBICOFF: I don't think this country is so incompetent that we can't devise a form, or a system, to take care of the person who's really poor, and hungry, and homeless, and uneducated.

DR. MacAVOY: But that's not the question. We are doing that, senator; but we're also taking care of a number more. Not my thirteen-year-old daughter; that was an exaggeration, of course.

SENATOR RIBICOFF: Well, you were the one that brought it up.

DR. MacAVOY: I'm sorry I did that. I made a mistake which gave you an opening that you didn't deserve. What I'm saying is that a check-writing program will not be able to distinguish, as the current programs do, between the wealth and earnings power of those who should be covered and the wealth and earnings power of those who should not.

MR. BORK: Let's suppose we instituted a program to provide income up to a fairly substantial level. I'd like to hear the congressman's views on whether work incentives would be so reduced that we'd really be paying for leisure, and be supplied with leisure?

CONGRESSMAN CONABLE: The problem is that our present system gives very little work incentive. As Wilbur mentioned, a large number of people on welfare are absolutely disqualified for it if they accept work. Although they have marginal skills, they get on welfare because, that way, they can take home as much as, or more than, they could if they went to work. Working costs them money.

This is one of the reasons why we've got to move toward the sort of thing the senator is talking about. Perhaps we won't be able to achieve it with today's technology. But we certainly aren't going to achieve it unless we have a plan, unless we start working toward consolidating food stamps with a cash program in order to reduce administrative complexity.

Now, I don't think we're going to save a lot of money this way. And I think we'll continue to have abuses, because in a democracy everybody is entitled to try to find his own rip-off, apparently. [Laughter.] But I do think that we can gradually improve the system; and it's terribly important that the system be conceptually sound and based on a long-range plan. The problem, right now, is that we seem to be "piece-mealing" everything. Somebody says, "Oh, that's a terrible problem, we ought to have a program for it." So we pile a new program right on top of all the others, making things so much more complicated that ultimately we throw up our hands in despair, and say, "What are we going to do? We've got to take care of the poor."

Of course, we don't want to brutalize society, to ignore the poor. In a competitive society, we have to accept the fact that some people are going to lose, and that they, too, are part of the society and have to be maintained in some way. But we've got to have a plan; and we must be sure that the concept we're working toward involves incentives, not disincentives as is true in the present hodgepodge.

DEAN COHEN: Can I rise to the defense of professors? [Laughter.]

MR. BORK: It's a losing fight, but—

DEAN COHEN: Professor MacAvoy has drawn attention to a fundamental question. No negative income tax proposal that I have seen deals with the question of assets. I think what we are both trying to say is that, inevitably, the matter of assets would come into play, even though Milton Friedman and other proponents of the negative income tax fail to recognize it in their plans. Once you include assets, you're right back to the same problem the present system poses of individualized analysis of assets in relation to a person's lack of income from work.

MR. BORK: Well, wouldn't that be easier than having 1,100 programs—giving food stamps, giving medicine, giving—

DEAN COHEN: Well, in the first place, there aren't 1,100 programs.

MR. BORK: I heard that number from an expert a moment ago.

SENATOR RIBICOFF: There are 1,150 separate federal, state, county, and city units administering welfare throughout the United States.

DEAN COHEN: But that's a gross exaggeration, senator. When you take the fundamental component of the welfare system, AFDC, which has 11 million recipients, you'll find only fifty states administer that program. It is under the complete control of the fifty states and the federal government.

There's no reason why we couldn't broaden AFDC to include the working poor and to provide a minimum. Doing that would solve about 75 percent of our current problems. It wouldn't be a perfect program, but it would meet two of the greatest unfulfilled needs. Then, after we'd done that, we could undertake your experimental and pilot programs on the work incentive to see what works best. Then, we might be able to select a better program than what we now have. But until we analyze and deal with this matter of assets, we're not going to solve the problem, because I don't think IRS could do it.

SENATOR RIBICOFF: Well, Wilbur, do you mean to say that Barber Conable an Abe Ribicoff couldn't take the asset factor into account in writing a welfare

251

bill? Certainly, if a man has $50,000 in the bank, he shouldn't be given $5,000 a year on a negative income tax check.

MR. BORK: What have been the results of the pilot programs on negative income tax?

DR. MacAVOY: Pilot programs were run in Seattle, Denver, and New Jersey. The New Jersey set of experiments came first; they were quite detailed and, incidentally, have been the subject of great controversy related to the construction of the sample and to the meaningfulness of the results given the short time frame of the experiment.

MR. BORK: Did we learn anything about the administrative costs of dealing with assets, with the young, and so forth?

DR. MacAVOY: No. The programs looked centrally at the question of whether work incentives were reduced as a result of receiving income through a negative income tax.

DEAN COHEN: But those were artificial programs. I don't think they really prove anything—

DR. MacAVOY: They got better, Mr. Cohen, as the program design was improved. The later of the pilot programs, those in Seattle and Denver, indicate that there are significant work disincentives under a negative income tax scheme.

MR. BORK: When you say "significant," do you mean that if the program were applied nationally, we'd have a serious problem of buying leisure for the population?

DR. MacAVOY: Many individuals with low income, male workers as well as women with children, would decide—for short- or medium-term periods, perhaps —not to go into the labor market, but to stay on the negative income tax instead.

MR. BORK: So that program is not a panacea in that sense either?

DEAN COHEN: I want to emphasize that those particular experiments were artificial and unreal, because they were short term and because the people who participated in them knew that.

DR. MacAVOY: That's true of the New Jersey experiment, but not the Seattle and Denver experiments.

DEAN COHEN: Well, the Seattle and Denver experiments are so limited and so small, and not necessarily representative of the wide range of income, racial, and family mixes, that—while I happen to agree with your general observation about the work incentive—I would not take them as the ultimate test.

What the senator and I are proposing is to allow several states—say, Delaware, Rhode Island, and Arizona, so that we would have both urban and rural states— to convert their present AFDC programs, plus SSI and the food stamp program, into a new program—say, a negative income tax, applied statewide. Then we would see if the work incentive, at different rates of income disregard and under very different but real conditions, would work. I think that's what the senator has in mind.

SENATOR RIBICOFF: That's exactly what I have in mind, because my feeling is that the last thirty years have proven that social programs don't always work out. [Laughter.] Everything looks good on paper, but when you're dealing with human beings, it's altogether different. I, personally, am convinced that I'll never vote to commit the nation to a multi-million dollar social program, unless it has first been tested and found to work.

MR. BORK: How would you conduct the state-by-state experiment?

SENATOR RIBICOFF: We'd take varied states—a small state, an industrial state—

MR. BORK: No. No. You let the state decide whether it wants to do it.

SENATOR RIBICOFF: That's right. We're not *telling* them. Never. In the first place, a state couldn't afford to do it.

MR. BORK: But you'd help them do it.

SENATOR RIBICOFF: Yes. We'd find a state that would be willing, because it couldn't be done without the cooperation of the federal government and the state.

DR. MacAVOY: Have any states come forward, senator?

MR. BORK: There's nothing to volunteer for, yet.

DEAN COHEN: There are two deficiencies now. There's no financial incentive for a state to do it, and it's not legal for them to do it under the present law.

DR. MacAVOY: Have you gone around and asked the states, Mr. Cohen, "At what price would you do it?"

DEAN COHEN: Well, they would do it if the federal government paid the additional cost for programs beyond what the states are doing now.

DR. MacAVOY: Have you tried auctioning it off to see who would do it for the least?

DEAN COHEN: If you recommend to the President that we auction if off, I'll be glad to help find the states.

CONGRESSMAN CONABLE: I think we're making a mistake here in over-emphasizing the value of work incentives, because the assumption is that the great proportion of people on welfare can work if only they wanted to, if only they had adequate incentives to do so. I suspect that there are a great many people—I'm sure Wilbur would know the statistics—who are going to be on welfare indefinitely —during their childhood, anyway—because they simply don't have the skills to work, or to get a job at all, whether or not they have the incentive.

DEAN COHEN: Well, it's even more difficult, Barber, because such a large pro-portion of both the people who are poor in this country and the people who are on welfare are in families headed by a woman. If they do want to go to work— and I'm sure many of them do—we would have to finance a child care program. That is another reason why costs would balloon—

MR. BORK: Well, now we're being told that work incentives aren't too important, because there aren't that many people in the welfare population who would respond to them.

DEAN COHEN: No. We're not saying they're not important for some people, but there's a group among the poor for whom work incentives are inoperative because of sickness, disability, education, or the number of children in the family.

MR. BORK: I was trying to find out whether, if we established such a plan, we would be risking a major loss of national efficiency by paying people not to work, and I can't get any estimate of the size of that problem, or find out even if it exists.

DR. MacAVOY: You can get different estimates from different members of the panel.

MR. BORK: Dr. MacAvoy thinks that the problem is substantial, and I gather some of the others do not; and I guess we'll never find out until we try it on a statewide basis.

DR. MacAVOY: But the results of the existing experiments are intimidating; they suggest that a statewide experiment could be extremely expensive. If you've got two or three good small-scale econometric studies, they can be sufficient to deter you from going to a statewide pilot program.

DEAN COHEN: I don't think the work incentive is really as important as it's been made out to be for the whole group of the 25 million who are poor, because 40 percent of them are children of the worker, or of the woman, who's the head of the family.

The issue turns on your philosophic view about encouraging, either by incentive or compulsion, the woman who's the head of the family to go to work, leaving her children in child care. That underlies this whole problem. If your point is that every woman ought to go to work and not take care of her own children, then you come to a different kind of conclusion from the one that follows from saying that only a small proportion of them—those who choose to—should go to work. And that's the difficulty in dealing with the problem.

MR. BORK: We're coming to the end of our time. I wonder, Congressman Conable, if you'd like to comment on this before we wrap up?

CONGRESSMAN CONABLE: Oh, I'll go along with Wilbur on what he just said.

DR. MacAVOY: Let me add a remark at this point. The AFDC program as now constructed appears to me, after some investigation, to be working well. The idea of making it over into a check-writing program applicable to the entire population and at the same time expecting strong work incentives to operate is absurd. The problem in designing a better approach rests with the additional people who would qualify under the low-income aspects of a comprehensive negative income tax scheme. They're not the working mothers without husbands who are already in the base load of our welfare system. We are talking about the addition of prospective beneficiaries who will alter their work status, or falsify it, to qualify for bigger benefits.

DEAN COHEN: Well, AFDC is a check-writing program at the present time. But what you mean by a check-writing program, I assume, is the same amount for every person—

DR. MacAVOY: Qualified only on self-reported income.

DEAN COHEN: Well, then you get back to the asset question and to the problem of excluding, or including, various groups. Until that's decided, you can't have a program.

MR. BORK: Thank you very much. We have concluded the first part of our program, and the panel is now open to questions from members of the press and the audience.

JAMES MILLER, assistant director of the Council on Wage and Price Stability: As I recollect, the New Jersey experiment was planned to be a decisive test of the feasibility and desirability of the negative income tax. Yet, I gather from the dis-

255

cussion tonight that the results of this test, and those in Denver and Seattle, have been inconclusive. Would the panelists give their views on the reasons why the experiments failed to give reliable answers and on the degree to which they showed that a negative income tax does not reach its objectives?

DEAN COHEN: My own view is that the various experiments were useful in indicating some of the problems that are involved. However, until we have experiments that cover large numbers of people under realistic conditions—where they will lose their welfare check, knowing that they will go off, or go on, in terms of a real situation—we will not be able to deduce the impact on working incentives and on entry and withdrawal of secondary workers in the labor market.

Second, I believe that we need to experiment with different kinds of income disregards. The one in the present law is $30 a month plus one-third of earned income. Well, I think we ought to experiment with $40 and 40 percent, and $50 and 50 percent, and other variations to see what impact they have on different levels of assistance. That has not really been done under the existing experiments.

MR. BORK: Dean Cohen, maybe you ought to explain what an "income disregard" is.

DEAN COHEN: Well, an income disregard, or a work incentive, refers to the amount of the work income of a welfare recipient that is subtracted from his or her welfare check. Under the present situation, two-thirds of earnings is subtracted; and people think that that practice, to some extent, acts as a disincentive to continue to work. Most of the negative income tax plans have proposed a work incentive, or income disregard, of 50 percent. Well, first, that immediately makes it more costly for people to go out to work. In my opinion, the pilot programs have not ascertained whether 40 percent or 50 percent or 60 percent is the right figure in relation to different levels of income.

So I wholeheartedly support the senator's proposal for realistic experiments involving people on welfare to determine who will go out to work under various levels of payment and various work incentives. We could then use the results to write general legislation.

I might add that I also favor experimenting with different incentives in different states. I would amend the present law, which provides for one work incentive for all fifty states, to allow different states to experiment with different levels. We might learn something from that.

MR. BORK: I gather that Dr. MacAvoy believes that we know more about the negative income tax than Dean Cohen thinks.

DR. MacAVOY: Dean Cohen's criticisms of these sample experiments would hold, I believe, for almost every sample survey that we make—of consumer expenditures, investment in plant and equipment, future outlays—

MR. BORK: Well, does that mean that they are all equally invalid?

DR. MacAVOY: No. It means that they're all equally valid. We're continually faced with a trade-off of larger expenditures in order to obtain larger samples against the careful design of a small-scale experiment that keeps costs down while still yielding valid results. The smaller the sample, the more likely it is that the results will be subject to error.

MR. BORK: Can you give us any idea of the magnitude of the disincentive to work in these negative income tax programs?

DR. MacAVOY: In the experiments done so far, criticisms like Dean Cohen's have been made of the sample size. I do not believe that a statistician would take those criticisms seriously. Of course, obtaining a valid inference from any one of these short-term experiments is hazardous, in terms of knowing what a specific individual would do if he received a payment on a negative income tax scheme versus payments from various welfare programs. However, we now have several experiments and can make inferences about how groups will behave.

MR. BORK: But I take it that you believe that these experiments have taught us something. Could you give any idea what they show about the likely loss to the labor force if we were to adopt a negative income tax scheme nationally?

DR. MacAVOY: You would not see the loss to the labor force in a sudden change in the labor force statistics. The effects of shifting to a negative income tax scheme would be seen in the outlays needed to cover hundreds of thousands more people than are currently assisted, who would receive an annual income of, say, $4,000 or $5,000, so that billions of dollars of additional outlay could go to those who otherwise would have worked more hours or weeks during the year. We're talking about transferring, through a government expenditure scheme, perhaps Mr. Cohen's $15 billion, perhaps $20 billion, and perhaps more.

MR. BORK: It's a cost problem, and not a loss of national efficiency.

DR. MacAVOY: I believe that it's fair to say that what comes out of these experiments is both that costs would rise and that work effort would fall. My point is that the change would be gradual as people learn about the new programs and adjust to the new incentives. The experiments put the burden of proof on those who suggest that a great deal more information will flow from large-scale, statewide experiments requiring much greater outlays.

STEPHEN TONSOR, University of Michigan: Senator Ribicoff and Dean Cohen, you have spoken eloquently as advocates of the poor, if albeit professionally, and

I think the focus of the meeting this evening has been on the poor. What in your opinion is the impact of these programs on the polity as a whole? Do you see any evidence that they have contributed to the demoralization of political life in the United States, that many people in the United States view these programs with hostility and perceive them as political failures?

SENATOR RIBICOFF: You come from the state of Michigan, where the unemployment rate is over 12 percent. How are people who don't have skills, or ability, or education going to get a job when people who have the skills and competence can't get a job? I think this is a compassionate country. If a person is disabled, if a person is incompetent, if a person must have someone to take care of him, do you throw him into Lake Michigan and forget he exists? What are you going to do with the poor person in Detroit who can't get a job?

PROFESSOR TONSOR: Well, Senator Ribicoff, I would remind you of the massive alienation of the public from politicians who have managed to use welfare as a ploy for political advancement.

SENATOR RIBICOFF: Professor, I think you know very little about politics, and I'll tell you why. Every politician knows that the people who don't vote are the poor and the black. They are not registered; they drift. They don't vote because they don't care. The people who vote in large numbers are the middle class. And that is why politicians play up to people like you as against the poor and black who don't vote.

CONGRESSMAN CONABLE: We've been talking about incentives here. In this country, the top 80 percent of our economic spectrum is on an incentive system, and the bottom 20 percent is on a disincentive system to some degree. It's interesting that the kinds of figures that have been bandied about up here imply a welfare plan that might increase the incentives for the bottom 20 percent, but would reduce them for the top 80 percent because of the increased taxes that would be needed to pay for it. Somehow, we must keep the program under enough control so that the average American will find it economically feasible for him to support it.

LESLIE LENKOWSKI, Smith Richardson Foundation: In his response to the previous question, Senator Ribicoff touched upon what I think is the main issue of welfare reform.

Prior to 1964, as the employment rolls went up, the welfare rolls always went down. After 1964, the employment rolls went up, but the welfare rolls also went up, very steeply, reaching about 3 million families about 1971 or 1972. As employment worsened after that, the welfare rolls stayed pretty much the same. In other words, it seems that the recent history of AFDC suggests that changes in national employment make very little difference to welfare enrollment. The question is, have we got a culture of dependency that may, indeed, be due to the AFDC program, and is your faith that better employment would reduce the rolls valid in view of history?

SENATOR RIBICOFF: I would say, sir, it's a combination. First, as Wilbur pointed out, when you're talking about AFDC, you are basically talking about women with children. If women are going to work, there must be some place to put those children. If a mother has a child of three or four and has to take care of it, obviously she can't work.

Perhaps what is needed is more family-planning programs so that women like that will have fewer illegitimate children. It's a factor of social deterioration. Our society does have flaws, and this is one of them. Again, you have the question: What does society do with a mother who is eighteen or nineteen years of age and has two or three illegitimate children? This is a great dilemma for a civilized society based upon the Judeo-Christian concept; and it is a dilemma that we are unwilling to face. It's easy to talk about welfare bums, but what would you do with that individual mother, and that individual innocent child who didn't ask to be brought into the world? Are you going to let him starve? Are you going to throw him into the gutter or trash heap?

BARRY CHISWICK, staff, Council of Economic Advisers: One of the issues that's raised is cashing out the in-kind programs—for example, converting the food stamp program into dollars, eliminating housing subsidies and giving the money in dollars rather than through housing vouchers. You have talked about combining these programs into a cash negative income tax, and the discussion of this scheme generally hinges around one program, one structure of benefits. The objections to this are twofold: one is the very large cost involved in covering all families under one structure, and the other is the problem of incentive effects. My question is: Since there are different demographic groups—the aged, AFDC-type families, intact families—who would respond differently to work incentives, would the panelists consider a negative income tax in which the structure of benefits was tailored to such demographic differences?

DEAN COHEN: That's exactly why I'd like to see some experiments that perhaps varied the work incentive in relation to different demographic and social conditions.

We talk very glibly about work incentives, but we know very little about them. Thousands of people on welfare have worked even when their welfare payments were reduced one dollar for each dollar of earnings. Economically, it didn't make sense; yet they went to work anyway. Why? I think it was because there are other work incentives beyond strictly economic ones. There is pride in working, for one thing. We don't know what a given work incentive, or one of different magnitudes, would do under different kinds of economic conditions. You have made a good suggestion. I think the senator and I would like to see how it worked out, in actual practice, in various regions, and in urban and rural areas of the country.

SENATOR RIBICOFF: That's a good common-sense approach you have, sir.

DR. MacAVOY: Let me add that Mr. Chiswick's question is brilliant, and just what one would expect from a senior staff member on the Council of Economic Advisers. [Laughter.]

SENATOR RIBICOFF: Why doesn't an idea like yours ever percolate through your bosses up to the President? [Laughter.]

DR. MacAVOY: It just percolated, but I am picturing an IRS form that requires a woman to check off a certain box depending on her demographic category, marital status, whether her husband is at home, or lives down the street, or hasn't been seen for years—a whole set of boxes of that nature. That would be a complication worth having in the IRS form: your tax schedule would depend on the box checked.

But then what is the IRS man going to do? Is he going to find out, in any definitive way, whether she checked the right box or just the box with the lowest tax schedule or the highest negative tax schedule?

MR. BORK: You'd have to have an audit system with high penalties.

DR. MacAVOY: High penalties would mean that you'd have an audit system with extremely high administrative costs. Mr. Chiswick, you answer this question: How would you do it? [Laughter.]

DEAN COHEN: I can tell you how. The IRS would employ social workers.

RITA RICARDO CAMPBELL, senior fellow, The Hoover Institution: I've enjoyed listening to the five gentlemen on the platform and Barry Chiswick in the audience discussing the important problems of demography and taxation, because two-thirds of the long-run actuarial imbalance of the social security system stems from the demographic changes. Barry really asked my question, but the answers he received, I believe, are inadequate. They do not discuss the major issues. Women engage in household activities for which they are not paid—that is, day care of children within the home, cooking, cleaning—and the value of these services is *not* in the gross national product. But when these services are performed by others than the homemaker and mother, they are paid for and are in the gross national product. Women's labor supply is, therefore, far more sensitive to their rate of anticipated earnings than men's labor supply. Women move in and out of the labor force more readily than men. If you are going to devise different systems for men and women and if then you are also going to have different categories for women—depending on whether the husband is there in the home (at least on the day when the welfare worker comes), whether the woman is a single head of household but happens to have two children whom she wishes to take care of herself or prefers to work and use a day care center—you will be weaving a very tangled web and still not solve the problem of the woman, a single parent, who has children to support and no other adult in her home, as might have been true in the past, to take care of her children. I'd like to hear you elaborate on these lines.

MR. BORK: I think Congressman Conable has a point that is raised by both of these last two questions.

CONGRESSMAN CONABLE: The only point I want to make is that somebody in Congress would raise the issue of privacy at some point. We are tugged in so many directions in this complicated society that it's fairly certain the sensitivities of the average American would be outraged by any poking and prying of this sort. That would likely become almost the dominant issue in any effort to reconstitute a system along such rational lines based on full information.

ROBERT WEINTRAUB, staff, House Banking and Currency Committee: All of you seem to agree that the present system involves a large bureaucracy. It excludes some deserving people, and it includes people with lots of assets and others who may be undeserving.

Let's suppose that we simply extended the present tax system to include a negative income tax, in the Friedman manner. Do you believe this would (a) involve a smaller or larger bureaucracy, (b) exclude more or fewer deserving people, (c) include more or fewer undeserving people? And if your answers are, "Smaller, fewer, and fewer," or two of those three, why don't you go for a negative income tax system? [Laughter.]

SENATOR RIBICOFF: Frankly, I don't know. That's why I would like to pilot that out. I would not, ever, vote for a negative income tax for the entire country as a substitute for the present welfare system. But I would like to see it tried in a couple of states.

DR. MacAVOY: I would respond, "None of the above, the same, and more for the following reasons which will take me ten minutes to enumerate." [Laughter.]

MR. BORK: On television, this program is going to be as comprehensible as an income tax form. [Laughter.]

DR. MacAVOY: If we were to use Dr. Weintraub's technique, we would be replacing the HEW division that deals with specific programs with an enlarged Internal Revenue Service, whereby checks would be sent to those who had such low levels

261

of income that, under the tax code, they would get payments rather than pay taxes. This negative income tax scheme would require a larger bureaucracy and a more complex surveillance system to try to find those who have no income than we have with an IRS that seeks out those who have large incomes and are not paying taxes. Perhaps this is what Senator Ribicoff was saying—that it's very difficult to envision the construction of that new bureaucracy in IRS. But I believe there would be one, and it would raise the problem that Representative Conable has raised about privacy.

Second, we have the matter of whether a negative income tax would cover more deserving people. I believe AFDC and the other programs—Medicaid, food stamps, and so on—are doing a good job in reaching deserving people. They are also reaching substantial parts of the population that might not be covered if the justification for these programs were strictly applied. Ten percent of those who receive food stamps have incomes roughly of $10,000 a year or more. That seems to me to be a little high. [Laughter.]

Third, given the general scope of an IRS form and the inability to differentiate well in a national negative income tax scheme, I believe more of the undeserving would receive the negative income tax than now receive welfare. So that's why I gave those three answers at the original point in this long answer.

PAUL FELDMAN, Public Research Institute: You gentlemen have been carrying on as if all we needed to do is discover a better welfare system, and then we'd immediately adopt it. But it's been a very long time since we've seen any government programs dispensed with. Professor MacAvoy has had some experience trying to do away with the Civil Aeronautics Board and several other regulatory agencies, and he hasn't yet managed it. Do you really believe that it would be possible to do away with many of these programs that you've been talking about if the cost was a reduction in benefits to some recipients and in jobs to some welfare workers?

MR. BORK: I think that question is tailored for you, congressman.

CONGRESSMAN CONABLE: I wish to note that one of the Senate's leading liberals has demonstrated tonight that he is quite conservative about change. And I think that makes an important point: government is a terribly conservative institution, and change comes with great difficulty.

Change with respect to a part of the government program as sensitive as welfare would obviously entail a great many labor pains, because of the sensitivities involved, because of the high visibility of the welfare system generally, and because of all the backlash that would come from the many people who would think the work ethic was being tampered with. There's no question that the political difficulties would be very great. Substantial change is not going to come about until we get a Congress and a President working in concert, until there is a sufficient mandate from the public to get us over the threshold of conservatism that affects such institutions. It's not going to come about until there are many programs of the sort we are having tonight that sensitize people to the difficulties involved in those changes—the complexity of the current system, the conceptual errors in it, and the problems of expense and philosophy that must be grappled with.

So I think your question is entirely appropriate. Welfare reform is going to take time, it's going to take effort, and it's going to come only with a major national effort. We aren't going to be able to do it piecemeal, either, in any significant way.

HOWARD TUCKMAN, Department of Economics, Florida State University: In listening to the conversation tonight, I am reminded of the passages in Pat Moynihan's book about the difficulty of explaining the formula of the negative income tax, both to the Congress and to the public.* Now, we know that, come January, there will be a new administration. And there's a reasonable probability that somewhere in that new administration a negative income tax will be proposed. If the public is not educated on this matter, what is your guess about what would happen to a proposal for negative income tax?

SENATOR RIBICOFF: It would never pass.

CONGRESSMAN CONABLE: We're quite capable of rejecting things quickly. [Laughter.]

Seriously, it's going to take a lot of groundwork, a lot of education, and a broad-based public perception of the need for change.

DR. MacAVOY: Are you capable of taking up things before adequate preparation has taken place?

SENATOR RIBICOFF: We often do, but that isn't right.

CONGRESSMAN CONABLE: Sometimes we're quite capable of not taking them up even after adequate preparation. [Laughter.]

SENATOR RIBICOFF: In answer to some of the questions this gentleman raises, this week the Committee on Government Operations, by a vote of seven to nothing, passed Senator Muskie's Zero Budgeting Act, which he called a "Sunset Bill." The bill provides that every program of the government must be reauthorized every five years. I expect to bring the bill out of committee this summer.

This proposal, if passed, would give us an opportunity to find out which programs work and which don't. The only way we could do that would be to have

---

* Editor's note: Daniel Patrick Moynihan, *Politics of a Guaranteed Income: The Nixon Administration and the Family Assistance Plan* (New York: Random House, 1973).

a real program evaluation—which is not done now, either in the executive branch or in Congress. Congress would then have to balance out what the situation would be with and without the program. Then it would have to accept the program, reject it, or come up with a substitute.

I think this is probably, prospectively, the greatest congressional reform since the Congressional Budget Act. I am confident that the Senate will pass it, but I don't know about the House. I would guess it will come out of the Government Operations Committee unanimously.

GERRY BRANNON, Georgetown University: I would like to ask Wilbur Cohen if he would comment on the fact that at present the food stamp plan seems to be structurally very good. It has a low marginal tax rate, it applies to the working poor, and so forth. One would almost think that the way to get to welfare reform would be gradually to increase the number of food stamps, then gradually make them bigger and greener, and finally put George Washington's picture on them. Then we could repeal the other programs.

DEAN COHEN: I do think the food stamp plan, and its extensive operation, has changed the entire nature of the welfare reform problem from what it was at the time of the family assistance proposal. It is much more difficult today than it was in 1970 and 1971 to talk about supplanting all the other programs with a negative income tax because the food stamp plan is now so extensive.

I don't believe, under present circumstances, that it is economically or politically acceptable to cash out the food stamp plan into any negative income tax that I know of. And that's very different from the situation in the early 1970s when the House and the Senate considered the family assistance plan. I think the food stamp plan represents an important development. I would only hope that, if we can get back to a period of full employment and if the food stamp plan could be narrowed down, it might be possible then to cash it out. But I must say, I am now very pessimistic about that. The food stamp plan is here, and it represents a very significant part of the total welfare picture. That makes cashing it out into a negative income tax much more difficult today than it would have been five years ago.

CONGRESSMAN CONABLE: It's interesting, in the light of Wilbur's remarks, to consider that the food stamp program is the one part of the welfare system that is likely to be reformed in the near future. There is a great deal of public discontent with it. One of the reasons is that virtually 40 million people are now eligible for food stamps, and the average American thinks that any welfare program for which so many people are eligible must have something conceptually wrong with it and must be potentially so expensive that the country can't carry it. So regardless of whether you think it's a good plan conceptually, it's under a great deal of political pressure now. Most people accept that it is going to be reformed in some way.

PHIL LYONS, staff, House Budget Committee: My question is, what provision do you think should be made in welfare reform for the individual's desire to work? In other words, what consideration, if any, should be given to qualifying the person for receipt of a benefit depending on whether he made an honest-to-goodness effort to work?

DEAN COHEN: That gets back to the problem I posed of how to deal with women who are heads of families. The question you ask is really based upon the expectation that the male head of family is the primary worker, an expectation that makes the question easy to handle. But what work are you going to offer at what wages to a woman who has three children, when the decision of whether she should stay home with her children or go to work is one which ultimately, in our society, she and not a government agency must make?

MR. BORK: In these programs, do we have any instances in which even the male head of the family is subjected to a test such as is proposed?

DEAN COHEN: In general, under our present program, the male member of the family is subjected to a work test. But as Senator Ribicoff said earlier, when there are no real jobs available in an area, that work test is very unreal. So I think that you'd have to pose that question for a full-employment economy. And it might well be answered in much the same way as we do in connection with unemployment insurance in terms of what is "suitable work."

Now, my answer to your basic question involves another proposal that we haven't discussed here and that I think has some merit. We could break this problem into two parts. First, there are the employable people, to whom we could apply the kind of work test and concepts that exist in unemployment insurance; these are mainly males, but also women who have no children under the age of six, or eight, or whatever age you want to set. Second, we would use the existing welfare program for the rest, and let them make their own choices about working or not. That would be one of the things that I would test out in selected states. I think there's a lot of merit to it, but I don't know whether it would work or not.

DR. MacAVOY: There's an additional element that Mr. Cohen has discussed before: once the opportunity for work is there, in a well-constructed program, how much of the additional income from work are you going to take away by reducing welfare payments? Now, I believe we all desire to provide not only the opportunity, but also the incentive, to work for those who are capable. That means we must take away very little of the income they would earn. On the other hand, if we do, the total amount of income received from welfare and work could be very substantial. I don't see how that trade-off can be made.

MR. BORK: We're going to have trouble with it, I think. But we have already discussed that.

JOHN TODD, Department of Health, Education, and Welfare: I work in the office that oversees the income maintenance experiments—which *do* have variable guarantees and tax rates. And, incidentally, we don't have final results from Seattle and Denver yet.

But my question concerns another matter. Everyone, with the possible exception of Dr. MacAvoy, seems to agree that the present distribution of benefits is inequitable—that the moneys that are currently flowing, at least from the federal Treasury and perhaps from state and local governments, are not distributed in the best way. Yet, there also seems to be wide agreement that a negative income tax would have a large price tag; very large numbers—$15 billion to $30 billion—have been mentioned. What would be your reaction to a more modestly priced negative income tax that, through the elimination of several in-kind programs and the utilization of longer accounting periods and asset periods, could in effect reshuffle much of the present money in a manner that would be, by your lights, more equitable?

DEAN COHEN: Let me make two comments on that, because I think a lot of people, even if they have different views, will agree with me on this point. I don't think that we can solve that problem until Medicaid no longer has to deal with the issue of eligibility. In other words, you've got to solve the so-called notch problem—

MR. BORK: Not all of us understand the notch problem.

DEAN COHEN: Let me put it very simply: it is the difficult problem of a person's becoming *eligible* under the negative income tax program, but becoming ineligible under the Medicaid program and thus losing more valuable medical benefits when he becomes eligible for relatively smaller income benefits.

Let me answer Mr. Todd's question this way: I don't think that his suggestion of a more modest negative income tax is realistically feasible under the present circumstances, because the lower we make the payment, the more we would have to have supplementation, either mandatory or voluntary, in California, Michigan, and New York; and we'd still confront the same problem of disparities.

SENATOR RIBICOFF: I'd like to ask Mr. Todd the same question I asked of Mr. Chiswick. When you have an idea like this, how do you get it up to the secretary of HEW? Does anybody listen to you? Whether the idea is good or not, I'm just curious about how, in the bureaucracy of the government, do young men like you bring your good ideas to the surface.

DEAN COHEN: Abe, when we were there, we used to have an open-door policy. They used to come to see us with their ideas.

MR. TODD: Well, I can speak, for example, of Secretary Weinberger, with whose management I have had more experience, and who, I think it's commonly known, supported the type of program I'm suggesting. I don't pretend that he did it solely on the basis of my urging. The program received mixed reviews, and the political climate existing at the time, plus budgetary considerations, led to an official postponement of the consideration of that idea. But I don't believe it's fair to say that it did not receive a hearing; nor do I think it's fair to say that the idea did not receive a testing out by people in IRS and others looking at its administrative feasibility.

GEORGE MERRILL, staff, Senate Budget Committee: You've all been talking about the little welfare programs, such as AFDC and food stamps, but no one has mentioned the biggest program of all—the social security program, which accounts for 20 percent of the federal budget now. Do you think that social security should be examined in this overall context of welfare reform?

DEAN COHEN: My answer is no. That's not what we're talking about in welfare reform. The social security program needs to be reexamined and changed fundamentally, but it has basically nothing to do with the welfare reform question that we're discussing today.

SENATOR RIBICOFF: You pose a basic problem, and I give you a political answer. To try to change the social security program will lead to revolution.

MR. BORK: In other words, Senator Ribicoff is not going to lose in New Hampshire in the next primary.

DR. MacAVOY: Won't the Sunset Law terminate the social security program?

SENATOR RIBICOFF: No. The Sunset Law does not apply to trust funds, pensions, social security—to programs in which there is a long-term investment and benefits.

DR. MacAVOY: You mean, there are already escape clauses.

SENATOR RIBICOFF: Well, it's altogether different. How are you going to terminate a retirement program that people have been paying into for decades with the expectation of receiving money back?

MR. BORK: This concludes our Round Table discussion, presented by the American Enterprise Institute and the Hoover Institution. I want to thank our distinguished panelists for a lively discussion—Dr. MacAvoy, Representative Conable, Senator Ribicoff, and Dean Cohen—and also the experts, members of the press, and guests who were kind enough to participate. Thank you. [Applause.]

Cover and book design: Pat Taylor